Bed &
Homes Directory

West Coast

8th Edition

Bed & Breakfast Homes Directory

West Coast

8th Edition

by

Diane Knight

KNIGHTIME PUBLICATIONS

Graphics by Diva Designs, Santa Cruz, California and Rainbow
Graphics, San Jose, California
Edited by Suzy Blackaby
Front cover photo by Michael Nikolich
Back cover photo by Raymond Miller
Maps by Eureka Cartography, Berkeley, California
Desktop publishing by Raymond Miller
Printed and bound in U.S.A. by Griffin Printing, Sacramento, California

Distributed in Canada by Whitecap Books Ltd., 1086 West 3rd Street,
North Vancouver, British Columbia V7P 3J6

Library of Congress Catalog Card Number: 93-061320

ISBN 0-942902-09-2

CONTENTS

As we have added more and more B&Bs in the Pacific Northwest to *BED & BREAKFAST HOMES DIRECTORY*, the emphasis has evolved from mostly California B&Bs to a well-balanced West Coast guidebook organized as follows: California, Oregon, Washington, and British Columbia are independent sections, each of which is introduced by a map that may be used to locate starred towns in which to find B&Bs. Selected towns may be located alphabetically within each section.

I must again address the controversy over the issue of guidebook authors charging B&B owners to be listed. Knighttime Publications *does* charge a listing fee of two times the average double rate charged by the B&B. While this may seem on the surface to be a questionable policy, a deeper look should put readers' minds at ease.

Every effort is made to seek out and include only those B&Bs that meet our criteria of cleanliness, comfort, hospitality, and value. I am one of the few bed and breakfast guidebook authors who actually visits each B&B and describes it from firsthand experience. The listing fee is accepted only after the B&B is visited and approved. Any B&B that is judged to be out of line in any of the above-mentioned areas is not included. Further, I do not list any B&B that I would not personally be pleased to stay in.

In addition to the expense of visiting every new B&B and occasionally re-visiting old ones, there are the substantial expenses of actual publication of *BED & BREAKFAST HOMES DIRECTORY*. In short, it would not be possible to produce the book without the income derived from the listing fees.

Readers, be assured that you are my foremost concern. The integrity of this book must remain high so that you will continue to buy and use it, and so that I can continue to do the work I love. No compromises are made in its creation.

B&B hosts have agreed to honor published rates for our readers at least until the end of 1994. In order for these rates to be honored, be sure to mention that you found their B&B in the current edition of this book. Some hosts offer a special discount to readers, as noted; you must have a copy of this edition to obtain the reader discounts.

Your feedback regarding your experiences while using this book is strongly encouraged. Comments and suggestions should be addressed to me at 890 Calabasas Road, Watsonville, CA 95076-0418.

As your travels take you to some of the places and people that have touched my heart, I continue to wish you the joy of serendipity.

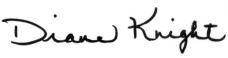

We are continuing the feature begun in 1988; that is, the addition of a listing of recommended restaurants for each state or province covered in *BED & BREAKFAST HOMES DIRECTORY*. This is not intended to be a comprehensive listing of good restaurants, nor does it contain extensive information about each one. It offers some assistance in finding suitable places for lunch or dinner as you travel through unfamiliar territory. You will have to call or drop by the establishment that you're considering to find out more about it.

I have selected many of the restaurants from my own happy dining experiences. I must admit that part of my motivation in compiling the listings is the marvelous convenience of having at my fingertips the names, addresses, and phone numbers of an excellent assortment of wonderful restaurants spanning the U.S. and Canadian west coasts. I have found myself using the listings constantly since the last compilation. The Dining Highlights have been substantially revised and expanded in this edition.

In addition to choosing restaurants myself, I've also asked hosts to name those in their areas that they can recommend without hesitation. Each was personally selected by someone who has had firsthand knowledge of it over a period of time. Restaurants range from a simple taco stand in Santa Barbara to a world-class restaurant in Sooke, B.C., and prices vary accordingly. There was no charge to restaurants for a listing.

Criteria for selection were good quality ingredients, careful preparation, a pleasant atmosphere, and (most important), superior value. The majority of restaurants included are gems -- really wonderful little places that tourists would be unlikely to discover on their own. While most offer good food at reasonable prices, some "splurge" restaurants are included -- and judged to be well worth the cost.

Although most of the restaurants have proven track records, no guarantees are possible. Your feedback on these recommendations is encouraged.

I want to emphasize that the number of restaurants listed for any given town is simply a product of information available to me. For example, since I live near the San Francisco Bay Area, my personal knowledge (as well as that of friends and colleagues) of its restaurants is much greater than that of, say, Santa Barbara or Portland. I apologize for the resulting lopsided coverage.

The B&Bs in this directory are, in most cases, strictly private homes, not commercial establishemnts. While some small, owner-occupied inns are also included, they are still the *homes* of the people who operate them. As a guest, remember to act with the same courtesy and consideration that you would expect of a guest in your own home.

Most *B&BHD* hosts don't consider themselves innkeepers. They are not in business full time -- and therein lies some of the appeal of being treated "like family." There may be occasions when hosts can't accommodate you because they'll be on vacation, or because Great Aunt Martha from Omaha will be using the guest room.

In many cases, daily maid service and room service are not provided. This varies a great deal from one B&B to the next, but, generally, the smaller and less expensive accommodations do not offer such services. However, it is at this type of B&B that you are likely to encounter the spontaneous personal favor at just the right moment.

A number of B&B hosts will accept only cash or traveler's checks in payment for accommodations. Over time, though, more and more hosts are accepting credit cards. This information is now included in the second paragraph of each description for your convenience. Be sure to verify what forms of payment will be accepted *before* your visit.

When reserving accommodations in B&B homes, it is very important to agree upon your time of arrival with the host. There is always some flexibility, but arrival time should be discussed. If it appears that you will be later than planned, it is only considerate (and most appreciated) that you call and let your host know.

Room rates include at least a Continental breakfast. In many cases, the rate includes a full breakfast; in a few situations, there may be an extra charge (as noted) for a full breakfast. If anything more than a Continental breakfast is served, it is so stated in each listing.

Many hosts look forward to having guests join them for a family-style breakfast. In some cases -- if the guest unit is totally separate and has cooking facilities -- the host(s) will simply leave the ingredients for breakfast so that guests may prepare it at their leisure. There are hosts who will be glad to serve you breakfast in your room, or even in bed. Morning may find you at a table of your own, or perhaps you'll breakfast at a large table with other B&B guests. As in many aspects of B&B travel, the accent is on *variety.*

For each listing:

The first line tells either the name(s) of the host(s) or the name given to the B&B and the phone number to call for reservations.

The second line gives the mailing address of the B&B to use if you're writing for reservations.

The third line, in parentheses, indicates the general location of the B&B. You should get specific directions from your host.

Next you'll find a descriptive paragraph about the B&B. It often tells something about the unique qualities of the home itself, the setting, the host(s), points of interest in the area.

The second paragraph indicates whether there are indoor pets and gives the host(s) preferences, such as "no smoking" or "children welcome." These appear in a consistent sequence in each listing. They are given only if the host(s) have indicated a specific policy on the subject. The paragraph also lists facilities or features available to guests, such as "laundry" or "hot tub."

Available transportation is sometimes indicated, as well as the host(s) willingness to pick up guests at a nearby airport (largely for the benefit of private pilots).

The following code refers to the headings at the end of each description:

ROOM
: Refers to a guest unit. The unit may be a room in the B&B home, an adjoining apartment,, or a separate cottage near the home. Each letter (A,, B,...) designates one guest unit, whether it has one, two, or more rooms.

BED
: Number and type(s) of bed(s) given for each guest unit. This means total beds per unit. T = twin, D = double, Q = queen, K = king

BATH
: Shd means you'll share a bath with the host(s). Shd* means the bath is shared by other guests,, if present. (You may have it all to yourself, especially midweek or off-season.) Pvt means the bath goes with the guest unit and is shared by no one else. It may be across the hall, but it is all yours.

ENTRANCE
: Main indicates you'll use the main entrance of the home. Sep means there is a separate entrance for guests.

FLOOR
: The floor of each guest room is indicated by number in most cases. LL means lower level, usually with steps down. 1G means a ground level room, with no steps.

DAILY RATES S refers to a single (one person); **D** refers to a double (two persons); **EP** refers to the rate charged for an extra person (above two) traveling with your party (generally, when there is an extra bed of some sort in the guest unit). Most of the rates quoted will have a local tax added. When this information is available, a plus sign (+) has been used by the **EP** rate. Some stated rates **include** the tax.

Example:

ROOM	BED	BATH	ENTRANCE	FLOOR	DAILY RATES	
					S - D	(EP) +
A	1K	Pvt	Main	2	$60-$65	($10)

Room (or unit) A has one king-sized bed, a private bath, uses the main entrance to the home, is on the second floor. One person will pay $60; two persons will pay $65; an extra person will pay $10. A local tax will be added.

NOTE TO TRAVELERS IN CANADA: Many Canadian B&Bs must charge a Goods and Services Tax (**G.S.T.**), which is fully refundable to travelers upon leaving Canada. Hosts will assist with procedure.

AC = Air Conditioning; VCR = Video Cassette Recorder;
BART = Bay Area Rapid Transit (in San Francisco Bay Area).

1. Try to plan your visit as far ahead as possible. This helps to ensure you'll get to stay at the B&B of your choice. It is a mistake, when planning less than six weeks ahead for peak seasons, to call or write for brochures from each B&B you are considering (particularly between the U.S. and Canada). Often, by the time you receive all the brochures, many B&Bs will be already booked.

2. Call your host(s) for reservations before 9 p.m. and after 10 a.m. (end of breakfast activity). Be sure to allow for the time difference if you're not on Pacific Time.

3. Carefully check details about the B&B you're considering before calling or writing. Confirm with your host anything that's not clear to you. Ask pertinent questions! One of the most important is the cancellation policy; these vary widely, and you must comply with it in order not to lose your deposit or have your credit card charged.

4. Check what form(s) of payment your host(s) will accept. Ask if a deposit is required.

5. Agree on time of arrival.

6. Notify your host(s) immediately of any change in plans!

Hosts listed in *BED & BREAKFAST HOMES DIRECTORY* have agreed to honor rates stated in the directory until the end of 1994.

The information contained in these listings has been prepared with great care, but we cannot guarantee that it is complete or in all cases correct. It is the user's responsibility to verify important information when making arrangements.

Wise, cultivated, genial con-
versation is the last flower of
civilization.... Conversation is
our account of ourselves.

—Ralph Waldo Emerson

What is pleasanter than the tie
of host and guest?

—Aeschylus

CALIFORNIA

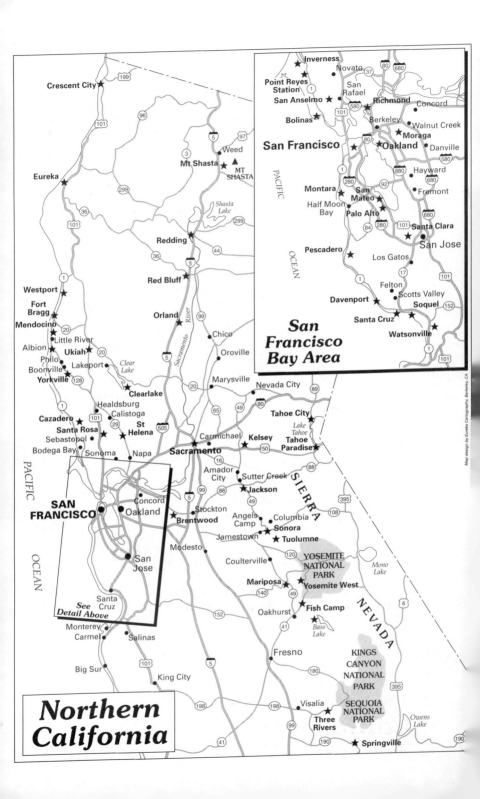

Northern California

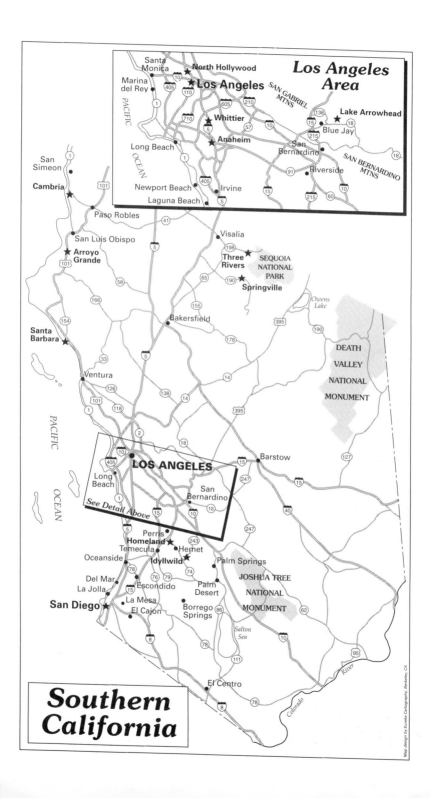

Los Angeles Area

Santa Monica
North Hollywood
Marina del Rey
Los Angeles
SAN GABRIEL MTNS
PACIFIC
405
110
10
1
605
210
Lake Arrowhead
138
Whittier
18
Blue Jay
710
5
57
10
15
Long Beach
Anaheim
215
San Bernardino
SAN BERNARDINO MTNS
1
Newport Beach
405
Irvine
91
Riverside
18
Laguna Beach
5
15
60
215
10
OCEAN

San Simeon
1
Cambria
101
Paso Robles
41
Visalia
San Luis Obispo
5
196
Three Rivers
SEQUOIA NATIONAL PARK
Arroyo Grande
101
58
65
190
Springville
166
155
Owens Lake
Santa Barbara
154
Bakersfield
395
190
178
33
DEATH
5
VALLEY
Ventura
126
138
14
NATIONAL
101
1
118
395
MONUMENT
2
18
10
Barstow
127
405
LOS ANGELES
15
Long Beach
247
1
San Bernardino
15
PACIFIC
See Detail Above
15
10
16
40
247
5
Perris
243
Homeland
Temecula
Hemet
Oceanside
Idyllwild
74
Palm Springs
78
76
79
JOSHUA TREE
Del Mar
La Jolla
15
Escondido
Palm Desert
NATIONAL
San Diego
La Mesa
El Cajon
Borrego Springs
86
MONUMENT
62
OCEAN
8
78
Salton Sea
111
10
95
El Centro
8
78
Colorado River

Map design by Eureka Cartography, Berkeley, CA

Southern California

The Wool Loft
(707) 937-0377

32751 Navarro Ridge Road, Albion, CA 95410
(Ten miles south of Mendocino)

The Wool Loft's setting overlooking the sea reminds me of some B&Bs in Ireland or Scotland. Sheep graze in nearby fields; the family garden and henhouse contribute food to the table. Jan and Sid offer three cheery guest rooms with private baths in the main house to guests who prefer traditional bed and breakfast; one of these (B) is a newer room with wonderful river and ocean views. The Wool Loft itself (A) is a separate accommodation. It's a spacious studio apartment with queen-sized bed, fully equipped kitchen, bath, wood-burning stove, and huge windows that afford magnificent vistas. Quiet and cozy seclusion on the famous Mendocino coast is yours if you choose The Wool Loft.

No pets, children, or smoking; gather eggs for breakfast if desired; large sun room, deck, and fireplace in main house; firewood provided in Wool Loft; off-street parking; two-night minimum; three-night minimum on holiday weekends; special weekly rate for Room A, $600; no breakfast served during week. *Open weekends for B&B (Friday-Sunday only).* Brochure available.

ROOM	BED	BATH	ENTRANCE	FLOOR	DAILY RATES S - D (EP) +
A	1Q	Pvt	Sep	2	$100
B	1Q	Pvt	Main	1	$85
C	1Q	Pvt	Main	1	$65
D	1Q	Pvt	Main	1	$65

Anaheim Bed & Breakfast   **(714) 533-1884**
1327 South Hickory, Anaheim, CA 92805
(Off Santa Ana Freeway)

Anaheim is the obvious headquarters for anyone planning to visit Disneyland or the convention center, both less than a mile away, or Knott's Berry Farm. Many people also find the location ideal for visiting beaches, L.A., as well as points to the south and east. Disneyland's nightly fireworks can be viewed in summer from the back yard of this suburban home. Margot Palmgren's home exudes a friendly welcome that puts visitors at ease right away. She speaks German fluently and loves meeting people from all over the world. You'll be in good hands with Margot; she knows the area intimately and can give you a real insider's view of things...for example, she remembers when the Knott family ran a little fruit stand nearby -- and the day Disneyland opened!

No pets or smoking; TV in each room; AC in Room A; ceiling fan in B and C; AC and fireplace in den; full breakfast; ample street parking; good public transportation and airport connections.

ROOM	BED	BATH	ENTRANCE	FLOOR	DAILY RATES S - D (EP) +
A	1D	Shd*	Main	1G	$30-$40
B	2T	Shd*	Main	1G	$30-$40
C	1D	Shd	Main	1G	$30-$40

The Guest House   **(805) 481-9304**
120 Hart Lane, Arroyo Grande, CA 93420
(Off U.S. 101, seventeen miles south of San Luis Obispo)

Homesick New Englanders, look no further than The Guest House at Arroyo Grande. It was built in the 1850s by a sea captain from the east and bears an unmistakable resemblance to the homes he left behind. Present owners Mark Miller and James Cunningham have kept the flavor of old New England alive in the house. Stenciled wall designs, American primitives, Oriental rugs, and family heirlooms add to the mellow, inviting atmosphere. A crackling fire in the hearth and comfortable places to sit make the living room a haven for easy conversation. The afternoon social hour often takes place in the bay-windowed sun room with French doors that lead out to the garden. Breakfast is appropriately hearty fare, served in the sun room or out in the garden. For traditional Yankee hospitality at the sign of the pineapple, The Guest House is a classic.

Cat in residence; no pet or children; full breakfast; afternoon refreshments; city park in turn-of-the-century village of Arroyo Grande; many antique shops in town and wineries in surrounding countryside; off-street parking.

ROOM	BED	BATH	ENTRANCE	FLOOR	DAILY RATES S - D (EP) +
A	1Q	Shd*	Main	2	$45-$60 ($10)
B	1D	Shd*	Main	2	$45-$60 ($10)

Bass Lake Bed & Breakfast   **(209) 642-3618**
53489 North Shore Drive, Bass Lake, CA 93604
(Overlooking north shore of Bass Lake)

Long-time residents Ken and Nita Kiehlmeier find living in the
Bass Lake community a pleasure in every season. It's a friendly place
with lots of natural beauty and wildlife, wonderful views of the lake,
water recreation galore, some fine restaurants, and easy access to the
wonder that is Yosemite. They delight in sharing their contemporary
wood home with B&B guests, who have the entire lower floor to
themselves. Guest accommodations have a separate entrance and a
front deck overlooking the lake. The open living space features
comfortable furnishings in earth tones and includes a cable TV/VCR
and an area to make snacks and hot and cold drinks. The two
attractive guest rooms are at the back. One has a queen bed, a futon,
and a large full bath. The other has a queen bed and a split bath with
shower only. Both have convenient closet and shelf space. Healthful
breakfasts are served upstairs in the hosts' spacious, relaxing dining
room. They can help you choose among the myriad ways to enjoy
their neck of the woods.

No pets; smoking outside only; TV/VCR; AC; boat rentals nearby;
fourteen miles from south entrance of Yosemite; off-street parking;
credit cards (V,MC); senior discounts. Brochure available.

ROOM	BED	BATH	ENTRANCE	FLOOR	DAILY RATES S - D (EP) +
A	1Q	Pvt	Sep	1	$65-$75 ($15)
B	1Q	Pvt	Sep	1	$60-$65

Thomas' White House Inn   **(415) 868-0279**
P.O. Box 132, Bolinas, CA 94924
(Between Stinson Beach and Point Reyes National Seashore)

The magic and mystery of Bolinas lies in its refusal to go the way of so many other seaside communities that nurture tourism at the expense of the natural environment. Bolinas is not easy to find; it's been said that if you want to find it, you will. Its startling beauty is nowhere more apparent than at this marvelous bluffside inn overlooking the Pacific. Just to breathe the fresh air here, to savor the panorama of blue sea, Stinson Beach, the foothills, and Mount Tamalpais, feels like a privilege. The New England-style home of Jackie Thomas is a crisp white with red trim. It has two stories and, at the top, an observation deck. Two large, artfully appointed bedrooms and a half-bath comprise the second floor. The first floor offers a full bath with an aviary for zebra finches, a living room with a fireplace accented by Mediterranean blue tile, a sun porch, and an open country kitchen with dried flowers hanging from the beams. From bedrooms, common rooms, and from the beautifully cultivated grounds, the view is omnipresent -- just as it should be.

No pets; no smoking on second floor; expanded Continental breakfast; off-street parking.

ROOM	BED	BATH	ENTRANCE	FLOOR	DAILY RATES S - D	(EP) +
A	1Q	Shd*	Main	2	$95	($10)
B	1D	Shd*	Main	2	$85	($10)

Diablo Vista
(510) 634-2396

2191 Empire Avenue, Brentwood, CA 94513
(Just east of Antioch, off Lone Tree Way)

This elegant ranch-style home is set on two acres of fruit and nut trees, with a view of Mount Diablo in the distance. It's an hour from San Francisco and ten minutes from the Sacramento River Delta. For hikers and cyclists, Black Diamond Regional Park, with its many trails and historic sites, is only four miles away, as is Contra Loma Lake for swimming, windsurfing, and fishing. Brentwood is famous for its many "U-Pick" fruit and vegetable farms, and maps are available from hosts Dick and Myra Hackett. Their main guest room (A) is located at one far end of the house. This huge room has its own entrance, bath, kitchenette, small library, TV, stereo system, and AC/heating units. Subtle colors, Oriental rugs, custom-made window cushions, and American antiques create a harmonious, soothing effect. Room B is a cozy room with twin beds; the bath is a few steps down the hall. Guests in this room, or the other two (C and D), enjoy reading or relaxing in the sitting room of the main residence. Take a swim in the pool, soak in the hot tub, sip a drink in one of the two gazebos, or relax in the lovely garden. Hosts have thoroughly searched out the best restaurants in the area, a boon to those of us who take our dining seriously.

No pets; children over eight (swimmers) welcome; smoking outside only; TV; stereo; swimming pool; hot tub; jogging and biking trails surround property; ample parking; some Spanish spoken.

ROOM	BED	BATH	ENTRANCE	FLOOR	DAILY RATES S - D	(EP)
A	1Q	Pvt	Sep	1G	$65	($10)
B	2T	Shd	Main	1G	$60	($10)
C	1D	Shd	Main	1G	$60	($10)
D	1T	Shd	Main	1G	$50	

21

PineStone Bed & Breakfast By The Sea (805) 927-3494
221 Weymouth Street, Cambria, CA 93428
(Overlooking Moonstone Beach)

From this new Victorian-style inn you can watch sunset and moonrise, hear the sounds of the surf, or take a walk on the beach. The lower floor is just for guests. The foyer is carpeted in mauve and attractively painted light green using a stippling technique. The carpeting and stippling are carried into one pink guest room and another that's blue. Each has a full private bath, a gas fireplace, cable TV, and a sliding glass door to an individual garden patio. The quiet, relaxing rooms as pretty as can be. On the second floor, there is another room for guests with a small private deck. Hosts Frank and Barbara Banner welcome people to enjoy the gorgeous view in the lounge by the large stone fireplace, in the dining area, or on the front deck. Their warm hospitality includes generous buffet breakfasts, afternoon refreshments, and anytime-coffee, tea, or chocolate. A sterling location plus all the comforts of home make staying at PineStone Inn By The Sea a total pleasure.

No pets, children, or smoking; walking distance to Cambria village shops and restaurants; off-street parking; credit cards (V,MC); for conversion to twin beds in Room B, $10 extra, first night only.

ROOM	BED	BATH	ENTRANCE	FLOOR	DAILY RATES S - D (EP) +
A	1Q	Pvt	Main	1	$80-$85
B	1K	Pvt	Main	1	$80-$85
C	1Q	Pvt	Main	2	$80-$85

SeaEscape   **(805) 927-3112**
340 Weymouth, Cambria, CA 93428
(Just east of Highway 1)

For an overnight stay while traveling the California coast or a weekend getaway, Cambria makes a wonderful stopping place. Just seven miles south of Hearst Castle, two blocks from Moonstone Beach, and within walking distance of charming Cambria village, Duane and Miriam Benell enjoy semi-retirement at their SeaEscape. The guest room of this lovely home is on the ground level, and the living-dining area is on the upper level with a view of the ocean. Having greatly enjoyed B&Bs abroad, hosts are pleased to extend hospitality to foreign visitors traveling in California. Though the Benells divide their time between Cambria and Whittier, B&B is available most of the year with *advance reservations* by calling (805) 927-3112, (310) 695-5431, or writing 12002 Beverly Drive, Whittier, CA 90601.

No pets or smoking; one or two children OK; full breakfast; TV and fireplace upstairs; off-street parking; Room B used only for people in same party as Room A; advance reservations *essential* year round for Hearst Castle tours.

ROOM	BED	BATH	ENTRANCE	FLOOR	DAILY RATES S - D (EP)
A	1K or 2T	Pvt	Main	1G	$45-$50
B	1Q		Main	1G	Inquire

Seaview Through the Pines   **(805) 927-3089**
570 Croyden Lane, Cambria, CA 93428
(East of Highway One, in pines overlooking coast)

The large, contemporary, cedar home of Audrey and Bill Mankey is perched on a hillside in the pines with a broad-range view to the sea. The entire lower level is a guest accommodation -- a clean, inviting place to unwind and settle into. The apartment has a full, well-stocked kitchen; a living room with a sitting area, cable TV and VCR, a fireplace, and a table for dining; a full bathroom; and a bedroom with an ocean view through the open doorway. A door from the kitchen leads to a private deck with a hot tub, a hammock, chairs, and view. Guests find refreshments upon arrival, plus a host of helpful information and a menu describing the wonderful breakfast choices. Neutral tones add to the tranquil environment, and it's obvious that everything, from bed to sofas to chairs, was built for comfort. Nestle into a beautiful world all your own at Seaview Through the Pines.

No pets; infants and children over thirteen welcome; no smoking; full breakfast; off-street parking.

ROOM	BED	BATH	ENTRANCE	FLOOR	DAILY RATES S - D (EP)
A	1Q	Pvt	Sep	LL	$85 ($15)

Whispering Pines
P.O. Box 326, Cambria, CA 93428
(1605 London Lane, off Ardath)

(805) 927-4613

For many, discovering Cambria is an added bonus to visiting the magical Hearst Castle at San Simeon. The quaint coastal town retains its homespun charm even though it becomes more arty and sophisticated each year. In a lovely, tranquil area just a short drive from the old Cambria village is Jack and Ginny Anderson's multi-level contemporary home with views of rolling hills and pines -- Whispering Pines, that is. Guests may retreat to the total privacy of a deluxe, tri-level apartment with its own entrance, and a flagstone patio and hot tub just outside. Light, immaculate, and tastefully decorated, the unit consists of a living room with fireplace, TV/VCR, dining area, kitchenette, full bath, and large loft bedroom. A tantalizing choice of breakfast entrees is offered, along with the luxury of delivery to your quarters, or perhaps the patio. Simply put, Whispering Pines is a great little hideaway on the central coast.

No pets; smoking outside only; full breakfast; off-street parking. Hosts also operate Bed & Breakfast Homestay, a reservation service listing $55-$85 rooms and apartments in the area. ****KNIGHTTIME PUBLICATIONS SPECIAL RATE: 10% discount with this book.** Brochure available.

ROOM	BED	BATH	ENTRANCE	FLOOR	DAILY RATES S - D (EP)
A	1K or 2T	Pvt	Sep	2 & 3	$85

House of a Thousand Flowers   **(707) 632-5571**
P.O. Box 369, Monte Rio, CA 95462
(Five miles east of Jenner-by-the-Sea)

It's obvious right away how the House of a Thousand Flowers got its name. Greenery, including fuchsias and other blossoming plants, bedeck the house and infuse it with cheer. Host Dave Silva takes pride in the family home that is now a remote country haven for harried city folk in need of escape. He and his border collie, Annie, greet guests upon arrival. (It's been said that this is the only B&B run by an old man and his dog; Dave says the dog is the one with the class.) The house is set high on a bluff above the Russian River and has two cozy guest rooms on its lower level. Each has its own deck, separate entrance, and access to an enclosed, plant-filled spa. Look toward the sea and you may witness the magical effect created as fingers of fog move through the redwoods. The main floor is also yours to enjoy, with grand piano, extensive library, and dining room where Chef David serves his famous omelettes. Coffee is ready by your room in the morning, and breakfast is served at your convenience. Discover a little slice of paradise at the House of a Thousand Flowers.

Dog and cat in residence; full breakfast; afternoon refreshments; rollaway bed available; spa; river and ocean activities, good restaurants and wineries nearby; off-street parking; credit cards (V,MC). Brochure available.

ROOM	BED	BATH	ENTRANCE	FLOOR	DAILY RATES S - D (EP) +
A	1Q	Shd*	Sep	LL	$90 ($15)
B	1Q	Shd*	Sep	LL	$80 ($15)

Big Canyon Bed & Breakfast   (707) 928-5631
P.O. Box 1311, Lower Lake, CA 95457
(Seigler Springs, at foot of Cobb Mountain)

The remote and woodsy mountain setting makes Big Canyon Bed & Breakfast a perfect place to escape to the quiet, natural world that inspires true relaxation. The Cape Cod-style home of John and Helen Wiegand has two spacious rooms for guests on its upper floor. One (A) has its own entrance, woodstove, skylight, and kitchenette, while the other (B) has a cozy alcove window seat. The entire floor makes an ideal family or group accommodation. In the immediate surroundings you may enjoy identifying spring wildflowers, gazing at bright stars, and finding Lake County diamonds. Or take a twenty-minute drive to Clear Lake and get into the swim of things. The casual country atmosphere of Big Canyon is conducive to doing simply whatever you please.

Smoking outside only; AC; (main) kitchen privileges; barbecue pit; bring mountain bikes; golf courses and tasting rooms with award-winning wines nearby; double sofa bed in Room A (no charge for use); off-street parking. **KNIGHTTIME PUBLICATIONS SPECIAL RATE: Two nights for the price of one Sunday-Thursday with this book. Brochure available.

ROOM	BED	BATH	ENTRANCE	FLOOR	DAILY RATES	
					S - D	(EP) +
A	1Q	Pvt	Sep	2	$65	
B	1Q	Pvt	Main	2	$65	

27

The Forbestown Bed & Breakfast Inn   (707) 263-7858
825 Forbes Street, Lakeport, CA 95453
(One block from Clear Lake in downtown Lakeport)

Jack and Nancy Dunne are pleased to own Lakeport's first bed and breakfast inn. The 1869 home was built when the town was known as Forbestown. Expert restoration has given the beautiful old home all its original charm. Each of the four luxurious guest rooms is a tasteful creation named after a historical figure of the Forbestown era. (A colorful cast of characters, I might add!) American oak antiques and designer fabrics highlight the decor, and gentle strains of music add to the calm elegance within. Outside, a secluded garden beckons one to relax in a lounge chair or to take a dip in the inviting pool or spa. Hosts can help with arrangements for visiting a gold mine, geothermal steam wells, wineries, and fine restaurants; water recreational equipment may be rented nearby. A rare glimpse of Lake County history coupled with splendid hospitality await you at The Forbestown Bed & Breakfast Inn.

No pets; no children under twelve; smoking outside only; full breakfast; afternoon refreshments; AC; swimming pool; spa; ample street parking; major credit cards; airport pickup (Lampson Field); off-season rates for business travelers. Brochure available.

ROOM	BED	BATH	ENTRANCE	FLOOR	DAILY RATES S - D (EP) +
A	1Q	Shd*	Main	1	$95
B	1K	Shd*	Main	1	$110
C	1Q	Pvt	Main	2	$110
D	1K	Shd*	Main	2	$95

Muktip Manor

(707) 994-9571

12540 Lakeshore Drive, Clearlake, CA 95422
(South shore of Clear Lake)

The home of Jerry and Nadine Schiffman (affectionately known as Muktip Manor) has an Early California charm all its own. The living quarters are all on the second floor, with doors opening onto a wrap-around veranda.   Located opposite the lake, it affords good views and a small, private beach.   The guest unit consists of a bedroom, living room, kitchen, and bath. While not luxurious, the decor is delightfully country. Jerry is a former actor. (Look for him on reruns of *Streets of San Francisco;* he always played a cop or a corpse.) Occasionally he enjoys an evening sail in his catamaran with guests who so choose. Whatever your particular pleasure might be, there's a host of activities to choose from: boating, windsurfing, swimming, canoeing, fishing, rock-hunting, and wine-tasting at Lake County wineries. The lifestyle at Muktip Manor is casual, unpretentious, and laced with humor -- a thoroughly engaging combination.

Cats in residence; no children; pets welcome ($5 extra); full breakfast; TV; kitchen; large deck; canoe available; launch ramp and public fishing piers nearby; ample street parking; airport pickup (Pearce); animal lovers preferred.

ROOM	BED	BATH	ENTRANCE	FLOOR	DAILY RATES
					S - D (EP)
A	1D	Pvt	Sep	2	$50

29

Pebble Beach Bed & Breakfast
1650 Macken Avenue, Crescent City, CA 95531
(Across from state beach)

(707) 464-9086
1(800) 821-9816

Experience an out-of-the-way surprise at this lovely home situated near a beautiful stretch of coastline you might not otherwise discover. Pebble Beach Bed & Breakfast is a quiet and gracious place. Watch sunsets from your room, relax in the guest lounge area, catch up on work at the desk and phone, or join Margaret Lewis for music and a glass of wine. The entire second floor is a suite for guests, with two bedrooms, a lounge, a bath, and an extra bedroom. It's only steps to that gorgeous beach, and Redwood National Park is within a few minutes' drive. Whatever brings you to this northwest corner of California, you'll remember it fondly after a stay at Pebble Beach Bed & Breakfast.

No pets; children by special arrangement; smoking downstairs only; full breakfast; lounge with telephone, desk, and refrigerator; cable TV/VCR; stereo system; CD library; VCR movie library; off-street parking; rate for three or four people, $150.

ROOM	BED	BATH	ENTRANCE	FLOOR	DAILY RATES S - D (EP) +
A	1K & 1Q	Pvt	Main	2	$100

New Davenport Bed & Breakfast   **(408) 425-1818** *or* **426-4122**
Davenport, CA 95017
(Nine miles north of Santa Cruz)

The New Davenport Bed & Breakfast is located in one of Davenport's original old buildings, just across the Coast Highway from the ocean. Four bright, comfortable rooms, furnished with antique beds and oak dressers, are available to B&B travelers. Delicious breakfasts are served in the sitting room and next door at the New Davenport Cash Store (pictured).   Breakfast, lunch, and dinner are served throughout the week. Weekend festivities often include live music and a lively crowd. This landmark also houses a gift and craft gallery. The New Davenport is an ideal getaway from the Bay Area. Though the trip is short, there's a wonderfully remote feeling about the place. And when you don't have to spend hours driving, there's much more time for fun.

No pets; no smoking in rooms; off-street parking; credit cards (V,MC); bus service from Santa Cruz; additional rooms available on the second story of the main (Cash Store) building, most with ocean views; some family rooms available; rates range from $90-$115 for two; 30% midweek discount in winter. Brochure available.

ROOM	BED	BATH	ENTRANCE	FLOOR	DAILY RATES	
					S - D	(EP) +
A	1D	Pvt	Main	1G	$60	
B	1D	Pvt	Main	1G	$70	
C	1Q	Pvt	Main	1G	$75	
D	1D	Pvt	Main	1G	$70	

An Elegant Victorian Mansion   (707) 444-3144 *or* 442-5594
1406 C Street, Eureka, CA 95501
(Convenient to downtown and Old Town attractions)

"An Elegant Victorian Mansion" -- that's what a local newspaper reported in 1888 when this Queen Anne-influenced Eastlake Victorian was being built for two-term Mayor and County Commissioner William S. Clark. The prestigious home, restored in every exquisite detail by owners Doug and Lily Vieyra, offers a glimpse of history, luxurious accommodations, and bountiful hospitality. Three individually decorated guest rooms feature beautiful antiques and artwork and enough amenities to make one feel totally pampered. Guests are invited to use the library, parlors, and sitting room as they wish. Lily's talents in the garden rival her skills in the kitchen; her roses are beautiful, as are palate-pleasing breakfasts and ice cream sodas. She and Doug want to bring alive the most gracious aspects of living at the turn of the century, to be a genteel, civilizing influence in an all-too-fast-paced world. They succeed marvelously.

No pets; no children under fifteen; no smoking; full breakfast; Finnish sauna; massage available; TV/VCR; stereo; robes provided; refrigerator; complimentary laundry service; bicycles available; secured off-street and garage parking; French and Dutch spoken; credit cards (V,MC); corporate and winter discounts. Brochure available.

ROOM	BED	BATH	ENTRANCE	FLOOR	DAILY RATES S - D (EP) +
A	1Q	Shd*	Main	2	$70-$80
B	1Q	Shd*	Main	2	$80-$90
C	1Q & 1T	Pvt	Main	2	$115-$125 ($35)

Old Town Bed & Breakfast Inn
1521 Third Street, Eureka, CA 95501
(Third near P, east end of Old Town district)

(707) 445-3951
1(800) 331-5098

Built in 1871, this historic home is one of the few remaining Greek Revival Victorians in the area. It was the original home of the local lumber baron until he built the Carson Mansion. Then it was moved to its present location, just a block and a half from the Mansion. Hosts Leigh and Diane Benson have kept the spirit of the past alive by furnishing the inn with antiques of the period. They've added their own whimsical touches, such as a teddy bear on each bed and rubber ducks and bubble bath for the clawfoot tubs. The result of their labors is the quintessential bed and breakfast inn. After a stroll around Old Town, relax by the fireplace in the Raspberry Parlor. Complimentary afternoon tea or wine and award-winning chocolates by the bedside await you. In the morning, sample one of Diane's country breakfast creations such as Eggs Derelict or Lumber Camp Breakfast Pie and homemade biscuits and jams. Old Town Bed & Breakfast Inn's warm atmosphere and convenient location will make your stay in Eureka a memorable experience.

Cats in residence; no pets; children over ten welcome; full breakfast; afternoon refreshments; outdoor hot tub on private patio; off-street parking; all major credit cards; extended stay and business traveler discounts; new guest wing features two deluxe accommodations with private baths, each $100-$125.

ROOM	BED	BATH	ENTRANCE	FLOOR	DAILY RATES S - D (EP) +
A	1K or 2T	Pvt	Main	2	$90-$100
B	1Q	Shd*	Main	2	$65-$75
C	1Q	Shd*	Main	2	$65-$75
D	1D	Pvt	Main	2	$70-$80
E	1Q	Pvt	Main	1	$95-$105

A Weaver's Inn   **(707) 443-8119**
1440 B Street, Eureka, CA 95501
(Convenient to downtown and Old Town attractions)

    Weaver Dorothy Swendeman and her husband Bob are the proud owners of one of Eureka's fine turn-of-the-century homes, built in 1883. Surrounded by a profusion of gardens and a picket fence, the inn has an authentic warmth created by old Victorian colors, handcrafted artworks, antique furnishings, and gracious, caring hosts. As a guest, you're invited to experiment with the looms, use the spinning wheel by the fireplace, enjoy sweet repose in a garden setting, or simply make yourself at home wherever you choose. Beautifully appointed accommodations include one room with a Japanese soaking tub in the bath, another that's perfect for a solo traveler, and an elegant suite. In the formal dining room or the sunlit porch, the Swendemans try to serve breakfast fare that "you won't get at home" -- just one aspect of their generous hospitality.

    Children and pets by arrangement; smoking outside only; full breakfast; sofa bed also in suite; fireplace in living room; piano in parlor; Japanese garden retreat; croquet on the lawn; major credit cards; off-street parking. Brochure available.

ROOM	BED	BATH	ENTRANCE	FLOOR	DAILY RATES	
					S - D	(EP) +
A	1Q	Pvt	Main	2	$70	
B	1K or 2T	Shd*	Main	2	$65	
C	1D	Shd*	Main	2	$45-$60	
D	1Q	Pvt	Main	2	$85	($15)

Karen's Bed & Breakfast Yosemite Inn   **1(800) 346-1443**
P.O. Box 8, Fish Camp, CA 93623
(Off Highway 41, two miles from south entrance to Yosemite)

Nestled in the trees in a quiet and lovely setting, this inn was built
with special attention to the needs of guests visiting Yosemite and
environs. Each room, delicately decorated in either soft pink, blue, or
peach, is fully carpeted, has a full ensuite bath, individual tempera-
ture control, and woodland view. Guests have their own entrance and
a sitting room with a gas fireplace and stocked teacart all to themselves; they are also welcome to enjoy the main living room, which
has a wood-burning stove, for visiting or for watching TV or videos.
Full breakfasts by candlelight are featured at Karen's. She helps
guests to sort out all the options Yosemite offers in each glorious
season; also close at hand are Bass Lake, the Mariposa Grove of Giant
Sequoias, and the unforgettable Scenic Narrow Gauge Railroad excur-
sion route. Nearby dining experiences range from simple to grand.
All the elements of a perfect holiday await you at Karen's Bed &
Breakfast Yosemite Inn.

Cat in residence; no pets; smoking outside only; full breakfast;
TV/VCR; off-street parking. Brochure available.

ROOM	BED	BATH	ENTRANCE	FLOOR	DAILY RATES	
					S - D	(EP) +
A	2T	Pvt	Sep	2	$80-$85	($15)
B	1Q	Pvt	Sep	2	$80-$85	($15)
C	1Q	Pvt	Sep	2	$80-$85	($15)

Old Stewart House Inn
511 Stewart Street, Fort Bragg, CA 95437
(Parallel to and one block west of Highway 1)

(707) 961-0775

Local historians can pinpoint where Fort Bragg got its start: Its premiere residence was built in 1876 by Calvin Stewart, founder of the lumber mill that is still the anchor of the area's economy. The three-story charmer, trimmed in blue, stands at the corner of Stewart and Pine, just a stone's throw from the Skunk Train Station (offering daily trips through the redwoods to Willits), Main Street restaurants, and the beach. In recent years, the house has been restored as a B&B by Darrell Galli. He has kept the Victorian flavor of the early days, carrying out a different theme in each room -- Queen Anne, European, Rose, and Garden. There is a private, romantic hot tub room for two, and separate family accommodations are available in the Carriage House (E). Darrell and Mondra have found myriad ways to cater to guests in this historic landmark.

Smoking outside only; full breakfast; common rooms, fireplace, TV/VCR available; hot tub room; off-street and street parking; Italian spoken; limited wheelchair access; major credit cards; off-season rates. In Room E, EP rate is for adults; 2T are bunk beds. Brochure available.

ROOM	BED	BATH	ENTRANCE	FLOOR	DAILY RATES S - D (EP)	
A	1Q	Pvt	Main	2	$95	
B	1Q	Pvt	Main	2	$85	
C	1Q	Pvt	Main	2	$75	
D	2T	Pvt	Sep	1	$65	
E	1Q & 2T	Pvt	Sep	1	$95	($15)

Rancho Kaeru   Reservations: (714) 894-5635
14452 Birmingham Drive, Westminster, CA 92683
(24180 Juniper Flats Road, Homeland; about five miles west of Hemet off Highway 74)

Glenn and Sharon Nakadate take refuge from their busy lives in
Orange County at their desert hideaway, Rancho Kaeru. In a terra
cotta landscape of mountains, valleys, and clear blue skies, the home
was built in the thirties by a man who created an exact replica of a
stone farmhouse he had seen in France. The original slate roof, finely
crafted woodwork and stonemasonry, walls three feet thick, and marvelous fireplaces add character and contribute to the comfortable
climate inside. The home's charming rusticity is augmented by beautiful antique and nostalgia pieces, plus all the comforts one could want
to enjoy either a brief getaway or a true vacation. Guests may choose
between two spacious, well-separated suites, and it is a tough deci-
sion! Outdoors, explore the twenty acres with its natural spring and
ponds, one of the largest eucalyptus trees in California, a profusion of
flowers and exotic fruit trees, and a night sky blanketed with stars.
It's hard to believe that just an hour or so from L.A. or Orange
County, the tranquil beauty of Rancho Kaeru awaits.

No pets; no children under ten; no smoking; full breakfast; home-
cooked dinners at extra charge by arrangement; VCR; ponds with
geese and ducks on property; Temecula wineries, good restaurants,
Ramona Outdoor Play (Hemet), Orange Empire Railway Museum
(Perris), air sports (Perris and Hemet), golfing, fishing, and factory
outlet shopping in vicinity; ample parking; one-night stays, $10 extra.
Information sheet available.

ROOM	BED	BATH	ENTRANCE	FLOOR	DAILY RATES S - D (EP)
A	1Q	Pvt	Main	1G	$75 ($20)
B	1Q	Pvt	Main	1G	$75

Wilkum Inn
(909) 659-4087

P.O. Box 1115, Idyllwild, CA 92549
(In mountains above Palm Springs at 26770 Highway 243)

That at-home feeling greets you as you enter Wilkum Inn. The warmth of pine, lace curtains, quilts, an organ, a large river rock fireplace, and cozy places to sit makes you want to don a bathrobe and curl up with a good book. The guest rooms are comfy and full of personality, too. One is on the main floor; others on the second floor include the Eaves, a two-room suite. Need a totally separate space where you can hole up in wooded seclusion? Try the inn's most private quarters: a self-catering unit (E) with its own entrance, kitchen, and loft. Wherever you stay, you'll be surrounded by trees and mountain vistas. And for your culinary pleasure, innkeepers serve an expanded Continental breakfast that might include crepes, Dutch babies, cheese-stuffed French toast, or *aebleskivers*.

No pets or smoking; some robes provided; complimentary beverages and snacks; hiking trails, a rock climbing school, Idyllwild School of Music and Arts, and good restaurants nearby; off-street parking; two-night minimum for Room E; discounts for two or more nights and for single travelers. Brochure available.

ROOM	BED	BATH	ENTRANCE	FLOOR	DAILY RATES S - D (EP) +
A	1D	Pvt	Main	1	$80
B	1Q	Pvt	Main	2	$85
C	1Q	Shd*	Main	2	$75
D	1K or 2T	Shd*	Main	2	$80
E	1Q	Pvt	Sep	2	$95

38

Rosemary Cottage
(415) 663-9338

75 Balboa Avenue, P.O. Box 619, Inverness, CA 94937
(Just south of village and west of Sir Francis Drake Boulevard)

A wall of windows overlooks a dramatic sylvan scene -- a sunlit wooded gulch that is sanctuary to many wild birds of the Point Reyes National Seashore. You lie on the deck at night and marvel at stars that never seemed so bright before. A romantic French-country cottage is your own private hideaway; luxuriate in its seclusion and the beauty surrounding it. Designed and built by owners Suzanne and Michel, Rosemary Cottage is about fifty yards through a forest from their home. It has many handcrafted details, a wood-burning stove, a full kitchen, and space that will comfortably sleep four. Under an old oak tree, the large deck overlooks an herb garden. It is a marvelous setting for alfresco meals. Settle into quiet relaxation or take off to enjoy the beaches, hiking trails, and prolific wildlife of the Seashore. Rosemary Cottage is near it all -- in a world of its own.

Families welcome; full breakfast; off-street parking; Spanish spoken; $35 extra for one-night stay on weekends; $15 discount to Knighttime readers Sunday-Thursday nights, not including holiday weeks or July and August.

ROOM	BED	BATH	ENTRANCE	FLOOR	DAILY RATES S - D (EP) +
A	1Q & 2T	Pvt	Sep	1	$115 ($15)

Terri's Homestay
P.O. Box 113, Point Reyes Station, CA 94956
(83 Sunnyside Drive, Inverness Park)

(415) 663-1289
1(800) 969-1289

High atop Inverness Ridge in a remote, "above it all" location adjoining Point Reyes National Seashore is Terri Elaine's comfortable redwood home. Here guests have plenty of space and privacy in quarters that include a large bedroom with a sitting area, a private bath, separate entrance, wood-burning stove, deck access, and an amazing view over ridges of Bishop pine toward the sea. Guatemalan artwork and fabrics add zest to the natural environment. Feel like exploring? Take a hike to the top of Mount Vision for a rewarding panorama; spend some time on secluded, bluff-lined beaches; see how many different species of wildlife you can spot. In the evening, enjoy a soak in the ozone-purified outdoor spa. To round out a thoroughly relaxing holiday, schedule a massage by Terri or her partner, who practice a variety of disciplines. This quiet, sunny spot offers an array of pleasures you won't soon forget.

Dogs on premises; children and outdoor dogs welcome; no smoking; expanded Continental breakfast; hammock, CD player, and futon in room; massage by appointment for one or two at a time (massuer also on hand); ample street parking; inquire about midweek, off-season, and extended stay rates.

ROOM	BED	BATH	ENTRANCE	FLOOR	DAILY RATES S - D (EP) +
A	1Q	Pvt	Sep	1	$100-$115($15)

The Wedgewood Inn
(209) 296-4300
11941 Narcissus Road, Jackson, CA 95642   **1(800) WEDGEWD**
(Six and one-half miles out of Jackson, off Highway 88)

Just ten minutes from bustling Jackson but hidden in a forested setting, The Wedgewood Inn comes as a heady discovery. The stunning Victorian replica is endowed with treasures collected over a lifetime by Vic and Jeannine Beltz. They have lovingly arranged each antique, collectible, family heirloom, objet d'art, handmade Victorian lampshade, and work of stained glass in its perfect place to create a rich haven of turn-of-the-century charm. Each romantic guest room has a distinct character expressed by colors, fabrics, furnishings, and nostalgia pieces. Three rooms have clawfoot tubs, balconies, and wood-burning stoves. A parlor grand piano carved in Austria graces the living room while beautiful tapestries enhance the formal dining room. Jeannine varies the table settings and the elaborate breakfast specialties that guests savor each morning. Vic and Jeannine offer a gracious welcome and a most comfortable stay in their dream-come-true, The Wedgewood Inn.

Cocker spaniel (Lacey) in residence; no children; smoking outside only; full breakfast; AC; terraced garden park with pathways, rose arbor, gazebo, fountains, hammocks, and croquet; off-street parking; credit cards (V,MC); Mobil Travel Guide 3-star rating. Lodging in Carriage House, two-room suite, $130; EP $20. Brochure available.

ROOM	BED	BATH	ENTRANCE	FLOOR	DAILY RATES	
					S - D	(EP) +
A	1D	Pvt	Main	2	$75-$85	
B	1Q	Pvt	Main	2	$80-$90	
C	1Q	Pvt	Main	3	$90-$100	
D	1Q	Pvt	Main	2	$95-$105	
E	1Q	Pvt	Main	2	$105-$115	

Mountainside Bed & Breakfast   **1(800) 237-0832**
P. O. Box 165, Kelsey, CA 95643
(Eight miles north of Placerville, off Highway 193)

   At the top of the Georgetown Divide between the South and Middle
Forks of the American River is the rustic family home of Mary Ellen
and Paul Mello. These former educators take pleasure in sharing their
comfortable abode on eighty acres of wooded paradise with guests
who always leave as friends.   There are decks galore and many
windows that take in a 180-degree view of the foothills and valley.
The Mellos have deep roots in the area and are most knowledgeable
about its wealth of outdoor recreation and mining history.   Three
pleasant guest rooms on the main floor have private baths. A large,
pine-paneled attic space with its own bath and deck can sleep up to
eight people. Weddings, receptions, and group functions work well at
Mountainside Bed & Breakfast, as do romantic holidays and family
vacations. Outstanding hospitality and country living at its best await
you at this wonderful mountain retreat.
   No pets; smoking outside only; full breakfast; TV, fireplace, and
piano in large parlor; hot tub; credit cards (V,MC); $5 discount to
Knighttime readers. Brochure available.

ROOM	BED	BATH	ENTRANCE	FLOOR	DAILY RATES S - D	(EP) +
A	1Q	Pvt	Main	1	$70	
B	1Q	Pvt	Main	1	$70	
C	1Q	Pvt	Sep	1	$75	
D	1K, 1Q, 4T	Pvt	Main	2	$75	($15)

Eagle's Landing
Box 1510, Blue Jay, CA 92317
(In San Bernardino Mountains on west shore of lake)

(909) 336-2642

This ingeniously designed home offers all the comfort and charm of a European mountain retreat, with many extra special touches. Finely crafted woodwork, plenty of view windows, and elements of Victorian styling make me think of a luxury tree house in a romantic Alpine setting. Each guest room is unique; all are private, quiet, and tastefully appointed with antiques, art, and handcrafted furnishings. Refreshments are served on a spacious deck or in the Hunt Room by a roaring fire, both with fantastic views of the lake. Breakfast at Eagle's Landing is a memorable event in the "Top of the Tower." Hosts Dorothy and Jack Stone provide unparalleled hospitality and attention to detail. In every respect, Eagle's Landing is a masterpiece.

No pets, children, or smoking; TV in Hunt Room; Room A has private deck; boutique shopping, ice skating, fine dining, and quaint towns of Blue Jay and Arrowhead Village nearby; off-street parking; credit cards (V,MC); also available is a 900-square-foot suite with fireplace, queen bed, TV, stereo, king sofa bed, and expansive lake view at $175; inquire about midweek discounts. Brochure available.

ROOM	BED	BATH	ENTRANCE	FLOOR	DAILY RATES	
					S - D	(EP) +
A	1Q	Pvt	Sep	3	$125	
B	1K	Pvt	Main	3	$95	
C	1K	Pvt	Main	2	$115	

43

Salisbury House
2273 West 20th Street, Los Angeles, CA 90018
(Near Santa Monica Freeway and Western Avenue)

(213) 737-7817
1(800) 373-1778

Experience a cozy kind of luxury at Salisbury House, located in the historic West Adams district of Los Angeles. Here you'll find all the amenities of a manor house in the country, yet you'll be only minutes from downtown and major freeways. This turn-of-the-century California Craftsman home is large and sturdy. An expert restoration job has left its original integrity intact. Graciously proportioned rooms are exquisitely furnished with antiques and collectibles. Colors, fabrics, and nostalgia pieces are imaginatively combined to give each room a distinct personality. The total effect is enchanting. The generous breakfasts served here are superb, the hospitality boundless. Hosts Sue and Jay invite you to treat yourself to the many charms of Salisbury House. I can't imagine a more relaxing or romantic intown spot.

No pets; smoking on porch only; full breakfast; sink in Room A; D is a 600-square-foot Attic Suite; E is a Sun Room Suite; ample street parking; major credit cards; inquire about weekly and monthly rates. Brochure available.

ROOM	BED	BATH	ENTRANCE	FLOOR	DAILY RATES S - D (EP) +
A	1Q	Pvt	Main	2	$90
B	1Q	Shd*	Main	2	$75
C	1Q	Shd*	Main	2	$75
D	1K & 1T	Pvt	Main	3	$100 ($10)
E	1D & 2T	Pvt	Main	2	$90 ($10)

Finch Haven Bed & Breakfast　　　Phone/FAX: **(209) 966-4738**
4605 Triangle Road, Mariposa, CA 95338
(1.6 miles off Highway 140)

Bruce and Carol Fincham offer two completely private, separate guest accommodations on the lower level of their quiet country home, where panoramic mountain views and visiting wildlife may be admired from one's own private patio or from the large, flower-studded upper deck. Each room -- the Bluebird and the Morning Glory -- has a tasteful, pretty, well-put-together decor that features an original work of art. Each also has a nook for drink and snack preparation. Tasty, nutritious breakfasts are served in your own quarters, on the upper deck, or in the upstairs kitchen. Hosts provide freshly ground coffee from an award-winning local coffee roasting company; guests are invited there for tours and tastings. Bruce, formerly a park ranger in Yosemite, can provide helpful, interesting tips for exploring the area, but be sure to allow enough time just to sit and stare at the view!

Smoking outside only; extended Continental breakfast; AC; picnic grounds, tennis courts, and community swimming pool at nearby town park; Yosemite Valley, Mariposa Grove of Giant Sequoias, important points of gold rush history, and California State Mining and Mineral Museum in area; ample parking; airport pickup (Mariposa County). Brochure available.

ROOM	BED	BATH	ENTRANCE	FLOOR	DAILY RATES S - D	(EP) +
A	2T	Pvt	Sep	1G	$65	($10)
B	1Q	Pvt	Sep	1G	$65	($10)

The Pelennor   **(209) 966-2832** *or* **966-5353**
3871 Highway 49 S, Mariposa, CA 95338
(Five miles south of Mariposa at Bootjack)

Dick and Gwen Foster follow the Scottish tradition of offering simple, low-cost accommodations, which are in a newer building adjacent to their home. They can provide tips on enjoying the area, a bit of hospitality, and even some bagpipe tunes on request. Hosts are pipers in two central California pipe bands; Dick and Gwen occasionally get out the telescope for some stargazing. No other B&B that I know of specializes in "Stars and Pipes," but guests who have sampled this unique combination are not likely to forget it. Each morning the Fosters serve what they term "a solid breakfast." For informal lodgings just off the main route of the Mother Lode and a short hour's drive from Yosemite, The Pelennor makes a welcome stop for the passing traveler.

Hosts have dogs, cat, and cockatiels; other animals roam the property; smoking outside only; lap pool; spa; sauna; kitchen in guest building available on a "you use, you clean" basis; off-street parking; at most, two rooms share one bath; two extra bedrooms in main house available as needed; available for outdoor weddings. Brochure available.

ROOM	BED	BATH	ENTRANCE	FLOOR	DAILY RATES S - D (EP)
A	1Q	Shd*	Sep	2	$35-$45 ($10)
B	1Q	Shd*	Sep	2	$35-$45 ($10)
C	1D	Shd*	Sep	2	$35-$45 ($10)
D	2T	Shd*	Sep	2	$35-$45 ($10)

Restful Nest Bed & Breakfast Resort   (209) 742-7127
4274 Buckeye Creek Road, Mariposa, CA 95338
(Five miles from town center, off Highway 49 S)

Many people use Mariposa as a home base for exploring Yosemite, but if you stay at the Restful Nest, it is possible to have a complete holiday right there, so try to allow enough time for both. Amidst beautiful mountain scenery, you may swim in the pool; fish in the pond; take a hike; have a barbecue or picnic; play tetherball, basketball, volleyball, or horseshoes; see a movie; or watch birds, including some rare species. Two accommodations comprise the ground floor of the main house, and another is in a private guest house next door. Each offers abundant space and privacy, plush carpeting and cushy places to sit, original oil paintings, and each is equipped with a microwave oven, a coffee and tea center, a fridge, and a TV/VCR with movies. Hugette and Armand Dubord are French Canadian, and the old-fashioned country breakfasts that Hugette prepares have a definite French influence. At the Restful Nest, you'll find a friendly atmosphere where your every need is catered to; leaving completely refreshed is virtually guaranteed.

Miniature poodle in residence; friendly lab outdoors; smoking on patio only; full breakfast; TV/VCR; swimming pool; fishing pond; picnic areas; barbecue facilities; various games; ample parking; major credit cards; French spoken; two-night minimum; AAA approved. Brochure available.

ROOM	BED	BATH	ENTRANCE	FLOOR	DAILY RATES
					S - D (EP) +
A	1Q	Pvt	Sep	1G	$65-$75 ($10)
B	1Q	Pvt	Sep	1G	$65-$75 ($10)
C	1Q	Pvt	Sep	2	$85 ($10)

47

Shiloh Bed & Breakfast (209) 742-7200
3265 Triangle Park Road, Mariposa, CA 95338
(Two and one-half miles off Highway 49 S)

The exact age of the original old farmhouse that is now Shiloh Bed
& Breakfast isn't known, but it has weathered well. In a peaceful
clearing surrounded by tall Ponderosa pines, cedars, and oaks, the
house has a screened front porch and a sun porch where breakfast is
often served. Just inside are a vintage country kitchen and a large,
full guest bathroom with shiny log walls. Up the stairway are two
adorable guest rooms with sloped ceilings, rustic woodwork, and a
gentle, cheery theme for each: Quilt and Sunflower. Accommodations
are fully carpeted just as they are in the Guest House (pictured) next
door. It is a self-contained unit, very roomy and private, with a
kitchen and sleeping space for up to five adults or four adults and two
children. From this quiet mountain retreat, a small country market
and a superb dining spot are just a short walk away. Hosts Ron and
Joan Smith, long-time residents and experienced hikers, can offer
many suggestions for enjoying the area.

Outdoor cats on property; no pets; smoking outside only; TV in
Quilt Room and Guest House; swimming pool; cot also in Room B;
sofa bed also in Guest House (C); ample parking; credit cards
(V,MC); off-season rates. Brochure available.

ROOM	BED	BATH	ENTRANCE	FLOOR	DAILY RATES S - D	(EP) +
A	1K	Shd*	Main	2	$65	($10)
B	1K	Shd*	Main	2	$55	($10)
C	2Q	Pvt	Sep	1	$85	($10)

Shirl's Bed & Breakfast (formerly Dick & Shirl's) **(209) 966-2514**
4870 Triangle Road, Mariposa, CA 95338
(Five miles from Mariposa enroute to Yosemite)

Shirl Fiester is quite contented living on her fifteen forested acres. It's a quiet, secluded setting where you can slow down, unwind, and tune in to nature -- most people leave completely refreshed. The home itself is rustic, commodious, and very relaxing. On the main floor, there's an open living area with a large, stone fireplace and cathedral ceilings of warm, polished redwood. An open kitchen is adjacent, and just off the dining area is a guest suite (A) that can be closed off for complete privacy. A cabin (B) on the property provides additional accommodations for up to four people. Large breakfasts and friendly conversation are part of the gracious hospitality to be found here. For country lodging on the way to Yosemite (forty miles away), Shirl's Bed & Breakfast is a fine choice.

Dog and cat in residence; no pets; TV; off-street parking; credit cards (V,MC); rollaway bed available in cabin.

ROOM	BED	BATH	ENTRANCE	FLOOR	DAILY RATES	
					S - D	(EP) +
A	1Q	Pvt	Sep	1G	$70	
B	1Q & 1T	Pvt	Sep	1	$70	($10)

Mendocino Farmhouse   **(707) 937-0241**
P.O. Box 247, Mendocino, CA 95460
(One and one-half miles from Mendocino village)

If you're seeking the quintessential farmhouse in Mendocino for your north coast getaway, look no further. The home of Marge and Bud Kamb provides superb accommodations in the quietest possible setting, so near and yet so far from the busy village scene. Here, there's a permanent warm glow to the interior that feels authentic to the core -- not "decorated." Sloped ceilings, pretty fabrics and rugs, and country antiques give the bedrooms an ambient coziness. Two of the rooms are quite spacious; Room A has a fireplace; a slightly smaller one (C), with a wood-burning stove, is irresistibly romantic. Newer quarters have been added in the converted barn overlooking the garden. Each has a separate entrance and a charm all its own, as well as such inviting features as stone fireplaces, coffee makers, and small refrigerators. In the morning, savor a sumptuous farmhouse breakfast in the sun room of the main house while taking in the views of redwood forest, beautiful gardens, a pond, and a meadow. The aura of this lovely home makes an indelible impression on those fortunate enough to stay here.

Children or pets by arrangement; smoking outside only; full breakfast; sofa sleeper extra in Room B; off-street parking; credit cards (V,MC).

ROOM	BED	BATH	ENTRANCE	FLOOR	DAILY RATES S - D	(EP) +
A	1K	Pvt	Main	2	$90-$95	($15)
B	1Q	Pvt	Main	2	$80-$85	($15)
C	1Q	Pvt	Main	2	$90-$95	($15)
D	1Q	Pvt	Sep	1	$100-$105	($15)
E	1Q	Pvt	Sep	1	$100-$105	($15)

The Goose & Turrets Bed & Breakfast   **(415) 728-5451**
P.O. Box 370937, Montara, CA 94037-0937
(Twenty-five miles south of San Francisco; one-half mile from beach)

Proximity to the Bay Area, a colorful history, and natural beauty
that hasn't been overtaken by development make the coastal hamlet of
Montara an ideal country escape. Raymond and Emily Hoche-Mong
welcome guests to The Goose & Turrets -- built around 1908 in the
Northern Italian villa style -- with "creature comforts, bonhomie, and
solitude." The wonderful old building has been refurbished and decorated to reflect the hosts' myriad interests and world travels. Each of the
five guest rooms has been fashioned with taste and imagination featuring
German down comforters, English towel warmers, and bathrobes. Step
out back to the old-fashioned gardens and "chat" with the resident
mascot geese, play bocce ball, hike down to beaches and rocky coves,
or lounge about at The Goose & Turrets where you can lose yourself in
a good book or practice the art of doing absolutely nothing.

No pets; smoking outside only; four-course breakfast; afternoon
tea; common room with woodstove, piano, game table, tape deck, and
eclectic library; Room A has sitting area with woodstove; Room E has
ecologically correct fireplace; major credit cards; French spoken;
airport pickup by host/pilots (Half Moon Bay, San Carlos, Palo Alto)
by prior arrangement; also, pickup for sailors at Pillar Point Harbor at
Princeton; twenty minutes from San Francisco International Airport.
Brochure available.

ROOM	BED	BATH	ENTRANCE	FLOOR	DAILY RATES S - D (EP) +
A	1Q	Pvt	Main	1	$100
B	1Q	Pvt	Main	1	$85
C	1Q or 2T	Pvt	Main	1	$90
D	1K	Pvt	Main	1	$90
E	1D	Pvt	Main	1	$85

Montara Bed & Breakfast   (415) 728-3946
P.O. Box 493, Montara, CA 94037
(Twenty-five miles south of San Francisco; one-half mile from beach)

Bill and Peggy Bechtell have remodeled their inviting country home to include a private guest suite on two floors. The bedroom, attractively decorated in a seaside motif, opens onto a redwood deck where you might catch a bit of morning sun. Upstairs, a sitting room has a woodstove and a distant view of the ocean through the trees. A full breakfast is served in a solarium overlooking the garden and waterfalls. This rustic, cozy retreat is just moments away from beaches, seaside dining, historic Montara Lighthouse, Fitzgerald Marine Reserve, and miles of hiking trails at the largely undiscovered McNee Ranch State Park. Other Coastside towns to the south offer further pleasures. The Bechtells want you to enjoy your privacy while feeling very much at home during your stay at Montara Bed & Breakfast. No problem.

Dog on premises; no children or smoking; full breakfast; ample street parking; credit cards (V,MC); airport pickup (Half Moon Bay); twenty minutes from San Francisco International Aiport; two-night minimum on weekends; seventh consecutive night free.

ROOM	BED	BATH	ENTRANCE	FLOOR	DAILY RATES S - D (EP)	
A	1K or 2T	Pvt	Sep	1	$80-$95	($20)

Ocean Villa Bed & Breakfast (415) 728-5417
P.O. Box 370971, Montara, CA 94037-0971
(Twenty-five miles south of San Francisco; one and one-half miles from beach)

You'll traverse some back roads leading away from the ocean and coastal Montara to reach Ocean Villa. Anticipation builds and is soon rewarded by your arrival at the Hollands' impressive bed and breakfast retreat. The massive white contemporary home with Spanish red tile roof and arresting views of sea and countryside is set on a hillside and has two-and-one-half acres of grounds. The luxurious B&B room is unimaginably huge. It has a cathedral ceiling, arched windows framing the stunning views, a king-sized brass bed plus an extra twin bed, a living area, TV, dining table, refrigerator, and even a pool table. You enter through the garden and ascend the stairway to this marvelously secluded hideaway. Breakfast, featuring eggs from the resident chickens, is delivered to your room at your convenience. At Ocean Villa, cares melt away, pressures cease, and your time is your own for a thoroughly relaxing country sojourn.

No pets; children welcome; full breakfast; smoking outside only. Information sheet available.

ROOM	BED	BATH	ENTRANCE	FLOOR	DAILY RATES S - D (EP)
A	1K & 1T	Pvt	Main	2	$95 ($10)

Frank & Virginia Hallman   **(510) 376-4318**
309 Constance Place, Moraga, CA 94556
(Five miles from Orinda BART station and Freeway 24)

At the Hallmans' Moraga home, you can have the best of both worlds while visiting the Bay Area. You can take off to "do" San Francisco in the ideal (car-less) fashion, then scoot back across the bay to the quiet luxury of this tastefully appointed home. The Hallmans will see that you have all the restorative comforts you need. There's a large pool and Jacuzzi spa in a private garden setting. Guest rooms are particularly pleasing. Moraga is usually sunny and is centrally located to many places of interest in the Bay Area. Hosts will help you find your way to the City, Berkeley, Napa Valley, Muir Woods, and elsewhere.

No pets or young children; no smoking preferred; full breakfast served at guests' convenience; robes provided; TV in each room; swimming pool; spa; living room with fireplace for guests; two miles from St. Mary's College, five from JFK University, ten from UC Berkeley, twelve from Mills College; network of hiking trails through Moraga and Lafayette, as well as other East Bay regional parks, nearby; bus and BART service; airport connections from San Francisco and Oakland; street parking; inquire about weekly and family rates.

ROOM	BED	BATH	ENTRANCE	FLOOR	DAILY RATES S - D (EP)
A	1Q	Shd*	Main	1G	$60
B	1Q	Shd*	Main	1G	$60

Ward's "Big Foot" Ranch B & B   **(916) 926-5170**
P.O. Box 585, Mount Shasta, CA 96067
(1530 Hill Road; two miles northwest of downtown Mount Shasta)

After their careers as educators in Saratoga, Barbara and Phil Ward returned to Phil's native Mount Shasta in 1980. Now they can bask in the glory of the splendid mammoth mountain every day; their rural ranch-style home is nestled among tall cedars and firs, but is situated for maximum views. A huge wrap-around deck is the scene of summer breakfasts, weather permitting. The beautifully maintained ranch has the feeling of a luxury resort with home-like warmth. There are two lovely guest rooms in the main house. The Wards are fond of entertaining and cooking for guests. (Phil's delicious *aebleskivers* have become a tradition.) On starry nights, gazing through a telescope from the deck is a sparkling experience. A restful atmosphere, generous hosts, and unprecedented views of Mount Shasta are yours at Ward's "Big Foot" Ranch.

Outdoor pets include dogs, llamas, and a burro; no visiting pets, please; full breakfast; refreshments; TV; living room for guests; trout stream; walking trails; horseshoes; Ping-Pong and croquet in summer; off-street parking. ****KNIGHTTIME PUBLICATIONS SPECIAL RATE: 10% discount with this book.** Informative brochure available.

ROOM	BED	BATH	ENTRANCE	FLOOR	DAILY RATES	
					S - D	(EP) +
A	1K	Pvt	Main	1	$65-$70	($10)
B	1Q	Pvt	Main	1	$55-$60	

Anna's Bed & Breakfast **(818) 980-6191**
10926 Hamlin Street, North Hollywood, CA 91606
(Two miles north of Hollywood Freeway)

Anyone desiring a quiet little spot convenient to some of L.A.'s main arteries (Ventura, Golden State, and Hollywood Freeways) will be pleased to discover Anna's Bed & Breakfast. It's a neat, Spanish-style bungalow offering one guest room attractively done in shades of blue. Anna's European background and love of travel are apparent in the decor. She enjoys serving breakfast in her delightful backyard garden on pretty days. From Anna's, it's a thirty-minute drive to downtown L.A. and just seven minutes to popular Universal Studios. Nearby Burbank offers a choice of new and noteworthy restaurants. For convenience, value, and homey accommodations, this B&B is a find.

Dog in residence; no children under twelve; no smoking; extra charge for full breakfast; fireplace, TV/VCR in living room; off-street or street parking; German spoken; inquire about weekly rates.

ROOM	BED	BATH	ENTRANCE	FLOOR	DAILY RATES S - D (EP)
A	1D	Shd	Main	1	$35-$40

Jessie & Pete Taylor (510) 531-2345
59 Chelton Lane, Oakland, CA 94611
(Oakland Hills)

The Taylors love sharing their home, which is set on a quiet lane in the hills above Oakland and the San Francisco Bay. Here you'll be assured of a gracious welcome and a good night's rest -- but that's only the beginning. For these generous-spirited hosts, taking special care of guests is a top priority. Two lovely guest rooms and a bath on the lower level of the house can be closed off for an extra measure of privacy. You may have breakfast on the front deck enclosed by a soothing Japanese garden, or on the rear deck facing the bay. View jewel-like San Francisco by night from your bedroom, the living room, or the deck. Three islands (Yerba Buena, Alcatraz, and Angel) and two bridges (Bay and Golden Gate) are visible by day. Need I say more?

Full breakfast; TV; decks; two parties traveling together may share the bath or use an additional bath at the top of the stairs; inquire about street parking; two-night minimum.

ROOM	BED	BATH	ENTRANCE	FLOOR	DAILY RATES S - D	(EP)
A	2T	Pvt	Main	LL	$35-$45	($10)
B	1D	Pvt	Main	LL	$35-$45	($10)

Tudor Rose Bed & Breakfast   **(510) 655-3201**
316 Modoc Avenue, Oakland, CA 94618
(Oakland Hills, off Broadway Terrace)

Anglophiles, rejoice! Corinne Edmonson keeps her memories of things British alive in the decor of the private guest quarters in her home. A large space with its own entrance, fireplace, sitting area, bath, and mini-kitchen occupies the second level of this three-level home in upper Rockridge overlooking San Francisco Bay. A certain English coziness is created by forest green carpeting, Laura Ashley wallpaper, and treasures from the Mother land. To this comfortable haven add the convenience of being near shopping areas, numerous restaurants, major hospitals, and public transportation (bus, BART, and ferry), and you have an ideal home base in the Bay Area.

No pets; no smoking preferred; cable TV; mini-kitchen; guests welcome on lovely deck; ample street parking. Brochure available.

ROOM	BED	BATH	ENTRANCE	FLOOR	DAILY RATES S - D (EP)
A	1Q	Pvt	Sep	2	$55-$65

The Inn at Shallow Creek Farm   **(916) 865-4093**
4712 Road DD, Orland, CA 95963
(North end of Sacramento River Valley; three miles west of I-5)

Who'd ever guess that just three miles away -- and worlds apart -- from I-5 you'd find a haven like The Inn at Shallow Creek Farm? The ivy-covered turn-of-the-century farmhouse is the centerpiece of this 3.5-acre citrus orchard where chickens, ducks, geese, and guinea fowl roam freely. It was revived in the early eighties by Kurt and Mary Glaeseman. The house and the hospitality have a genuine old-fash-ioned quality. Common rooms solely for guests' use include a large living room with a fireplace, a sitting room overlooking the orchard, and a cheery dining room. A large, airy suite on the first floor offers space and privacy; two nostalgic rooms on the second floor are perfect for two couples. A separate four-room cottage offers extra privacy. It has a wood-burning stove, a sun porch, and a full kitchen. In every season, The Inn at Shallow Creek Farm delights city-weary folks who relish its quiet rural atmosphere.

No pets; smoking outside only; full breakfast featuring farm fresh eggs and produce; guest refrigerator; excellent area for walking, cycling, exploring, birdwatching, stargazing, and photography; poul-try, produce, and homemade jams and jellies available for purchase; off-street parking; French, German, and Spanish spoken; credit cards (V,MC); airport pickup (Orland). Brochure available.

ROOM	BED	BATH	ENTRANCE	FLOOR	DAILY RATES	
					S - D	(EP)
A	1Q	Pvt	Main	1	$65	
B	1Q	Shd*	Main	2	$55	
C	2T	Shd*	Main	2	$55	($15)
D	1Q	Pvt	Sep	1	$75	($15)

59

Adella Villa   **(415) 321-5195**
P.O. Box 4528, Palo Alto, CA 94309   **FAX: 325-5121**
(Thirty miles south of San Francisco between I-280 and U.S. 101)

   Surround yourself with old-world luxury when you enter this pri-
vate, one-acre country estate.   The spacious, pale pink, twenties
Italian villa offers tranquility in a park-like setting of beautiful gar-
dens with a fountain, a koi pond, and a solar-heated swimming pool.
Inside, guests may enjoy a variety of common areas: the Fireside
Room, with fireplace, large-screen TV/VCR and selected videos, and
shiatsu massage lounge chair; the Dining Room, featuring an antique
Louis XVI dining set; the Music Room, accented by a mahogany
Steinway antique baby grand piano.   Each tastefully appointed guest
room is exceptional for its comfort and its singularity.   The Grey
Room has a Jacuzzi tub; the French Room has a French deep soaking
tub with Jacuzzi; the Champagne Room has a kitchenette and its own
entrance overlooking the pool.   To stay at Adella Villa is to "Go First
Class."
   No pets; no children under twelve; smoking outside only; full
breakfast; refreshments always available; radio, telephone, TV, and
sherry in each room; laundry room, dry cleaning, copier, and FAX
machine available; swimming pool; patio; bicycles; off-street parking;
major credit cards.   **KNIGHTTIME PUBLICATIONS SPECIAL
RATE: 10% discount with this book.   Brochure available.

ROOM	BED	BATH	ENTRANCE	FLOOR	DAILY RATES S - D (EP)
A	1Q	Pvt	Main	1	$105
B	1Q	Pvt	Main	1	$105
C	1Q	Pvt	Sep	LL	$105

Creekside Guest Cabin
(415) 879-0319

P.O. Box 478, Pescadero, CA 94060
(Adjacent to Butano State Park)

A narrow country road winds its way into Butano Canyon and a small community of homesites alongside Butano Creek. Here, nestled in the ferns and redwoods, the Rynders' creekside cabin offers respite from the hectic pace of today's world. Bob and Jane have recently enlarged the cabin's living area and created a new dining space overlooking a private garden. A new kitchenette is fully equipped for easy meal preparation. A bedroom with a queen-sized bed has an adjacent bathroom, and a twin sofa unit provides extra sleeping in the living room. At your leisure, peruse the eclectic collection of books, magazines, tapes, CDs, and movies on hand. Redwood beams and panelling, together with soft, restful colors, bamboo blinds, easy-living furnishings, and a pot-bellied woodstove on a brick hearth contribute to an atmosphere especially conducive to rest, relaxation, and a good night's sleep. From the cabin, a creekside trail leads to Butano Falls, a half-mile upstream. An eight-mile drive takes you to the ocean and the lovely beaches of San Mateo County's south coast. In nearby Pescadero, country markets and fruit stands can supply your larder. And some very good local restaurants can handle your dining out needs.

No pets; children over ten welcome; TV/VCR; AM/FM-CD-tape player; charbroiler; sun deck; heated community swimming pool nearby; one-night stays, $10 extra; two-night minimum on holiday weekends; inquire about extended stays.

ROOM	BED	BATH	ENTRANCE	FLOOR	DAILY RATES S - D (EP)
A	1Q & 2T	Pvt	Sep	1G	$85-$95 ($20)

The Country House   **(415) 663-1627**
P.O. Box 98, Point Reyes Station, CA 94956
(On Mesa overlooking village of Point Reyes Station)

On an acre at the end of a quiet street where old-time houses share
the landscape, The Country House stands surrounded by an apple
orchard and English-style flower gardens. You'll get a wonderful
view of Inverness Ridge from the property, as well as frequent
glimpses of resident wildlife. The Main House itself exudes a casual,
let-your-hair-down version of "Welcome home!" A hearth with a
wood-burning Franklin stove is the focal point of the spacious living
area that includes the dining area and kitchen. Cook pots hang from
the open rafters, and an old Oriental rug covers the floor by the stove
-- a heartwarming, comfortable scene. The Main House is reserved as
a unit and can accommodate either a romantic twosome or a larger
party. There are two antique-furnished bedrooms with queen beds and
private baths. Located in a separate wing is the Sunday Best Suite,
with fireplace and private bath. There is a queen bed in a loft with a
picture window view. You will be treated as a favored house guest in
Ewell McIsaac's relaxing country retreat.

No pets; children welcome; smoking outside only; full breakfast;
cable TV; Tomales Bay, villages of Point Reyes Station and Inverness,
and many the many natural wonders of the Point Reyes National
Seashore nearby; off-street parking; excellent for families and reun-
ions; extended stay rates. Brochure available.

ROOM	BED	BATH	ENTRANCE	FLOOR	DAILY RATES	
					S - D	(EP) +
A	2Q	2 Pvt	Main	1G	$100	($15)
B	1Q	Pvt	Sep	1G	$85	($15)

Thirty-nine Cypress　　　　　　　　　　　**(415) 663-1709**
P.O. Box 176, Point Reyes Station, CA 94956
(Near Point Reyes National Seashore)

Thirty-nine Cypress is on 3.5 acres of land a mile north of the village of Point Reyes Station. Drive down the long driveway, park, and walk through a rose-covered arch into a secret garden. The house itself is on a bluff overlooking a 500-acre ranch, the upper reaches of Tomales Bay, and the ridge that is the beginning of the Point Reyes National Seashore. Host Julia Bartlett has cleverly tucked an inviting spa halfway down the bluff where, while you're soaking, you can watch cattle graze and egrets and herons hunt. The valley is part of a major flyway and, particularly during fall and winter, the site of lots of bird activity. The house is natural and rustic. The redwood walls are hung with original art, and there are shelves of books and a cozy reading corner for rainy days. The antiques and aging Oriental rugs are from Julia's family home in Illinois. Breakfast is served in front of sliding glass doors that are open in fine weather.

Gardens; patios; spa; off-street parking; credit cards (V,MC); mid-week rates, $5 less.

ROOM	BED	BATH	ENTRANCE	FLOOR	DAILY RATES	
					S - D	(EP) +
A	1Q	Pvt	Main	1G	$120	($20)
B	1D	Pvt 1/2	Main	1G	$100	($20)
C	1Q	Pvt 1/2	Main	1G	$110	($20)

The Faulkner House   **(916) 529-0520**
1029 Jefferson Street, Red Bluff, CA 96080
(North downtown area)

Its setting beside the Sacramento River and the diverse styles of Victorian architecture to be found here make Red Bluff a unique community. It's also the home of the William Ide Adobe, where California's first and only president lived. A great place to stay while soaking up some local history is The Faulkner House, a gracious Queen Anne home on a quiet, shady street where you'll find four inviting guest rooms and a hospitable welcome from Mary and Harvey Klingler. The decor for each room is exactly fitting and the look uncontrived, like an elegant lady aging ever so gracefully. The Arbor Room has a European carved bedroom set, while the sunny Wicker Room has an iron bed and wicker accessories. The Tower Room is small but charming, and the spacious Rose Room features a brocade fainting couch. A satisfying and relaxing stop is certain to be yours at The Faulkner House.

No pets or children; smoking outside only; AC; fireplace; ample street parking; major credit cards; airport pickup (Red Bluff, Redding). Brochure available.

ROOM	BED	BATH	ENTRANCE	FLOOR	DAILY RATES S - D (EP) +
A	1D	Pvt	Main	2	$53-$55
B	1Q	Pvt	Main	2	$73-$75
C	1Q	Pvt	Main	2	$78-$80
D	1Q	Pvt	Main	2	$78-$80

Palisades Paradise   (916) 223-5305
1200 Palisades Avenue, Redding, CA 96003   1(800) 382-4649
(Central Redding, at edge of Sacramento River)

The name Palisades Paradise isn't an exaggeration. What else would you call a beautiful, newly decorated contemporary home of exceptional comfort with a panoramic view of city lights and river bluff? From the Sunset Suite (B), glass doors open onto a patio with a garden spa where you can watch day turn to evening and soak your cares away. Both the suite and the Cozy Retreat (A) are restful indeed, with soft, muted colors and comfortable beds. The work of some local artists adds to the pleasant decor. Gail Goetz welcomes business and pleasure travelers, making them feel totally at home in the relaxed atmosphere of her Palisades Paradise.

Small dog in residence; children welcome when reserving both rooms; no smoking in bedrooms; living room with fireplace, wide-screen TV and VCR; AC; spa; off-street parking; credit cards (AE). Brochure available.

ROOM	BED	BATH	ENTRANCE	FLOOR	DAILY RATES S - D (EP) +
A	1D	Shd*	Main	1G	$60
B	1Q	Shd*	Main	1G	$70

Ruth Simon & Hy Rosner   **(510) 237-1711**
2723 Esmond Avenue, Richmond, CA 94804-1375
(Off San Pablo Avenue)

In this quiet Richmond neighborhood, a new contemporary home that fits in agreeably with the older homes around it was recently built. The lot is small, but the house was cleverly designed to seem spacious inside. The owners are Ruth Simon, a writer and seismologist, and Hy Rosner, who's retired. Their home is filled with books, art, and music, making the ambiance one of civility and comfort. The large upstairs guest room is light and airy, with a crewel-embroidered bedspread, a sofa bed, and a private half-bath. While you're in Richmond, explore picturesque Point Richmond Historical District. All the bridges across San Francisco Bay are visible from the waterfront, and you'll find some beautifully restored buildings and good restaurants there as well.

No pets or smoking; TV; VCR; crib and single rollaway bed available; shared full bath; garden hot tub; swimming at nearby municipal indoor pool; good public transportation; ample street parking; two-night minimum.

ROOM	BED	BATH	ENTRANCE	FLOOR	DAILY RATES S - D (EP)
A	1D	Pvt 1/2	Main	2	$30-$35 ($5)

Abigail's   **(916) 441-5007**
2120 G Street, Sacramento, CA 95816
(Central downtown location)

Besides being at the pulse of California politics and government, Sacramento is a pleasant city in which to live, to vacation, or to do business. Manageable in size and layout, it is also rich in history, culture, and dining opportunities. On a tree-lined street graced with fine old mansions, Abigail's opens its doors to those seeking a refined, home-like atmosphere in a most convenient location. Guests are welcomed into the large, attractive living room of the beautifully maintained 1912 Colonial Revival mansion. A fireplace, comfortable places to sit, and a spirit of friendliness help to put one at ease. A particular charm distinguishes each lovely guest room: Solarium, Uncle Albert, Aunt Rose, Anne, and Margaret. Delicious breakfasts featuring a different entree each morning are served in the sunny dining room. The neighborhood is great for walking; it's a snap to find your way to the state Capitol and other important attractions. Innkeepers Susanne and Ken Ventura offer an oasis of hospitality in the midst of the bustling city.

Two cats in residence; no pets; older children by arrangement; smoking outside only; full breakfast; AC; rollaway bed available; games and piano available; garden patio with hot tub; public transpo-ration and airport connections; off-street parking; all major credit cards; single midweek rates. Brochure available.

ROOM	BED	BATH	ENTRANCE	FLOOR	DAILY RATES S - D (EP) +
A	1Q	Pvt	Main	2	$95
B	1Q	Pvt	Main	2	$105
C	1Q	Pvt	Main	2	$115
D	1K	Pvt	Main	2	$135 ($35)
E	1Q	Pvt	Main	2	$135 ($35)

The Studio   **(916) 481-1142**
P.O. Box 1574, Carmichael, CA 95609
(5346 Kenneth Avenue, in Sacramento suburb of Carmichael)

Open the wrought iron gate, go a few steps on the walkway alongside the home of Mary Lucile and Bruce Johnson, and you're in for a beautiful surprise. Tucked back from the older, established residential street is The Studio, a caramel-hued garden hideaway filled with fine art, books, antiques, and soothing comfort. The quiet and private space features a sitting area, a unique bathroom that opens out to a hidden patio, a fully-equipped kitchenette, and a queen-sized bed made up with fine linens. Guests also have access to a handsome library, a desk, a phone, and a word processor (by arrangement). Artists or writers in need of a restorative getaway or a tranquil haven in which to work will find The Studio a nurturing shelter; business travelers or vacationers will find it an ideal home base while in the Sacramento area.

No pets; smoking outside only; full breakfast served in library or on patio; AC; lots of games and books; 5-minute walk to bus, then light rail into town (30 minutes total); airport pickup by arrangement; two-week maximum stay.

ROOM	BED	BATH	ENTRANCE	FLOOR	DAILY RATES S - D (EP)
A	1Q	Pvt	Sep	1G	$65

Judy's Bed & Breakfast (707) 963-3081
2036 Madrona Avenue, St. Helena, CA 94574
(One-half mile west of Main Street, or Highway 29)

You'll get a warm, wine-country welcome at Judy's. Bob and Judy
Sculatti have enjoyed their vineyard setting for many years. They've
converted a spacious, private room at one end of their home to a B&B
accommodation of great charm and comfort.   The large space is
furnished with lovely antiques, Oriental rugs, and a romantic brass
bed. There is also a wood-burning stove with a glass door. Complimentary beverage and cheese are offered upon your arrival. Breakfast
is served in your room or outside by the pool. Judy's is a gracious
place to return to after a day of touring and tasting. To round out your
perfect day, dine at one of the Napa Valley's superb restaurants.

No pets; no smoking preferred; TV; AC; off-street parking; Italian
spoken. **KNIGHTTIME PUBLICATIONS SPECIAL RATE: 10%
discount with this book. Brochure available.

ROOM	BED	BATH	ENTRANCE	FLOOR	DAILY RATES S - D (EP) +
A	1Q	Pvt	Sep	1G	$85

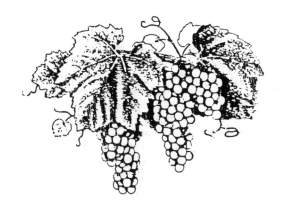

Judy's Ranch House   **(707) 963-3081**
701 Rossi Road, St. Helena, CA 94574
(Just west of Silverado Trail in Conn Valley)

The Sculatti family operates an additional B&B home on the opposite side of the Napa Valley but just as accessible to it. The spacious, comfortable California ranch-style home is situated on seven acres with a three-acre Merlot vineyard. Everywhere you look, there are idyllic views of the Conn Valley countryside. Guests have use of an inviting living room with fireplace and TV, a large country kitchen, and a Jacuzzi spa -- a marvelous place to unwind while watching cattle, deer, and quail feed in neighboring pastures and vineyards. Relax on the front patio, which looks out upon century-old oak trees lining a seasonal creek. Each bedroom has a ceiling fan, air conditioner, private bath, and hillside view. Your hosts can help you with plans for enjoying the Napa Valley's many attractions.

Farm animals on property; no pets; smoking outside only; round-the-clock hot beverages available; Jacuzzi spa; ample parking. **KNIGHTTIME PUBLICATIONS SPECIAL RATE: 10% discount with this book. Brochure available.

ROOM	BED	BATH	ENTRANCE	FLOOR	DAILY RATES S - D (EP)+
A	1K or 2T	Pvt	Main	1G	$105
B	1Q	Pvt	Main	1G	$95

Mario & Suellen Lamorte   **(415) 456-0528**
45 Entrata Drive, San Anselmo, CA 94960
(Walking distance from central San Anselmo)

To stay at the Lamortes' three-story brown-shingled house is to savor the taste of old Marin. It's on a quiet, tree-lined lane that was cut into a hillside long ago; from here, the views of the hilly terrain are a visual feast. The lower floor of the house is a private guest suite that can accommodate up to four people. Natural wood paneling and floors, Oriental rugs, unique paned windows, and a curved redwood sleeping alcove give the interior a warm rustic charm. French doors lead to a private deck where sunlight filters through a canopy of fruit and oak trees. The home is within walking distance of fine restaurants, shops, hiking trails, and lakes. San Anselmo is less than an hour from the wine country and Point Reyes National Seashore, yet only fourteen miles from the Golden Gate Bridge. Whether you plan to do the town or explore the country, the Lamortes' is a good place to start.

Children welcome ($10 extra for one or two); no smoking; full breakfast; kitchen; TV; phone; rollaway bed available; off-street parking; Italian spoken.

ROOM	BED	BATH	ENTRANCE	FLOOR	DAILY RATES	
					S - D	(EP)
A	1D & 1T	Pvt	Sep	LL	$70	($10)

Bears at the Beach Bed & Breakfast   **(619) 272-2578**
1047 Grand Avenue, San Diego, CA 92109
(Pacific Beach)

Long-time resident Doña Denson welcomes B&B guests to a small vintage complex of lodgings owned for many years by her Aunt Ruth, who collected bears and other stuffed animals. The furry friends stayed on to serve as the welcoming committee, and they delight visitors almost as much as the superb location, just two blocks from the Pacific Ocean and three from Mission Bay. Guest quarters include two lovely bedrooms, Bay and Beach, done in soft pinks and greens with handmade quilts and other comforting touches. A full bath, a refrigerator, a cozy sitting area, and a private patio complete the accommodations. Doña is on hand each morning with a different creative, homemade breakfast. To find a place this quiet, clean, attractively decorated, hospitable, and reasonably priced so near the beach and San Diego's many attractions is remarkable, so don't pass up a visit with the Bears at the Beach!

Children or pets by arrangement; smoking outside only; extended Continental breakfast; robes provided; bicycle and skate rentals nearby; restaurants and nightlife within walking distance; inquire about extra bed; October-May rate, $55; ample street parking. Brochure available.

ROOM	BED	BATH	ENTRANCE	FLOOR	DAILY RATES S - D (EP) +
A	1D	Shd*	Main	1G	$60
B	1Q	Shd*	Main	1G	$60

Blom House Bed & Breakfast　　　　　　**(619) 467-0890**
1372 Minden Drive, San Diego, CA 92111
(Mission Heights)

Its location overlooking Hotel Circle, Fashion Valley Mall, and the intersection of Highways 8 and 163 gives Blom House the advantages of easy access to most any of San Diego's highlights and absolute knockout views from its windows, deck, and hot tub. Only when you step inside this warm, elegant home do you see what a find it is. Enter an invitingly comfortable living and dining area where guests gather for conversation, refreshments, and breakfast; at other times enjoy the expansive deck or hot tub, or spend time ensconced in one of three luxurious suites, tastefully appointed and stocked with every imaginable amenity. For a dreamy, romantic environment, choose the Honeymoon Suite (A) facing the deck. A family or two couples may choose the two-bedroom family suite (B), while visitors in town for an extended stay might settle happily into the split-level Lovers' Suite (C). Bette Blom loves cooking for and pampering her treasured guests.

Small dog in residence; no pets; smoking on deck only; full breakfast; TV/VCR, stocked fridge, and phone in each suite; AC; fireplace in living room; off-street and street parking; from one to three miles to most attractions; Dutch and Spanish spoken; rollaway bed in Room C, $7; Sunday-Thursday night rate, $49; weekend package (two nights), $135. Information sheet available.

ROOM	BED	BATH	ENTRANCE	FLOOR	DAILY RATES	
					S - D	(EP) +
A	1Q	Pvt	Main	1	$75	
B	1Q & 1K or 2T	Pvt	Main	1	$75	($25)
C	1Q	Pvt	Main	1	$75	

Carole's Bed & Breakfast　　　　　　　　　**(619) 280-5258**
3227 Grim Avenue, San Diego, CA　92104
(Near northeast edge of Balboa Park)

　　Host Carole Dugdale is just as keen on preserving her home's history as she is her own. A designated historical site, the 1904 home captures the flavor of the days when San Diego was a "frontier port." Enhanced by a lovely rose garden, the Vernacular Craftsman-style home typically features a gabled dormer roof; leaded glass in some windows; interior wood paneling, ceiling beams, and built-in cabinetry. But it is Carole's appreciation of the past -- her home, interesting antiques, and family mementoes -- that inspired her to create an environment of old-fashioned warmth, comfort, and friendliness. The bedrooms are furnished with queen-sized beds, handmade quilts, and some antiques. Feel free to take a dip in the large swimming pool, play a tune on the piano, or enjoy TV or a movie in the spacious living room. From such a convenient location, you'll explore San Diego with ease.

　　No pets; no children under sixteen; two and one-half baths; ceiling fans; Jacuzzi; walking distance to Balboa Park, zoo, and museums; public transportation; off-street and street parking; Spanish spoken; inquire about reserving Room B with private bath.

ROOM	BED	BATH	ENTRANCE	FLOOR	DAILY RATES S - D　(EP) +
A	1Q	Shd*	Sep	2	$55
B	1Q	Shd*	Sep	1	$55
C	1Q	Shd*	Main	2	$55
D	1Q	Shd*	Main	2	$55

The Cottage   **(619) 299-1564**
3829 Albatross Street, San Diego, CA 92103
(Hillcrest area, near San Diego Zoo)

The Hillcrest area is characterized by old homes and canyons, offering an unhurried, isolated atmosphere. Conveniently located on a quiet cul-de-sac, this private cottage (A) recreates the feeling of a Victorian country home. It is furnished with beautiful antiques, including such pieces as an oak pump organ and an old-time coffee grinder that still works. The accommodation includes a living room with a wood-burning stove, a bedroom, a bath, and a fully equipped kitchen; each is uncommonly charming. The Garden Room (B) is a bedroom in the main house with its own entrance and bath. Your hosts, Bob and Carol Emerick, have thought of everything a traveler might need while in residence, and their vast collection of information about the area is yours to peruse (history, architecture, menus, maps, directions, etc.). If ever a place could inspire affection, The Cottage does just that. You may find yourself returning sooner than you think.

TV; public transportation; inquire about parking; major credit cards. Brochure available.

ROOM	BED	BATH	ENTRANCE	FLOOR	DAILY RATES	
					S - D	(EP) +
A	1K & 1T	Pvt	Sep	1	$65	($10)
B	1K	Pvt	Sep	1	$49	

San Diego Hideaway   (619) 460-2868
8844 Alpine Avenue, La Mesa, CA 91941
(Ten miles east of downtown, between Highways 8 and 94)

After years as B&B hosts, first at The Lamplighters in Downey, then at Magnolia House in Redlands, Jim and Doris Gentry have retired to the quiet, established San Diego suburb of La Mesa. Here they continue their gracious hospitality in the southern tradition. The lower level of the home they call San Diego Hideaway serves as one of the guest accommodations. It is a very large suite with its own den, a bath, and a lovely bedroom -- exceptional for its privacy, comfort, and tranquility. Another attractive bedroom on the main floor has twin beds and a private bath. From the spacious living area, where guests are always welcome, vistas of wide open skies with a mountain backdrop add to the relaxing atmosphere. Furnishings here, as in the rest of the house, lean toward the traditional, with selected antiques and family heirlooms. Enjoy breakfast with a gourmet touch in the formal dining room or the sun room. Fresh flowers and fruit, decanters of wine, and other thoughtful amenities add to the pleasure of staying at the Gentrys' wonderful hideaway.

Small dog in residence; no pets; no children under sixteen; smoking outside only; full breakfast, if desired; afternoon refreshments; 35" TV/VCR available; AC; off-street parking; some Spanish spoken.

ROOM	BED	BATH	ENTRANCE	FLOOR	DAILY RATES S - D (EP)
A	1Q	Pvt	Main	LL	$50-$55
B	2T	Pvt	Main	1	$50-$55

Casa Arguello   (415) 752-9482
225 Arguello Boulevard, San Francisco, CA 94118
(Presidio Heights, between California and Lake)

Mrs. Emma Baires makes her B&B guests feel right at home in Casa Arguello, a large, two-floor flat located in a safe residential area; it's within easy walking distance of shops and restaurants on Sacramento Street, Clement Street, and in Laurel Village. Spacious, immaculate rooms feature brass or iron beds with comfortable mattresses. The view from each room and the artwork adorning the walls are constant reminders that you couldn't be anywhere *but* San Francisco. Casa Arguello celebrates its sixteenth year as a B&B home in 1994, and, not surprisingly, it has more return visitors than ever. People appreciate the cheerful, home-like accommodations that Mrs. Baires so graciously provides.

No pets or smoking; TV in each room; large living room for guests; inquire about street parking; Spanish spoken; good public transportation and airport connections; one-night stays, $5 extra; two-night minimum preferred.

ROOM	BED	BATH	ENTRANCE	FLOOR	DAILY RATES	
					S - D	(EP) +
A	1D	Shd*	Main	3	$55	
B	1K	Shd*	Main	3	$55	
C	1K	Pvt	Main	3	$70	
D	1K	Pvt	Main	3	$72	
E	1T	Shd*	Main	2	$43	

77

The Garden Studio   (415) 753-3574
1387 Sixth Avenue, San Francisco, CA 94122
(Two blocks from Golden Gate Park and U.C. Medical Center)

John and Alice Micklewright are the second owners of this 1910 Edwardian-style home. It is quite handsome in appearance, from the unusual sloped roof to the extensive interior woodwork. The house feels rich, solid, and handcrafted. The Garden Studio is at garden level; it has a separate entrance from the street and a fully carpeted interior. The peach and green color scheme accents the fully equipped kitchen with slate floor and marble counters, and is carried throughout the bath and dressing rooms. The queen-sized iron bed has a down comforter and a cover with a Marimeko green and white motif. The light and airy apartment opens onto a compact city garden with lawn, flowering border, and a private, serene feeling. Well-traveled guests appreciate the attention to detail hosts have shown in providing many conveniences to enhance their stay in the City.

No pets or smoking; no breakfast provided, but neighborhood cafes nearby; TV; iron and ironing board; private telephone (with deposit); rollaway bed; information and maps for neighborhood and City attractions provided; good public transportation and airport connections; inquire about parking; French spoken. Brochure available.

ROOM	BED	BATH	ENTRANCE	FLOOR	DAILY RATES	
					S - D	(EP) +
A	1Q	Pvt	Sep	1G	$65-$70	($10)

The Herb'n Inn   (415) 553-8542
525 Ashbury Street, San Francisco, CA 94117   FAX: 553-8541
(Haight-Ashbury District)

Brother-sister team Pam and Bruce Brennan are proud of their neighborhood's rock 'n' roll roots. The Haight is still a colorful, lively part of the City, and the hosts can guide you to some of its interesting spots. They are glad to own a handsome Victorian in the midst of it all and are taking pains to restore it to its turn-of-the-century grace while adding modern conveniences, such as a beautiful open kitchen/dining area that overlooks an attractive back yard, complete with garden and decking. Herbs growing in the kitchen window enliven the delicious full breakfasts, and the guest rooms are named for four of them: Cilantro, which overlooks the garden; Coriander, a front room that serves as a bridal suite; Rosemary, which has its own sink; and Tarragon, which has a private deck. There are private and shared baths, a variety of bed sizes and decor, and thoughtfully selected quality furnishings. The Brennans' Herb'n Inn is indeed a homey urban retreat.

No pets; smoking outside only; full breakfast; TV/VCR upon request; good public transportation and airport connections; specialized tours arranged; off-street and street parking. Brochure available.

ROOM	BED	BATH	ENTRANCE	FLOOR	DAILY RATES S - D (EP)
A	1Q	Pvt	Main	2	$70-$75
B	1Q	Shd*	Main	2	$60-$65
C	1D	Shd*	Main	2	$60-$65
D	2T	Shd*	Main	2	$60-$65

Moffatt House   **(415) 661-6210**
431 Hugo Street, San Francisco, CA 94122   **FAX: 564-2480**
(Between Fifth and Sixth Avenues near Golden Gate Park)

This pale blue Edwardian home is in close proximity to the popular neighborhood haunts of Ninth and Irving, Golden Gate Park, and U.C. Medical Center. Ruth Moffatt knows the area well and offers assistance with just about anything her guests might need. The four guest rooms are neat and cheerful, with artistic touches in the decor and, typically San Franciscan, shared split baths. The quiet, safe location of Moffatt House makes walking a pleasure -- neighborhood shops, cafes, bakeries, and markets invite browsing. The new exercise discount really pays off in a form most everyone can enjoy. Moffatt House pays a quarter a mile for any running or walking guests do in Golden Gate Park. Yes, Ruth puts the cash right in your hand! Moffatt House puts San Francisco at your feet -- the possibilities are endless....

Cat in residence; kitchen privileges; crib available; one-night stays and late arrivals OK; Spanish, Italian, and French spoken; good public transportation and airport connections; inquire about parking; credit cards (V,MC).

ROOM	BED	BATH	ENTRANCE	FLOOR	DAILY RATES S - D	(EP) +
A	2T	Shd*	Main	2	$39-$49	
B	1D	Shd*	Main	2	$39	
C	1Q & 1T	Shd*	Main	2	$49-$59	($10)
D	1Q	Shd*	Main	2	$49-$59	

Ed & Monica Widburg   **(415) 564-1751**
2007 Fifteenth Avenue, San Francisco, CA 94116
(South of Golden Gate Park and U.C. Medical Center)

The Widburgs' home has an individual charm of its own, both inside and out. Their wide, quiet street is elevated to allow striking views of the ocean and the Golden Gate. The white stucco home and landscaped yard have a look of understated elegance. European and Indonesian art objects, antiques, maps, and family heirlooms fit well into an interior graced with exquisite finishing details. At the front of the main floor, a bedroom and adjacent bath are available to guests. Hosts sleep downstairs, so there's an extra degree of privacy. Large view windows across the back of the house make the dining and living rooms unusually pleasant. The Widburgs' European background contributes to their unfailing graciousness: they are not only well traveled but accustomed to hosting visitors from other countries. Bed and breakfast is a way of life to them, and sharing their special city by the sea is second nature.

No pets, children, or smoking; TV in guest room; European languages spoken; good public transportation and airport connections; ample street parking.

ROOM	BED	BATH	ENTRANCE	FLOOR	DAILY RATES S - D (EP)
A	1Q	Pvt	Main	2	$70-$75

The Palm House   **(415) 573-7256**
1216 Palm Avenue, San Mateo, CA 94402
(A block east of El Camino Real, between 12th and 13th Avenues)

Alan and Marian Brooks have enjoyed creating The Palm House, and they're justifiably proud of it. Built in 1907, it's a picture-book, Craftsman-style home in a quiet residential area of San Mateo. The interior has a warm, European ambiance created by multi-paned windows and dark wooden panels and beams. Some of the stunning works of art on the walls were done by Alan, an accomplished and successful painter. B&B guests are treated to gracious breakfast service and sun-dried, 100% cotton sheets and towels. The Palm House is located within walking distance of shops and restaurants; San Francisco International Airport is a short ride away by bus or taxi. You can get to San Francisco, Stanford University, or the Pacific Ocean in less than thirty minutes, and all can be reached by public transportation. Alan and Marian wish to convey the spirit of British bed and breakfast to their guests -- and you'll see a surprising bit of evidence to prove it.

Children welcome; ample street parking.

ROOM	BED	BATH	ENTRANCE	FLOOR	DAILY RATES S - D (EP)
A	1Q	Pvt	Main	2	$55-$60 ($10)
B	1D	Shd	Main	2	$50-$55
C	1T	Shd	Main	2	$50

Bed & Breakfast at Valli's View   **(805) 969-1272**
340 North Sierra Vista, Montecito, CA 93108
(Foothills of Montecito)

Valerie Stevens has fashioned the house of her dreams in a gorgeous spot. She has reason to be proud: Valli's View is a beauty inside and out. Its ambiance of tranquility and comfort will soothe even the most frazzled nerves. There's a variety of places to relax outdoors -- a spacious patio with lounge chairs, a porch swing, or a deck with a view of the mountains. In the evening, it's a pleasure to sit in the living room around the grand piano and fireplace. Soft-colored fabrics and rich carpeting enhance the charming decor. A choice of tempting breakfasts (using seasonal fruits and vegetables from the garden) may be served to you in bed, on the patio, or by the fireplace. As a guest of Valerie and her husband, Larry, you'll feel that your every need has been anticipated -- a satisfying experience indeed.

No indoor pets or smoking; full breakfast; TV; off-street parking; train or airport pickup (Santa Barbara); seventh consecutive night free.

ROOM	BED	BATH	ENTRANCE	FLOOR	DAILY RATES	
					S - D	(EP)
A	1Q	Pvt	Main	1G	$75	($30)

Ocean View House   (805) 966-6659
P.O. Box 3373, Santa Barbara, CA 93130
(Three blocks from the ocean)

Bill and Carolyn Canfield offer guests an attractive private suite in their home. It has a bedroom, a bath, and an adjoining paneled den with a sofa bed. Interesting books and collections may be perused at your leisure. A generous Continental breakfast featuring fruit from backyard trees is served on the patio, a good vantage point for viewing sailboats and the Channel Islands with a background of vivid blue. Close by are beaches and lovely Shoreline Drive, a popular place for joggers, skaters, cyclists, and sightseers. The harbor and downtown Santa Barbara are within three miles. The playhouse in the back yard is a big favorite with children. If you need a relaxing spot that the whole family can appreciate, Ocean View House has all the necessary ingredients.

Dog and cat in residence; smoking on patio preferred; two TVs; refrigerator; ample street parking; two-night minimum.

ROOM	BED	BATH	ENTRANCE	FLOOR	DAILY RATES S - D (EP)
A	1Q	Pvt	Sep	1G	$55-$60 ($10)

Madison Street Bed & Breakfast   (408) 249-5541
1390 Madison Street, Santa Clara, CA 95050
(Near Santa Clara University and San Jose Municipal Airport)

One doesn't necessarily associate the Santa Clara Valley with historic homes and genteel living, but that is exactly what you'll find at Theresa and Ralph Wigginton's completely restored Victorian on Madison Street. The result of their painstaking work is a unique lodging establishment with turn-of-the-century style and personal service. The high-ceilinged rooms are appointed with wallcoverings of authentic Victorian design, Oriental rugs, antique furnishings, brass beds, and one romantic four-poster. Deluxe breakfasts are served in a dining room that overlooks landscaped grounds with a pool, spa, and barbecue area. Hosts will try to accommodate your business or personal needs; they can arrange for such things as private meetings and intimate, home-cooked dinners. A most pleasant atmosphere for work or relaxation is yours at Madison Street Bed & Breakfast.

No smoking; full breakfast; TV and movies available; sink in Rooms C and D; robes provided; telephones in rooms; dry cleaning services; tantalizing dinners for four to sixteen guests by arrangement; Winchester Mystery House and Great America Amusement Park ten minutes away; ample street parking; major credit cards.

ROOM	BED	BATH	ENTRANCE	FLOOR	DAILY RATES S - D	(EP) +
A	1Q	Pvt	Main	1	$85	
B	1D	Pvt	Main	1	$75	
C	1D	Shd*	Main	1	$60	
D	1D	Shd*	Main	1	$60	
E	1D	Pvt	Sep	LL	$85	

Jasmine Cottage   **(408) 429-1415**
731 Riverside Avenue, Santa Cruz, CA 95060
(Near downtown, beach, and Boardwalk)

The attractions that most people come to colorful Santa Cruz to see -- Pacific Garden Mall (the pulse of downtown), the Santa Cruz Beach Boardwalk, and Santa Cruz Beach -- can all be easily reached on foot from Dorothy Allen's snug little 1910 bungalow, where she offers one comfy, cozy room for guests. Conveniences such as a private bath, stereo, TV/VCR, and phone are appreciated by people traveling for business or pleasure. Dorothy serves complimentary beverages and snacks and the choice of a full or Continental breakfast. Her easygoing, helpful hospitality makes Jasmine Cottage a delighful place to call home while sampling the unique pleasures of Santa Cruz.

No pets; smoking outside only; full or Continental breakfast; TV/VCR; good restaurants, Shakespeare Santa Cruz, Cabrillo Music Festival, theaters, museums, wineries, Santa Cruz Municipal Wharf, UCSC, and more nearby; off-street parking; credit cards (V,MC). Brochure available.

| ROOM | BED | BATH | ENTRANCE | FLOOR | DAILY RATES |
					S - D (EP) +
A	1D	Pvt	Main	1	$45-$60

Felton Crest Guest House (408) 464-1013
780 El Solyo Heights Drive, Felton, CA 95018   FAX: 462-3697
(Off Highway 9)

Felton Crest, a redwood Victorian nestled in an acre of redwoods in the mountains above the San Lorenzo Valley, beckons the true romantic in search of the perfect retreat.   You will be welcomed with champagne, have the option of breakfast in bed, and be left to savor the sweet privacy of your own quarters as well as the outdoor decks. Each spacious guest room is loaded with amenities and has peaceful redwood views; beds are beautifully made up with Battenberg lace coverlets and lots of pillows.   The downstairs Master Suite has a Jacuzzi tub and its own living room. The Treetop Penthouse is a huge space with a vaulted ceiling, ample windows, plush carpeting, a fireplace, a deck, and a big screen projection TV with VCR and many laser discs; the bathtub has a portable Jacuzzi element. Hanna Peters is the caring host at Felton Crest, and she enjoys setting the stage for the ultimate romantic getaway.

Dogs and cats in residence; no pets; smoking on deck only; full breakfast; TV/VCR in each room; interesting mountain towns with shops and good restaurants nearby; off-street parking; *available weekends only.* Brochure available.

ROOM	BED	BATH	ENTRANCE	FLOOR	DAILY RATES S - D (EP) +
A	1Q	Pvt	Main	1	$100
B	1K	Pvt	Sep	LL	$150
C	1K	Pvt	Main	2	$175

Inn Laguna Creek
(408) 425-0692

2727 Smith Grade, Santa Cruz, CA 95060
(In Santa Cruz Mountains, twenty minutes from downtown)

An architecturally unique contemporary home, Inn Laguna Creek is a peaceful retreat set amid coastal redwoods and oriented toward a rippling creek. Fern and wildflower, raccoon and deer, blue jay and hawk may be seen from any of the decks or while meandering through acres of natural gardens surrounding the house. The primary guest area is located on the home's lower level. A cozy sitting room with a wet bar, stereo, VCR, and games separates the two guest rooms, which are spacious, comfortable, and most attractive. Each has a down comforter and a private deck overlooking the creek; there is also a large sun deck with a hot tub just outside the sitting room. The main floor living room, like the rest of the house, is warm and inviting, and you're welcome to come up and help yourself to snacks or beverages or just visit most any time. This floor also features a Master Suite with a private bath, a solarium, and a tiled soaking tub. Hosts Gay and Jim offer a quiet, nurturing environment in the enchanted setting of their redwood mountain paradise.

No pets or smoking; full country breakfast; robes provided; extensive book and video library; hiking along creek or nearby trails; bicycling, beachcombing, whale watching, wine tasting, and more in Santa Cruz area; off-street parking; major credit cards; off-season rates. Brochure available.

ROOM	BED	BATH	ENTRANCE	FLOOR	DAILY RATES S - D (EP) +
A	1Q	Shd*	Main	LL	$95
B	1Q	Shd*	Main	LL	$95
C	1Q	Pvt	Main	1	$125

Valley View
P.O. Box 66593, Santa Cruz, CA 95067
(Santa Cruz Mountains, off State Highway 17)

(415) 321-5195
(Reservations)
FAX: 325-5121

Total privacy and seclusion, a fabulous view, all the comforts of home, and only about a minute from Highway 17 and another twelve from the beaches of Santa Cruz? Indeed. This un-hosted B&B can make your fantasy getaway a reality. The home was designed with many elements of Frank Lloyd Wright's style by his protege, John Taggart. Walls of glass on the back side of the house bring in the beauty of the more than 20,000 acres of redwood forest that the home overlooks. A large deck has the same view, a spa, and comfortable places to relax. The interior features a unique kitchen-in-the-round, mirrored walls, luxurious carpeting throughout, and a large stone fireplace. Imaginatively shaped rooms offer wide vistas of the valley of redwoods. Unwind in country splendor, take a hike along redwood-lined paths, or head for Santa Cruz and the beach. It's all here to be savored by a fortunate few.

No children or pets; smoking outside only; stocked refrigerator, including provisions for a light Continental breakfast; small barbeque; cable TV; stereo; piano; off-street parking; German spoken; major credit cards; house used for one couple at a time; two-night minimum.

ROOM	BED	BATH	ENTRANCE	FLOOR	DAILY RATES S - D (EP)
A	1K	Pvt	Sep	1G	$125

Pygmalion House   **(707) 526-3407**
331 Orange Street, Santa Rosa, CA 95407
(Convenient to downtown and historic Railroad Square)

How fittingly named is Pygmalion House, a rare Santa Rosa survivor of the 1906 earthquake. Once a fading Queen Anne Victorian, it underwent a painstaking transformation to its present beauty. Everything about the home speaks a heartfelt welcome, from the (seasonal) glow of the parlor fire to the presentation of afternoon refreshments to the multi-course breakfast. Most of all, it is Lola Wright who makes her home feel like your home. She is ever ready to help guests in any way and has many who return again and again. Each of five guest rooms, mostly on the ground floor with its own entrance, is an individual creation. Selected antiques and an abundance of handwork -- needlepoint, quilting, embroidery, and lace -- lend warmth and personality to the decor. Pygmalion House, notable for its history and hospitality, is a treasure.

No pets; smoking outside only; full breakfast; AC; showers and clawfoot tubs available; off-street parking; major credit cards. Brochure available.

ROOM	BED	BATH	ENTRANCE	FLOOR	DAILY RATES S - D	(EP) +
A	1Q & 2T	Pvt	Sep	1G	$65-$70	($15)
B	1K	Pvt	Main	1	$65-$70	
C	1Q	Pvt	Sep	1G	$55-$60	
D	1Q	Pvt	Sep	1G	$55-$60	
E	1Q	Pvt	Sep	1G	$55-$60	

Barretta Gardens Inn   **(209) 532-6039**
700 South Barretta Street, Sonora, CA 95370
(Central Sonora)

As you approach this turn-of-the-century gem, you will notice the long, inviting, old-time front porch and lots of foliage. Further exploration of the house and grounds reveals additional delights. Situated at the top of a terraced hillside of gardens, trees, and lawns, Barretta Gardens Inn has various levels and common areas where, even when the inn is full, you are sure to find places for quiet repose. The home's basic integrity has been honored with only the most appropriate furnishings and decorative motif for each room. At the back of the house, the Dragonfly room has two walls of paned windows facing greenery and sunsets and features a stunning water lily and dragonfly stained-glass panel, vintage light fixtures and door hardware, and a wonderful jetted bathtub for two. Another room, Periwinkle, is a Victorian confection in whites and blues with a ten-foot ceiling. Distinctive antiques, fine pieces of silver, and fresh flower arrangements punctuate the decor of the elegant historical home. Early coffee and tea are served by the parlor fireplace, and the breakfast that follows in the formal dining room is truly sensational.

No pets; smoking on front porch only; full breakfast; central AC; porch, solarium, two parlors, gardens (common areas); off-street parking; major credit cards; one-bedroom suite at $105; two-bedroom suite at $215. Full-color brochure available.

ROOM	BED	BATH	ENTRANCE	FLOOR	DAILY RATES S - D (EP) +
A	1Q	Pvt	Main	1	$85
B	1Q	Pvt	Main	1	$95
C	1Q	Pvt	Main	2	$80
D	1K	Pvt	Main	2	$90
E	1Q	Pvt	Main	2	$90

Lavender Hill Bed & Breakfast   **(209) 532-9024**
683 South Barretta Street, Sonora, CA 95370
(Central Sonora)

Set on a hill overlooking town and countryside, Lavender Hill Bed & Breakfast is a turn-of-the-century Victorian with period furnishings and plenty of old-fashioned comfort. Alice Byrnes presides with good humor and an easy manner that make for a relaxing stay. On the main floor there are spacious common areas where guests are welcome, as well as a formal dining room where three-course breakfasts are graciously served. Bedrooms on the second floor vary in size and combine the charm of sloped ceilings, papered walls, quilts, and floral themes. To visit Lavender Hill Bed & Breakfast is to enjoy the unhurried pace and abundant hospitality that make staying here an unqualified pleasure.

No pets or smoking; full breakfast; TV, stereo, books, and games available; porch swing; lawn furniture under shade trees; walk to shops and restaurants; off-street parking.

ROOM	BED	BATH	ENTRANCE	FLOOR	DAILY RATES S - D (EP) +
A	1Q	Pvt	Main	2	$80
B	1Q	Shd*	Main	2	$70
C	1Q	Shd*	Main	2	$70
D	1Q	Pvt	Main	2	$80

Lulu Belle's, A Bed & Breakfast
85 Gold Street, Sonora, CA 95370
(Central Sonora)

(209) 533-3455
1(800) 538-3455

This vintage home captures the many faces of the gold rush days as few places do. Lulu Belle's, circa 1886, is chock-full of character, offering rooms to satisfy a diversity of tastes. In the main house, The Parlor Suite (B) with its theme of red velvet and crystal has the sizzle of a fancy bordello. In the adjacent carriage house, The Calico Room (C) has a cozy, rustic appeal, while the rose-toned Suite Lorraine (E) features four-poster, canopied beds. Full country breakfasts may be served in your private quarters, in the dining room, or outdoors in the garden. Guests find the living area of the main house a warm and welcoming place to gather. Hosts Janet and Chris Miller have taken care to preserve the colorful slice of history that is Lulu Belle's.

No pets; smoking outside only; full breakfast; TV and fireplace in living area; music room with many instruments; AC; walk to shops and restaurants; street parking; some German and Spanish spoken; major credit cards; theater packages and ski discounts.

ROOM	BED	BATH	ENTRANCE	FLOOR	DAILY RATES S - D	(EP) +
A	1Q	Pvt	Sep	1	$70-$85	($20)
B	1Q	Pvt	Sep	1	$80-$95	($20)
C	1Q	Pvt	Sep	1	$70-$85	($20)
D	1K	Pvt	Sep	2	$70-$85	($20)
E	2D	Pvt	Sep	2	$80-$95	($20)

The Blue Spruce Inn   **(408) 464-1137**
2815 Main Street, Soquel, CA 95073
(Edge of Soquel Village, mid-Santa Cruz County)

Located within easy walking distance of antique shops and restaurants of historic Soquel Village, The Blue Spruce Inn is comprised of two fully refurbished neighboring houses. Five individually decorated rooms emphasize Lancaster County quilts, specially commissioned local artwork, and a host of luxurious appointments. Most rooms have their own entrances, and some have private spas and/or gas fireplaces. Enjoy the inn's lovely sitting room with a bay window and a wood-burning fireplace or the private patio garden with a grape arbor and a hot tub -- that is, when you're not out exploring the Monterey Bay Area that stretches from Santa Cruz to Monterey. It's all here: beaches, wineries, shops, hiking trails, quaint coastal towns, and the first-rate hospitality of innkeepers Pat and Tom O'Brien.

No pets; smoking outside only; full breakfast; Spanish spoken; off-street parking; major credit cards; senior and corporate discounts. Brochure available.

ROOM	BED	BATH	ENTRANCE	FLOOR	DAILY RATES S - D (EP) +
A	1Q & 1T	Pvt	Sep	1	$115-$125 ($20)
B	1Q	Pvt	Sep	1	$95-$100
C	1Q	Pvt	Main	2	$75-$80
D	1Q	Pvt	Sep	1	$115-$125
E	1Q	Pvt	Sep	1	$90-$95

Annie's Bed & Breakfast   **(209) 539-3827**
33024 Globe Drive, Springville, CA 93265
(In Sierra foothills off Highway 190)

Annie Bozanich and her husband, John, offer B&B guests something delightfully unusual in lodging. Oh, all the comforts are here in abundance, but then...well...about the hosts...John is a horse trainer and saddlemaker. Annie, who takes dancing lessons, happens to love pigs; her pet, Blossom, who lives in a pen in the side yard, weighs in at around 1,000 pounds and loves to be fed and have her picture taken. The newest addition is Boo, a pot belly pig who performs assorted tricks. When John and Annie had their swimming pool built, they equipped it with spouting fountains all around, inside jets, and a place to install a volleyball net. Staying at Annie's is just plain fun -- and each individually decorated room is just plain gorgeous. Full country breakfasts are beautifully served. Here *everything* is a special treat.

No pets, children, or smoking; full breakfast and afternoon refreshments; swimming pool; golf, fishing, boating, tennis, and hiking nearby; off-street parking; major credit cards; inquire about weddings, receptions, and small business meetings and dinner parties. Brochure available.

ROOM	BED	BATH	ENTRANCE	FLOOR	DAILY RATES S - D (EP)
A	1D	Pvt	Sep	1	$85-$95
B	2T	Pvt	Sep	1	$75-$85
C	1D	Pvt	Sep	1	$75-$85

Chaney House   **(916) 525-7333**
P.O. Box 7852, Tahoe City, CA 96145
(Overlooking west shore of Lake Tahoe)

Few homes around Lake Tahoe possess the unique sense of history that Chaney House has. Some of the Italian stonemasons who built Vikingsholm at nearby Emerald Bay in the twenties also worked on this impressive home. Eighteen-inch-thick stone walls, elaborately carved woodwork, Gothic arches, and a massive stone fireplace reaching to the top of the cathedral ceiling give the interior an old-world European flavor. Stone arches and walls outline the paths around the three patios; on one of these, superb breakfasts are served on mild days. Across the road, enjoy the private pier that juts out into the crystal clear water or take a bike ride on the path alongside the lake; in winter, choose from the many ski areas close at hand. Hosts Gary and Lori Chaney love the territory around them and they are well-versed on its wealth of outdoor and indoor activities for year-round pleasure. Let the warmth of their hospitality enhance your next visit to spectacular Lake Tahoe.

Dog and cat in residence; no pets; children over twelve welcome; smoking outside only; full breakfast; sofa bed extra in Room C; TV/VCR; barbecue; off-street parking; additional lodging in quaint, European-style honeymoon hideaway (D) with kitchen and extra futon; two-night minimum on weekends.

ROOM	BED	BATH	ENTRANCE	FLOOR	DAILY RATES S - D (EP) +
A	1Q	Pvt	Main	1	$95
B	1Q	Shd*	Main	2	$95
C	1K	Shd*	Main	2	$105 ($20)
D	1D	Pvt	Sep	2	$110 ($20)

Chalet A-Capella

(916) 577-6841

P.O. Box 11334, Tahoe Paradise, CA 95708
(Near intersection of Highways 89 and 50)

Richard and Suzanne Capella's chalet-style home blends well with the Alpine scenery that surrounds it. You can go cross-country skiing from the doorstep, drive to a number of ski touring trails or downhill slopes in about thirty minutes, or fish right across the street in the Upper Truckee River. South Shore casinos are a short distance away. The interior woodwork and sloped ceilings of the upstairs guest quarters create a snug, rustic feeling. A bedroom and a private bath are just right for a couple. Summer or winter, Chalet A-Capella is a picture-perfect vacation spot.

No pets; no smoking preferred; TV; deck; off-street parking; Italian spoken; one-night stays, $5 extra; two-night minimum preferred.

ROOM	BED	BATH	ENTRANCE	FLOOR	DAILY RATES S - D (EP)
A	1Q	Pvt	Sep	2	$50

Cort Cottage

(209) 561-4671 *or* **561-4036**

P.O. Box 245, Three Rivers, CA 93271

(East of Visalia, near entrance to Sequoia National Park)

The setting for this B&B is breathtaking. The inviting private cottage with a panoramic view of mountain and sky was built by architect/owner Gary Cort to fit snugly into a hillside near the Corts' home. At sunrise and sunset, colors play off the rocks in a constantly changing show. In the spring, wildflowers bloom in profusion along the path you'll probably want to take down to seasonal Salt Creek. A private outdoor hot tub is located, as Cathy Cort says, "directly under the Milky Way." The cottage is a splendid home base for exploring Sequoia, where you can witness trees that are the largest living things on earth. You'll feel dwarfed by their size and awed by their beauty -- and love every minute of it. Those with an interest in art will want to visit the hosts' Cort Gallery in Three Rivers; it is "dedicated to the ideal that art is a part of every moment."

No pets; smoking outside only (deck); sunken bathtub; kitchen; sofa bed in living room; hot tub; off-street parking; two-night minimum except for last-minute availability.

ROOM	BED	BATH	ENTRANCE	FLOOR	DAILY RATES S - D (EP)
A	1Q	Pvt	Sep	1	$70-$75 ($10)

The Garden Room   **(209)561-4853**
43745 Kaweah River Drive, Three Rivers, CA 93271
(East of Visalia, near entrance to Sequoia National Park)

Set among large oak trees at the end of a private road near the
Kaweah River, The Garden Room is a self-contained guest accommodation that was architecturally designed to blend with the vintage
home of Mike and Celeste Riley. Connected by a breezeway to their
home, the unit was built partially around a large boulder that was
integrated into the design and serves as a base for a free-standing
fireplace. Cascading plants thrive among rocks that extend from the
boulder. The total effect is ingeniously organic, with built-in furnishings and everything perfectly coordinated, from the forest green floral
chintz fabric right down to the dishes. Mike's artistic touches highlight the decor: lovely oil paintings of rural scenes on the walls and
stenciled designs on the wooden doors, dining table, and headboard.
Above the bed, there's a large skylight, and beyond the sliding glass
doors, a rock-enclosed garden patio. The Garden Room was custom-
crafted for comfort; it's a place to bask in country seclusion surrounded by art and nature.

No pets; smoking outside only; full breakfast; TV; patio with
chairs; coffee/tea-making area with small fridge; extra sleeping space
on built-in seating; off-street parking; excellent hiking nearby; summer recreation at Lake Kaweah.

ROOM	BED	BATH	ENTRANCE	FLOOR	DAILY RATES	
					S - D	(EP)
A	1Q	Pvt	Sep	1G	$75	($10)

MICHAEL E. RILEY

Oak Hill Ranch   **(209) 928-4717**

P.O. Box 307, Tuolumne, CA 95379
(Ten miles southeast of Sonora, off Highway 108)

Even though I knew this Victorian ranch home was built in 1980, I had to keep reminding myself that it wasn't here at the turn of the century. Sanford and Jane Grover conceived of the home some thirty-five years ago and began collecting authentic Victorian building materials. Two years of restoring the pieces preceded construction of the home, which was the Grovers' son's senior architectural project in college. Today it stands on fifty-six of the most beautiful acres imaginable. The silence is broken only by the sounds of local fauna, and each room of the home exudes a quietly elegant personality. Oak Hill Ranch is tailored "for a perfect sojourn into the past," to quote an early guest. The superb hospitality offered by the Grovers takes many forms (including a breakfast fit for a gourmet) -- I suggest you relax and enjoy the total experience.

No pets; young people over fourteen welcome; smoking outside only; full breakfast; fireplaces; porches, balcony, and gazebo; bicycles available; hiking trails on and off property; tennis courts and swimming pool nearby; one and one-half hours to Yosemite; off-street parking; airport pickup (Columbia); Victorian honeymoon cottage with fireplace, $115; EP rate with rollaway bed, $18. Brochure available.

ROOM	BED	BATH	ENTRANCE	FLOOR	DAILY RATES S - D (EP) +
A	1D	Shd*	Main	2	$70
B	1Q	Shd*	Main	2	$75
C	1Q	Pvt	Main	2	$85
D	1Q	Pvt	Main	1	$85

Oak Knoll Bed & Breakfast   **(707) 468-5646**
P.O. Box 412, Ukiah, CA 95482
(Seven miles south of Ukiah)

Surrounded by classic wine country scenery of rolling hills and vineyards, Oak Knoll is a contemporary home of generous proportions and sweeping views. Shirley Wadley, a former college music teacher, keeps an immaculate house that's both elegant and comfortable. Guests are invited to enjoy the piano in the living room, a fire in the fireplace and perhaps a movie on the 40-inch screen in the family room, and games, reading, or television in the study/sitting room adjacent to the bedrooms. Snacks and breakfast are often served on the spectacular 3,000 square-foot deck. Oak Knoll's location is central to many attractions: the coast, the redwoods, Lake Mendocino, and wineries of Mendocino County. It's an altogether satisfying bed and breakfast stop.

No pets or children; smoking outside only; TV/VCR; AC; study; deck; off-street parking; airport pickup (Ukiah). Brochure available.

ROOM	BED	BATH	ENTRANCE	FLOOR	DAILY RATES	
					S - D	(EP) +
A	1Q	Shd*	Main	2	$65-$70	
B	1Q	Shd*	Main	2	$65-$70	

Knighttime Bed & Breakfast   **(408) 684-0528**
890 Calabasas Road, Watsonville, CA 95076
(Upper Monterey Bay Area)

Our well constructed custom home is set in a clearing on twenty-six acres of eucalyptus, redwood, and manzanita just a few minutes from the beaches between Santa Cruz and Monterey. Built with conventional wood siding in the style of a New England log home, it has a pitched roof and wide porches. The bright interior is filled with art, pine and walnut cabinetry, and creature comforts. Eclectic furnishings include some antiques as well as reproductions, wicker, and new pieces tucked into inviting nooks and crannies. The main floor has a country French flavor, and the decor of the upper floor -- the guests' private area -- is strongly influenced by shells and the sea. Luscious shades of pink and peach prevail in the sitting room, large bath, commodious bedroom, and second bedroom that can sleep two additional persons in the same party. My husband, Ray, and I enjoy guests from all walks of life.

No smoking; pets by arrangement; off-street parking.

ROOM	BED	BATH	ENTRANCE	FLOOR	DAILY RATES S - D (EP)	
A	1T, 1D, 1Q	Pvt	Main	2	$50-$60	($20)

Howard Creek Ranch   **(707) 964-6725**
P.O. Box 121, Westport, CA 95488
(Three miles north of Westport on Highway 1)

   Sally and Sonny invite you to retreat to the romance of yesteryear at
Howard Creek Ranch. Their ranch house was built in 1872 by Alfred
Howard, newly arrived from the coast of Maine. At one time a
stagecoach stop, it is now a quaint and cozy home filled with collectibles and antiques. The guest suites allow privacy, and the old
fireplace inspires conversation and fun. The house is set in a wide,
secluded valley at the mouth of Howard Creek. It faces the ocean and
a wide, sandy beach where you can walk for miles at low tide. Several
private, handcrafted redwood guest units on the forty-acre property
offer additional accommodations. At this bed and breakfast resort,
you can find your own pace and tune in to the natural beauty all
around you.
   Various animals on property; full ranch breakfast; kitchen privileges by arrangement; barbecue; ornamental pool; hot tub; sauna;
massage by reservation; off-street parking; credit cards (V,MC); sinks
in all guest units; skylights in most units; A has a balcony; Unit D is
a boathouse; E and F are cabins; both have woodstoves and electricity;
off-season and midweek rates. **KNIGHTTIME PUBLICATIONS
SPECIAL RATE: 10% discount with this book. Brochure available.

ROOM	BED	BATH	ENTRANCE	FLOOR	DAILY RATES S - D	(EP) +
A	1Q	Pvt	Sep	2	$95	
B	1K & 1D	Pvt	Sep	1	$95	($10)
C	1Q	Shd	Main	2	$69	
D	1D	Pvt	Sep	1	$95	
E	1D	Pvt	Sep	1	$55	
F	1K & 1D	Pvt	Sep	1	$125	($10)

Coleen's California Casa   **(310) 699-8427**
P.O. Box 9302, Whittier, CA 90608
(Five minutes from I-605; thirty minutes east of downtown L.A.)

   Staying at Coleen Davis's contemporary hillside home is one pleasant surprise after another. Park in front, then make your way through
the lush foliage to the back where you'll find a delightful patio/garden
and the entrance to the private guest quarters. After settling in, join
Coleen on the patio for wine and hors d'oeuvres. After dark you can
view the lights of Whittier, and maybe the fireworks of Disneyland,
from the large front deck (pictured) where ample breakfast specialties
are served. If you're inclined to watch TV, write, or read in bed, the
adjustable king-sized bed in Room A will please you. The Casa is a
quiet retreat where families can share a private space and get all the
help they need to plan a day's adventure in the booming L.A. area.
You may even wind up with a little memento from Coleen to remind
you of your wonderful visit; she's great with surprises.
   No pets; full breakfast; TV, robes in each room; use of fridge and
microwave; off-street parking; wheelchair access; C is a room off
front deck with king bed and sitting room with sofa bed, $85 as a
suite; two-night minimum; one-night stays, $10 extra. Host operates
a B&B reservation service: CoHost, America's Bed & Breakfast, with
listings throughout California.

ROOM	BED	BATH	ENTRANCE	FLOOR	DAILY RATES	
					S - D	(EP)
A	1K	Pvt	Sep	1G	$55	($15)
B	2T	Pvt	Sep	1G	$55	
C	1K	Pvt	Sep	1G	$55	

Redwood House   **(707) 895-3526**
21340 Highway 128, Yorkville, CA 95494
(Twenty miles from Cloverdale and U.S. 101)

I call Redwood House a buried treasure. It's tucked into the woods in a part of the wine country which is currently being discovered -- a real "find." The Hanelts have a private guest cottage that's all redwood and glass. It has a living room with a woodstove, a fully equipped kitchen, a bath, a spiral staircase leading to a sleeping loft, and a screened-in porch. There are views from the cottage of trees, sky, and a creek you can swim or row in during the summer. There are wooded paths to explore, a small children's beach, a dock, and two decks overlooking the creek. The Hanelts take pleasure in sharing this heavenly spot with their guests, whose options include wine-tasting at fine Anderson Valley wineries, side-tripping to the Mendocino coast (thirty-five miles away), or simply settling into the freedom and joy of country living.

Children welcome; no smoking; no breakfast provided; double futon and crib available; fridge, stove, microwave, and dishes in kitchen; sauna; off-street parking; EP rate is for adults; two-night minimum.

ROOM	BED	BATH	ENTRANCE	FLOOR	DAILY RATES
					S - D (EP)
A	1D & 1T	Pvt	Sep	2	$70 ($10)

Sheep Dung Estates   **(707) 894-5322**
P.O. Box 49, Yorkville, CA 95494
(One mile north of Yorkville, two miles off Highway 128)

"With a name like Sheep Dung Estates..." Yes, and it is not just good, but great! Perched on the side of a hill in the company of old oak trees, two new and compact private cottages offer vistas across the coastal range of mountains that surround the Anderson Valley. Here you may bask in sweet isolation from the rest of the world, hike to your heart's content on hosts Anne and Aaron's 160 acres, swim in the pond, or even traverse the old country roads through 3,000 acres of the original sheep ranch. There are wineries, restaurants, and other attractions of the Anderson Valley to explore -- and Mendocino is about forty miles away. But the cottages are so enticing for their functional comfort, serene ambiance, quality craftsmanship, and close proximity to nature that staying put may be the biggest temptation of all. Each cottage has its own private road, a nifty little kitchenette stocked with provisions, a modern bathroom, a wood-burning stove with a tiled hearth, and heavenly views from the bed, sitting area, and porch. Alternative energy sources are used. Sheep Dung Estates offers a unique experience in lodging, to say the least.

Dogs welcome; no smoking; provisions for full breakfast provided; two-night minimum; weekly rate, $375. Brochure available.

ROOM	BED	BATH	ENTRANCE	FLOOR	DAILY RATES S - D (EP)
A	1Q	Pvt	Sep	1	$75

Waldschloss Bed & Breakfast   **(209) 372-4958**
7486 Henness Circle, Yosemite West, Y. N. P., CA 95389
(Midway between Wawona and Yosemite Valley)

Many who visit John and Betty Clark envy their unique location. Surrounded on three sides by the national park, their property is in a private development at 6400 feet, well away from the congestion of the valley yet ideally poised for exploring a variety of wonders. Waldschloss is a beautifully appointed mountain home with two distinctive accommodations. A spacious room done in ivory and lace features a collection of fine old quilts; it has a large bath with oak cabinetry. A detached two-floor suite has a sitting room with a free-standing circular stairway leading to the sleeping quarters: a twin-bedded room with oak and brass furnishings, a ceiling fan, lace curtains, and fluffy bedspreads in ivory, pink, and blue. A full bath completes the suite. Country silence, starry night skies, home cooking, freshly ironed cotton sheets, cozy comforters, a brick fireplace, and old toys tucked discreetly about enhance Waldschloss -- a real Yosemite experience.

No pets; children by arrangement; smoking on deck only; full breakfast; TV/VCR; off-street parking; some German spoken; credit cards (V,MC); *closed December-February*. Brochure available.

ROOM	BED	BATH	ENTRANCE	FLOOR	DAILY RATES	
					S - D	(EP) +
A	1Q	Pvt	Main	1	$78	($15)
B	2T	Pvt	Sep	1 & 2	$88	($15)

The only things I own which are still worth what they have cost me are my travel memories, the mind-pictures of places which I have been hoarding like a happy miser for more than half a century.

—Burton Holmes

The whole object of travel is not to set foot on foreign land; it is at last to set foot on one's own country as a foreign land.

—G.K. Chesterton

Please read "About Dining Highlights" on page *vii*.

ALAMEDA

Courtyard Cafe Gallery, 1349 Park Street; (510) 521-1521; Continental/California

Kamakura, 2549 Santa Clara Avenue; (510) 2549 Santa Clara Avenue; Japanese

Le Bouc Restaurant Francais, 2424 Lincoln Avenue; (510) 522-1300

AMADOR CITY

Ballads, 14220 Highway 49; (209) 267-5403; California

Imperial Hotel, Highway 49; (209) 267-9172; Continental

ANGELS CAMP

Utica Mansion Inn, 1090 Utica Lane; (209) 736-4209; changing eclectic menu

APTOS

Cafe Sparrow, 8042 Soquel Drive; (408) 688-6238; French-style home cooking

Chez Renee, 9051 Soquel Drive; (408) 688-5566; French/Continental

Manuel's, 261 Center Street; (408) 688-4848; casual Mexican

The Veranda, 8041 Soquel Drive; (408) 685-1881; American/California

Palapas, 21 Seascape Village, Seascape Boulevard and Sumner Avenue; (408) 662-9000; Mexican seafood

ARCATA

Folie Douce, 1551 G Street; (707) 822-1042; French/innovative pizzas

BASS LAKE

Ducey's on the Lake, 39255 Marina Drive; (209) 642-3131; varied menu

BEN LOMOND

Ciao Bella!, 9217 Highway 9; (408) 336-9221; Italian

The Tyrolean Inn, 9600 Highway 9; (408) 336-5188; Austrian

BERKELEY

Ajanta, 1888 Solano Avenue; (510) 526-4373; Indian

Cafe at Chez Panisse, 1517 Shattuck Avenue; (510) 548-5525; California

Cafe Fanny, 1603 San Pablo Avenue; (510) 524-5447; fresh, simple breakfasts/lunches

Caffe Venezia, 1799 University Avenue; (510) 849-4681; Italian

The Dining Room, 2086 Allston Way, Shattuck Hotel; (510) 845-9756; American

Enoteca Mastro, 933 San Pablo Avenue, Albany; (510) 524-4822; Northern Italian/ nouvelle Northern California

Fatapple's, 1346 Martin Luther King Jr. Way; (510) 526-2260; American/burgers

Gertie's Chesapeake and Bay Cafe, 1919 Addison Street; (510) 841-2722; Maryland and Louisiana seafood dishes

Ginger Island, 1820 Fourth Street; (510) 644-0444; Asian/California

Kirala Japanese Restaurant, 2100 Ward Street; (510) 549-3486

Lalime's, 1329 Gilman Street; (510) 527-9838; Mediterranean French

Plearn Thai Cuisine, 2050 University Avenue; (510) 841-2148

Rick & Ann's, 2922 Domingo Street; (510) 649-8538; American

Yujean's Modern Cuisine of China, 843 San Pablo Avenue; (510) 525-8557

BIG SUR

Deetjen's Big Sur Inn, Highway 1; (408) 667-2377; vegetarian/fish/meat

Glen Oaks Restaurant, Highway 1; (408) 667-2623; seafood/Continental

Nepenthe, Highway 1; (408) 667-2345; American

BOLINAS

Bolinas Bay Bakery & Cafe, 20 Wharf Road; (415) 868-0211; eclectic menu

BOONVILLE

The Boonville Hotel, Highway 128; (707) 895-2210; California

BOULDER CREEK

Scopazzi's Restaurant & Lounge, 12200 Big Basin Highway; (408) 338-6441

CALISTOGA

All Seasons Cafe & Wine, 1400 Lincoln Avenue; (707) 942-9111; bistro/ wine

Calistoga Inn, 1250 Lincoln Avenue; (707) 942-4101; fresh seafood/American

Valeriano's Ristorante, 1457 Lincoln Avenue, Mount View Hotel; Italian

CAMBRIA

The Brambles Dinner House, 4005 Burton Drive; (805) 927-4716; prime rib/seafood

Ian's Restaurant, 2150 Center Street; (805) 927-8649; American/extensive wine list

Main Street Grill, 603 Main Street; (805) 927-3194; excellent fast food and take-out orders

Robin's, 4095 Burton Drive; (805) 927-5007; breakfast/lunch/dinner/varied ethnic and vegetarian dishes

The Sow's Ear, 2248 Main Street; (805) 927-4865; ribs/chicken/fish

CAPITOLA

Balzac Bistro, 112 Capitola Avenue; (408) 476-5035; informal Continental

Caffe Lido Bar & Ristorante, 110 Monterey Avenue, Capitola Village at the beach; (408) 475-6544; casual Italian

Country Court Tearoom, 911 B Capitola Avenue; (408) 462-2498; breakfast/ lunch/afternoon tea/ brunch served in quaint English/southern style

Coyote Cafe, 201 Esplanade; (408) 479-4695; grill/taqueria

Fiorella's, 911 Capitola Avenue; (408) 479-9826; fine authentic Italian

Gayle's Bakery & Rosticceria, 504 Bay Avenue; (408) 462-1200; baked goods/salads/hot entrees

Masayuki's, 427 Capitola Avenue; (408) 476-7284; sushi/Japanese

Shadowbrook Restaurant, 1750 Wharf Road; (408) 475-1511; Continental

Sophie's, 200 Monterey Avenue; (408) 479-8695; Greek/seafood

CARMEL

Casanova Restaurant, Fifth Street between San Carlos and Mission; (408) 625-0501; country French/Italian

La Boheme Restaurant, Dolores Street near Seventh; (408) 624-7500; country European

L'Escargot, Mission Street at Fourth; (408) 624-4914; French

Pacific's Edge, Highway 1, four miles south of Carmel at Highlands Inn; (408) 624-3801; ocean view fine dining/regional California

Rio Grill, 101 Crossroads Boulevard; (408) 625-5436; creative American

CASTROVILLE

Central Texan Barbecue, 10749 Merritt Street; (408) 633-2285; "A Vegetarian's Nightmare"

La Scuola, 10700 Merritt Street; (408) 633-3200; Italian/Tuscan specialties

CATHEYS VALLEY

The Chibchas, 2747 Highway 140; (209) 966-2940; Colombian/American

COLUMBIA

City Hotel Restaurant, Main Street; (209) 532-1479; nouvelle California

CONCORD

Grissini, 1970-A Diamond Boulevard; (510) 680-1700; Northern Italian

Yvonne Thi's, 2118 Mount Diablo Street; (510) 680-1656; Vietnamese

CORTE MADERA

Il Fornaio, 233 Corte Madera Town Center; (415) 927-4400; Italian

Savannah Grill, 55 Tamal Vista Boulevard; (415) 924-6774; American

DANVILLE

Blackhawk Grille, 3540 Blackhawk Plaza Circle; (510) 736-4295; contemporary Mediterranean

Bridges Restaurant and Bar, 44 Church Street; (510) 820-7200; California with Asian influence

Cafe de Paris, 3407 Blackhawk Plaza Circle; (510) 736-5006; crepes

Faz, 400 South Hartz Avenue; (510) 838-1320; Mediterranean/Greek/Italian

Florentine Restaurant and Pasta Market, 3485 Blackhawk Plaza Circle; (510) 736-6060; Italian

Sen Dai, 101-C Town & Country Drive; (510) 837-1027; Japanese

DAVENPORT

New Davenport Cash Store Restaurant, Highway 1; (408) 426-4122; fresh home cooking, California style

EMERYVILLE

Bucci's, 6121 Hollis Street; (510) 547-4725; Italian

Colors, 59th and Hollis; (510) 655-7100; cafe/rotisserie/Italian

Townhouse Bar & Grill, 5862 Doyle Street; (510) 655-5929; American

EUREKA

Bay City Grill, 508 Henderson Street; (707) 444-9069; light, imaginative meals/casual atmosphere

Bristol Rose Cafe, Eureka Inn, Seventh and G Streets; (707) 442-6441; upscale European cafe

Michael's Steak House, 909 Fifth Street; (707) 443-0877; steaks/prime rib

The Rib Room, Eureka Inn, Seventh and G Streets; (707) 442-6441; Continental

Samurai, 621 Fifth Street; (707) 442-6802; Japanese

The Sea Grill, 316 E Street, Old Town; (707) 443-7187; seafood/steaks

Tomo Japanese Restaurant, 2120 Fourth Street; (707) 444-3318

FISH CAMP

The Narrow Gauge Inn, Highway 41; (209) 683-6446; Continental

FORESTVILLE

Topolos Russian River Vineyards, 5700 Gravenstein Highway North; (707) 887-1562; Greek/California

FORT BRAGG

Egghead Omelettes of Oz, 326 North Main Street; (707) 964-5005

The Wharf, overlooking Noyo Harbor on the Noyo River; (707) 964-4283; seafood/steaks

GREENBRAE

Joe Lo Coco's, 300 Drake's Landing Road; (415) 925-0808; Italian

HALF MOON BAY

San Benito House, 356 Main Street; (415) 726-3425; French/Northern Italian

Pasta Moon, 315 Main Street; (415) 726-5125; homemade pasta and sauces

Waves, 4230 Cabrillo Highway; (415) 726-9500; Northern Italian/pasta/seafood/view dining

HEALDSBURG

Bistro Ralph, 109 Plaza Street; (707) 433-1380; American

Samba Java, 109-A Plaza Street; (707) 433-5282; Caribbean

Tre Scalini, 241 Healdsburg Avenue; (707) 433-1772; fine Italian cuisine

HEMET

Joe's The Sicilian, 41525 East Florida; (909) 766-JOES; Italian

IDYLLWILD

Hidden Village, 25840 Cedar Street; (909) 659-2712; Mandarin Chinese

Pastries by Kathi, 54360 North Circle Drive; (909) 659-4359; specialty bakery/restaurant/breakfast/lunch/rural mountain ambiance

Restaurant Gastrognome, 54381 Ridgeview Drive; (909) 659-5055; elegant dining/fresh fish/steaks/cocktails

INVERNESS

Drake's Beach Cafe, Kenneth C. Patrick Visitor Center, Drake's Beach; (415) 669-1297; grilled fish/oysters/snacks/chowders

Manka's, Argyle at Callender Way; (415) 669-1034; Continental/game

JACKSON

Buscaglia's, 1218 Jackson Gate Road; (209) 223-9992; Italian/American

Teresa's, 1235 Jackson Gate Road; (209) 223-1786; Italian/American

JAMESTOWN

Bella Union Dining Saloon, 18242 Main Street; (209) 984-2421; game dishes and a variety of specials

Michelangelo, 18228 Main Street; (209) 984-4830; Italian trattoria

KELSEYVILLE

Konocti Klines Oak Barrel, 6445 Soda Bay Road; (707) 279-0101; seafood

Lakewood Restaurant & Bar, 6330 Soda Bay Road; (707) 279-9450; French/American

Loon's Nest, 5685 Main Street; (707) 279-1812; American

LAFAYETTE

Spruzzo! Ristorante, 210 Lafayette Circle; (510) 284-9709; Italian

Duck Club, Lafayette Park Hotel; (510) 283-3700; regional American

Miraku, 3740 Mount Diablo Boulevard; (510) 284-5700; Japanese

Tourelle, 3565 Mount Diablo Boulevard; (510) 284-3565; Mediterranean bistro

Uncle Yu's Szechuan, 999 Oak Hill Road; (510) 283-1688

LAKE ARROWHEAD

Casual Elegance, 26848 Highway 189, Agua Fria; (909) 337-8932; American/ Continental

Chef's Inn & Tavern, 29020 Oak Terrace, Cedar Glen; (909) 336-4487; American/Continental

LAKEPORT

Park Place Cafe, 50 Third Street; (707) 263-0444; homemade pasta/on the lake

Rainbow Restaurant & Bar, 2599 Lakeshore Boulevard; (707) 263-6237; American/lake view

LARKSPUR

Lark Creek Inn, 234 Magnolia Avenue; (415) 924-7766; American

LITTLE RIVER

Little River Restaurant, 7750 Highway 1; (707) 937-4945; seafood/ meat/poultry

LIVERMORE

Wente Brothers Restaurant (Champagne Cellars), 5050 Arroyo Road; (510) 447-3696; California/summer concerts

LOS ANGELES

Al Amir, 4356 Woodman Avenue, Sherman Oaks; (818) 784-3469; Middle Eastern

Anarkali Indian Tandoori Restaurant, 7013 Melrose Avenue; (213) 934-6488

Angeli Caffe, 7274 Melrose Avenue; (213) 936-9086; Italian

Authentic Cafe, 7605 Beverly Boulevard; (213) 939-4626; Southwestern

Bice, 301 North Canon Drive; (213) 272-BICE; Italian

Cafe des Artistes, 1534 North McFadden Place, Hollywood; (213) 461-6889; French (simple, bistro-style)

Cafe La Boheme, 8400 Santa Monica Boulevard; (213) 848-2360; California

Cafe Gale, 8400 Wilshire Boulevard; (213) 655-2494; eclectic menu

Cafe Morpheus Bistro & Bakery, 180 North Robertson Boulevard; (310) 657-0527; Franco-Italian

Campanile, 624 South La Brea Avenue; (213) 938-1447; Italian

Cha Cha Cafe, 656 North Virgil Avenue; (213) 664-7723; Caribbean

Chan Dara, 1511 North Cahuenga Boulevard; (213) 464-8585; Thai

Chopstix, 7229 Melrose Avenue; (213) 937-1111; Chinese

Cicada, 8478 Melrose Avenue; (213) 655-5559; country French

El Cholo, 1121 South Western Avenue; (213) 734-2773; Mexican

El Floridita, 1253 North Vine Street; (213) 871-8612; Cuban

El Mercadito, 3425 East First Street, East L.A.; (213) 268-3451; authentic Mexican

Emilio's Ristorante, 6602 Melrose Avenue; (213) 935-4922; Italian

Empress Pavilion, 988 North Hill Street, Chinatown; (213) 617-9898; Chinese

Engine Company Number 28, 644 South Figueroa Street; (213) 624-6996; American

Flora Kitchen, 460 South La Brea Avenue; (213) 931-9900; California

Georgia, 7250 Melrose Avenue; (213) 933-8420; Southern

Giorgio, 114 West Channel Road, Santa Monica; (310) 459-8988; bustling cafe with lighter Italian cuisine

The Greek Connection, 133 North La Cienega Boulevard, Beverly Hills; (310) 659-2271

The Grill on the Alley, 9560 Dayton Way; (310) 276-0615; American

Harold and Belle's, 2920 West Jefferson Boulevard; (213) 735-9918; Creole

Hop Li Restaurant, 526 Alpine Street, Chinatown; (213) 680-3939; Chinese

Il Fornaio Cucina Italiana, 301 North Beverly Drive; (310) 550-8330

Il Piccolino, 641 North Highland Avenue; (213) 936-2996; Italian

Indigo, 8222-1/2 West Third Street; (213) 653-0140; California

Intermezzo, 6919 Melrose Avenue; (213) 937-2875; French

Jake & Annie's, 2702 Main Street, Santa Monica; (310) 452-1734; American

Kachina Grill, 330 South Hope Street; (213) 625-0956; Southwestern

Katsu, 1972 North Hillhurst Avenue; (213) 665-1891; Japanese

Knoll's Black Forest Inn, 2454 Wilshire Boulevard, Santa Monica; (310) 395-2212; German

L.A. Trattoria, 8022 West Third Street; (213) 658-7607; Italian

La Luna, 113 North Larchmont Avenue; (213) 962-2130; Italian

Locanda Veneta, 8638 West Third Street; (310) 274-1893; Italian

Managua, 1007 North Alvarado Street; (213) 413-9622; Central American

Matsuhisa, 129 North La Cienega Boulevard, Beverly Hills; (310) 659-9639; Japanese

McCormick & Schmick's Seafood Restaurant, 600 Hope Place; (213) 629-1929

Mezzaluna, 9428 Brighton Way; (310) 275-6703; Italian

Mon Kee, 679 North Spring Street; (213) 628-6717; Chinese seafood

Monica's on Main, 2640 Main Street, Santa Monica; (310) 392-4956; American

Moustache Cafe, 8155 Melrose Avenue; (213) 651-2111; French

North Beach Bar & Grill, 111 Rose Avenue at Main Street, Venice; (310) 399-3900; old-fashioned steakhouse/contemporary California

The Original Sonora Cafe, 445 South Figueroa Street; (213) 624-1800; Mexican

Paru's Indian Vegetarian Restaurant, 5140 Sunset Boulevard; (213) 661-7600

Pazzia, 755 North La Cienega Boulevard; (310) 657-9271; Italian

Pho 79, 9200 Bolsa Avenue, Westminster; (714) 893-1883; Vietnamese

Plum Tree Inn, 937 North Hill Street; (213) 613-1819; Chinese

Rosalind's, 1044 South Fairfax Avenue; (213) 936-2486; Ethiopian

Rose Cafe and Market, 220 Rose Avenue, Venice; (310) 399-0711; Continental

Rosso e Nero, 7371 Melrose Avenue; (213) 658-6340; Italian

Sher-E Punjab Restaurant, 5370 Wilshire Boulevard; (213) 933-2031; Indian

17th Street Cafe on Montana, 1610 Montana Avenue, Santa Monica; (310) 453-2771; California

Simply Thai, 1850 North Hillhurst Avenue; (213) 665-6958

Tokyo Kaikan, 225 South San Pedro Street; (213) 489-1333; Japanese

West Beach Cafe, 60 North Venice Boulevard, Venice; (310) 823-5396; upscale California

Ye Olde King's Head, 116 Santa Monica Boulevard, Santa Monica; (310) 451-1402; English pub fare

Yamashiro, 1999 North Sycamore Avenue, Hollywood; (213) 466-5125; fine dining with spectacular view/Japanese

Zumayas, 5722 Melrose Avenue; (213) 464-0624; Mexican

LOS GATOS

Andale Taqueria, 21 North Santa Cruz Avenue; (408) 395-8997; light, healthy Mexican

Cafe Marcella, 368 Village Lane; (408) 354-8006; Italian trattoria

Pigalle, 27 North Santa Cruz Avenue; (408) 395-7924; French

Sweet Basil Thai Cuisine, 25 East Main Street; (408) 399-5180

Valeriano's Ristorante, 160 West Main Street; (408) 354-8108; Italian

MARIPOSA

Charles Street Dinner House, Highway 140 and Seventh Street; (209) 966-2366; Continental

Ocean Sierra, 3125 Triangle Road; (209) 742-7050; varied menu

MENDOCINO

Bay View Cafe, Main Street; (707) 937-4197; breakfast/lunch/dinner/ocean view

Chocolate Mousse Cafe, 390 Kasten Street; (707) 937-4323; eclectic menu

MacCallum House Restaurant and the Grey Whale Bar & Cafe, 45020 Albion Street; (707) 937-5763; Continental/fresh local ingredients; bistro menu

955 Ukiah Street, 955 Ukiah Street; (707) 937-1955; American

MENLO PARK

Carpaccio, 1120 Crane Street; (415) 322-1211; Italian

Fontana's Italian Restaurant, 1850 El Camino Real; (415) 328-0676

MILLBRAE

Hong Kong Flower Lounge, 51 Millbrae Avenue; (415) 878-8108, and 1671 El Camino Real; (415) 873-3838; Chinese

MILL VALLEY

The Avenue Grill, 44 East Blithedale Avenue; (415) 388-6003; American

Buckeye Roadhouse, 15 Shoreline Highway; (415) 321-2600; American

MONTARA

The Foglifter Restaurant, Corner of Eighth Street and Highway 1; (415) 728-7905; eclectic menu

MONTEREY

Tarpy's Roadhouse, Highway 68 at Canyon Del Rey; (408) 647-1444; creative American country food

MORAGA

Chez Maurice, 360 Park Street; (510) 376-1655; French/Continental

MOSS LANDING

Maloney's Harbor Inn, Highway 1 at the bridge; (408) 724-9371; California/ seafood

MT. SHASTA

Bellissimo, 204-A West Lake Street; (916) 926-4461; eclectic menu

NAPA

Pasta Prego Trattoria, 3206 Jefferson Street, The Grape Yard; (707) 224-9011

NICASIO

Rancho Nicasio, in Nicasio, off Sir Francis Drake Boulevard; (415) 662-2219; meat specialties in western atmosphere

NOVATO

Dalecio, 340 Ignacio Boulevard; (415) 883-0960; Italian

OAKHURST

Crystal Falls Inn, 42424 Road 222; (209) 683-4242; fine dining

Erna's Elderberry House, Victoria Lane off Highway 41; (209) 683-6800; fine European dining

OAKLAND

Bay Wolf Restaurant, 3853 Piedmont Avenue; (510) 655-6004; California/ Mediterranean

Cactus Taqueria, 5525 College Avenue; (510) 547-1305; Mexican

Chef Paul's, 4197 Piedmont Avenue; (510) 547-2175; French

Citron, 5484 College Avenue; (510) 653-5484; Mediterranean-influenced California

Creme de la Creme, 5362 College Avenue; (510) 420-8822; California/ country French

Fana, 464 Eighth Street; (510) 271-0696; Ethiopian

Fornelli, 5891 Broadway Terrace; (510) 652-4442; Italian

Jade Villa, 800 Broadway; (510) 839-1688; Chinese/dim sum

La Brasserie, 542 Grand Avenue; (510) 893-6206; traditional French

Little Shin Shin, 4258 Piedmont Avenue; (510) 658-9799; Chinese

Nan Yang, 301 Eighth Street; (510) 465-6924, and 6048 College Avenue; (510) 655-6385; Indian/Chinese/Burmese home cooking

New Sunshine Ristorante, 3891 Piedmont Avenue; (510) 428-2500; pizza/Italian

Olivetto, 5655 College Avenue; (510) 547-5356; Mediterranean

Piemonte Ovest, 3909 Grand Avenue; (510) 601-0500; Italian

Sorabal, 372 Grand Avenue; (510) 839-2288; Korean

Ti Bacio Ristorante, 5912 College Avenue; (510) 428-1703; heart-healthy Italian

Zachary's, 5801 College Avenue; (510) 655-6385; Chicago pizza

OLEMA

Olema Inn Restaurant, 10000 Sir Francis Drake Boulevard at Highway 1; (415) 663-9559; Continental

PACIFIC GROVE

Fish & Basil, American Tin Cannery Outlet Center; (408) 649-0707; fresh fish with an Oriental touch

Taste Cafe & Bistro, 1199 Forest; (408) 655-0324; Franco-Italian

PALM SPRINGS

Alfredo's, 292 East Palm Canyon Drive; (619) 320-1020; Italian

Cedar Creek Inn, 1555 South Palm Canyon Drive; (619) 325-7300; American

Las Casuelas Terraza, 222 South Palm Canyon Drive; (619) 325-2794; Mexican

Original Thai Cuisine Siamese Gourmet, 4711 East Palm Canyon Drive at Gene Autry Trail; (619) 328-0057

Otani, A Garden Restaurant, 266 Avenida Caballeros; (619) 327-6700; Japanese

PALO ALTO

Fresco, 3398 El Camino Real; (415) 493-3470; California

Gordon Biersch Brewing Company, 640 Emerson Street; (415) 323-7723; brewpub/ California

PERRIS

Chicago Pasta House, 24667 Sunnymead Boulevard, Moreno Valley; (909) 924-5777

PESCADERO

Duarte's Tavern, 202 Stage Road; (415) 879-0464; seafood/local specialties

PHILO

The Flood Gate Store & Grill, 1810 Highway 128; (707) 895-3000; regional dishes/grilled items

POINT REYES STATION

Station House Cafe, 11180 Main Street (Highway 1); (415) 663-1515; American regional

Taqueria La Quinta, corner of Third Street and Highway 1; (415) 663-8868; Mexican

RED BLUFF

Brian's, 320 Walnut; (916) 527-3990; dinner Friday/Saturday night

The Green Barn, 5 Chestnut Avenue; (916) 527-3161; prime rib/fish/salads
REDDING
Jack's Grill, 1743 California Street; (916) 241-9705; steakhouse
Nello's Place, 3055 Bechelli Lane; (916) 223-1636; Italian
River City Bar & Grill, 2151 Market Street; (916) 243-9003; Cajun/Creole/Continental/American
REDWOOD CITY
Barbarossa European Restaurant, 3003 El Camino Real; (415) 369-2626
RICHMOND
Hidden City Cafe, 109 Park Place, Point Richmond; (510) 232-9738; California
SACRAMENTO
Aldo's, Fulton & Marconi; (916) 483-5031; fine dining/opera/piano bar
Biba, 2801 Capitol Avenue; (916) 455-2422; Northern Italian/Bolognese
Boulevard Coffee Roasting Company, 5901 Fair Oaks Boulevard, Carmichael; coffee house
Cafe La Salle, 1028 Second Street, Old Sacramento; (916) 442-4775; fine dining in old-world ambiance
Danielle's Village Creperie & Gallery, Fulton & Marconi; (916) 972-1911
Fat Frank's, 808 L Street; (916) 442-7092; Chinese
Mace's, 501 Pavillion's Lane; (916) 922-0222; fine dining
Pilothouse Restaurant, aboard Delta King, historic Sacramento waterfront; (916) 441-4440
ST. HELENA
Pairs, 1420 Main Street; (707) 963-7566; California/Southwest
Terra, 1345 Railroad Avenue; (707) 963-8931; California
Tra Vigne, 1050 Charter Oak; (707) 963-4444; rustic Italian
Trilogy, 1234 Main Street; (707) 963-5507; American
SAN ANSELMO
Comforts, 337 San Anselmo Avenue; (415) 454-6790; eclectic menu
SAN DIEGO
Anthony's Seafood, 9530 Murray Drive, La Mesa; (619) 463-0368; fresh seafood in lake-side setting
Alexis Greek Cafe, 3863 Fifth Avenue; (619) 297-1777
The Blue Crab Restaurant, 4922 North Harbor Drive; (619) 224-3000; seafood/lunch/dinner
Brigantine, 9350 Fuerte Drive, La Mesa; (619) 465-1935; varied menu
Busalacchi's Ristorante, 3683 Fifth Avenue; (619) 298-0119; Sicilian
California Cafe Bar & Grill, Horton Plaza; (619) 238-5440; California
California Cuisine, 1027 University Avenue; (619) 543-0790
Calliope's Greek Cafe, 3958 Fifth Avenue; (619) 291-5588
Canes California Bistro, 1270 Cleveland Avenue; (619) 299-3551
Celadon, a Thai Restaurant, 3628 Fifth Avenue; (619) 295-8800
Chez Odette, 3614 Fifth Avenue; (619) 299-1000; French

Chinese Garden Restaurant, 3057 Clairemont Drive, Clairemont Village; (619) 275-2888

Cilantros, 3702 Via de la Valle; (619) 259-8777; Mexican/Southwest

Dansk Tea Room, 8425 La Mesa Boulevard, La Mesa; (619) 463-0640

El Bizcocho, 17550 Bernardo Oaks Drive, Rancho Bernardo; (619) 277-2146; Spanish

Esperanto, 4462 Mission Boulevard, Pacific Beach; (619) 274-3904; pasta

Fairouz Cafe & Gallery, 3166 Midway Drive #102; (619) 225-0308; Middle Eastern

The French Side of the West, 2202 Fourth Avenue; (619) 234-5540; French

La Gran Tapa, 611 B Street; (619) 234-8272; Spanish

Lader's, 5654 Lake Murray Boulevard, La Mesa; (619) 463-9919; Italian

Lamont Street Grill, 4445 Lamont Street, Pacific Beach; (619) 270-3060; California/French

La Tour Eiffel, 412 University Avenue; (619) 298-5200; French

Little Tokyo, 501 University at Fifth; (619) 291-8518; Japanese

Mandarin Plaza, 3760 Sports Arena Boulevard, Sports Arena Village; (619) 224-4222; Chinese

Montana's American Grill, 1421 University Avenue; (619) 297-0722

The Old Ocean Beach Cafe, 4967 Newport Avenue, Ocean Beach; (619) 223-2521; eclectic menu/casual dining

Osteria Panevino, 722 Fifth Avenue; (619) 595-7959; Tuscan

Petro's Place, 6618 Mission Gorge Road; (619) 280-4888; Greek

Qwiig's, 5091 Santa Monica, Ocean Beach; (619) 222-1101; seafood

Rosaria Pizza, 1801 Morena Boulevard, Bay Park; (619) 275-0460 or 275-0474; New York-style pizza

Saska's, 3768 Mission Boulevard, Mission Beach; (619) 488-7311; steak/seafood/late night dining

The Study, 3847 Fourth Avenue; (619) 296-4847; coffee specialties

Thai Chada, 527-G University Avenue; (619) 297-9548

Tremors, 1400 Camino De La Reina, Mission Valley; (619) 293-7861; casual family dining from 11:00 a.m. on

Vesuvio, 3412 - 30th Street, North Park; (619) 291-3230; Southern Italian

SAN FRANCISCO

Aqua, 252 California Street; (415) 956-9662; contemporary seafood

Baker Street Bistro, 2953 Baker Street; (415) 931-1475; neighborhood French

Brasserie Savoy, 580 Geary Street; (415) 474-8686; French/seafood

Buca Giovanni, 800 Greenwich Street; (415) 776-7766; Italian

Boulevard, 1 Mission Street; (415) 543-6084; cutting-edge American

Cafe For All Seasons, 350 West Portal Avenue; (415) 665-0900; American

Cafe Kati, 1963 Sutter Street; (415) 775-7313; international

Caffe Delle Stelle, 330 Gough Street; (415) 252-1110; informal Italian/live opera some evenings

Casa Aguila, 1240 Noriega; (415) 661-5593; Mexican

Cha Cha Cha, 1801 Haight Street; (415) 386-5758; Caribbean

China House Bistro, 501 Balboa Street; (415) 752-2802; Chinese

Citrus North African Grill, 2373 Chestnut Street; (415) 563-7720; Moroccan

City of Paris, 101 Shannon Alley, Shannon Court Hotel; (415) 441-4442; Parisian-style brasserie

Cleopatra Restaurant, 1755 Noriega Street; (415) 753-5005; Middle Eastern

Compass Rose, Westin St. Francis Hotel, Union Square; (415) 774-0167; lunch/ high tea/cocktails in splendid surroundings

Cypress Club, 500 Jackson Street; (415) 296-8555; contemporary regional American

Des Alpes, 732 Broadway; (415) 391-4249; Basque

Elka, 1611 Post Street; (415) 922-7788; upscale seafood with French and Japanese touches

Fog City Diner, 1300 Battery Street; (415) 982-2000; contemporary American

The Flying Saucer, 1000 Guerrero Street; (415) 641-9955; neighborhood French

Fringale, 570 Fourth Street; (415) 543-0573

Geordy's, 1 Tillman Place; (415) 362-3175; healthy American

Geva's, 482-A Hayes Street; (415) 863-1220; contemporary Caribbean

Hana Restaurant, 408 Irving Street; (415) 665-3952; neighborhood Japanese/ sushi bar

Harry Denton's, 161 Steuart Street; (415) 882-1333; American

The Helmand, 430 Broadway; (415) 362-0641; Afghanistani

Hong Kong Flower Lounge, 5322 Geary Boulevard; (415) 668-8998; Chinese

Hyde Street Bistro, 1521 Hyde Street; (415) 441-7778; California

Ironwood Cafe, 901 Cole Steet; (415) 664-0224

Jackson Pavilion, 640 Jackson Street; (415) 982-2409; inexpensive prime rib/daily specials

Julie's Supper Club, 1123 Folsom Street; (415) 861-0707; American

Kabuto, 5116 Geary Boulevard; (415) 752-5652; sushi/Japanese

Kuleto's, 221 Powell Street (adjacent to Villa Florence Hotel); (415) 397-7720; Italian

La Bergerie, 4221 Geary Boulevard; (415) 387-3573; neighborhood French

La Folie, 2316 Polk Street; (415) 776-5577; upscale French

Le Central, 453 Bush Street; (415) 391-2233; French bistro/brasserie

L'Olivier, 465 Davis Street; (415) 981-7824; lighter classic French

Lulu, 816 Folsom Street; (415) 495-5775; Mediterranean

Manora's Thai Restaurant, 1600 Folsom Street; (415) 861-6224

McCormick & Kuleto's, Ghirardelli Square; (415) 929-1730; upscale seafood/California

Michelangelo Cafe, 579 Columbus Avenue; (415) 986-4058; hearty Italian

Moose's, 1652 Stockton Street; (415) 954-0792; American

Noe's Cook, 3782 - 24th Street; (415) 826-3811; neighborhood German

One Market, 1 Market Street; (415) 777-5577; American

Oriental Pearl, 760/778 Clay Street, Chinatown; (415) 433-1817; Chinese

PJ's Oyster Bed, 737 Irving Street; (415) 566-7775

Palio D'Asti, 640 Sacramento Street; (415) 395-9800; regional Italian

Panos', 4000 - 24th Street; (415) 824-8000; Greek

Rosemarino, 3665 Sacramento Street; (415) 931-7710; neighborhood Mediterranean

Roosevelt Tamale Parlor, 2817 - 24th Street; (415) 550-9213; no-frills Mexican

Royal Thai, 610 Third Street; (415) 485-1074

Square One, 190 Pacific Street; (415) 788-1110; multi-ethnic cuisine

Stars Cafe, 555 Golden Gate Avenue; (415) 861-7827; light food/fish & chips

The Stinking Rose, 325 Columbus Avenue; (415) 781-7673; garlic specialties

Stoyanof's Cafe & Restaurant, 1240 Ninth Avenue; (415) 664-3664; Greek/Mediterranean/seafood

Suppers, 1800 Fillmore Street; (415) 474-3773; homestyle American

Suzie Kate's, 655 Union Street; (415) 981-5283; Southern home cooking

Tart to Tart, 641 Irving Street; (415) 753-0643; neighborhood cafe/coffees/baked goods

Thep Phanom Restaurant, 400 Waller Street; (415) 431-2526; Thai

Tuba Garden, 3634 Sacramento Street; (415) 921-TUBA; California

Tung Fong, 808 Pacific Avenue; (415) 362-7115; dim sum

Wu Kong Restaurant, 101 Spear Street, 1 Rincon Center; (415) 957-9300; Shanghai Chinese

Zuni Cafe, 1658 Market Street; (415) 552-2522; Mediterranean

SAN JOSE

Eulipia Restaurant & Bar, 374 South First Street; (408) 280-6161; California

Gordon Biersch Brewing Company, 33 East San Fernando Street; (408) 294-4052; brewpub/California

Il Fornaio, 302 South Market Street, Hotel Sainte Claire; Italian

SAN LUIS OBISPO

Cafe Roma, 1819 Osos Street; (805) 541-6800; cucina rustica Italiana

SAN MATEO

Bella Mangiata Caffe, 233 Baldwin Avenue; (415) 343-2404; Italian

Buffalo Grill, 66 - 31st Avenue; (415) 358-8777; American home cooking

Cafe for all Seasons, 50 East Third Avenue; (415) 348-4996; American

Capellini Ristorante, 310 Baldwin Avenue; (415) 348-2296; Italian

Eposto's Four Day Cafe, 1119 South B Street; (415) 345-6443; Italian

Jo Ann's B Street Cafe, 30 South B Street; (415) 347-7000; American

Max's Bakery and Kitchen, 111 East Fourth Avenue; (415) 344-1997; American

SAN RAFAEL

Cafe 901, 901 Lincoln; (415) 457-0450; Southwest

La Bergerie, 1130 Fourth Street; (415) 457-2411; classic French

Milly's, 1613 Fourth Street; (415) 459-1601; vegetarian

Pacific Tap and Grill, 812 Fourth Street; (415) 457-9711; American grill and beer garden

Rice Table, 1617 Fourth Street; (415) 456-1808; Indonesian

SANTA BARBARA

Citronelle, 901 Cabrillo Boulevard; (805) 966-2285; California/French

Cold Spring Tavern, 5995 Stagecoach Road; (805) 967-0066; American/game

La Super-Rica, 622 North Milpas Street; (805) 963-4940; tacos/Mexican

Mousse Odile, 18 East Cota; (805) 962-5393; French

Paradise Cafe, 702 Anacapa; (805) 962-4416; seafood/California

SANTA CLARA

Birk's, 3955 Freedom Circle; (408) 980-6400; classic American grill

SANTA CRUZ

Cafe Bittersweet, 2332 Mission Street; (408) 423-9999; Italian/French/American home cooking/desserts/espresso/wine bar

Casablanca Restaurant, overlooking beach at 101 Main Street; (408) 426-9063; Continental cuisine/elegant atmosphere

Crow's Nest, by beach at Santa Cruz Yacht Harbor; (408) 476-4560; seafood/steaks/oyster bar

Hollins House, 20 Clubhouse Road; (408) 425-1244; Continental

India Joze, 1001 Center Street; (408) 427-3554; Asian/Middle Eastern

Linda's Seabreeze Cafe, 542 Seabright; (408) 427-9713; varied menu/breakfast/lunch

Memphis Minnie's, 1415 Pacific Avenue; (408) 429-6464; Southern

O'mei Restaurant, 2361 Mission Street; (408) 425-8458; Chinese

The Swan/Heavenly Goose, 1003 Cedar Street; (408) 425-8988; Szechwan Chinese

SANTA ROSA

John Ash & Co., 4330 Barnes Road at U.S. 101 and River Road; (707) 527-7687; wine country cuisine

La Gare, 208 Wilson Street; (707) 528-4355; Swiss/French

Mixx, 135 Fourth Street; (707) 573-1344; Continental

Ristorante Siena, 1229 North Dutton Avenue; (707) 578-4511; Italian

SAUSALITO

Arawan, 47 Caledonia Street; (415) 332-0882; Thai

Casa Madrona Restaurant, 801 Bridgeway; (415) 331-5888; California

Coconuts, 3001 Bridgeway; (415) 331-7515; Caribbean

North Sea Village, 300 Turney; (415) 331-3300; Chinese

SCOTTS VALLEY

Zanotto's Pasta & More, 5600 Scotts Valley Drive; (408) 438-0503; pasta/Italian dishes

SEBASTOPOL

Mom's Apple Pie, 4550 Gravenstein Highway N; (707) 823-8330; American home cooking

SONORA

Carmela's, 21 South Stewart; (209) 532-8858; homestyle Italian

Coyote Creek Cafe, 177 South Washington; (209) 532-9115; international/healthy preparations

Diamondback Grill, 110 South Washington; (209) 532-6661; great burgers and innovative daily specials

Hemingway's Cafe, 362 South Stewart; (209) 532-4900; American/French

La Tortuga, 11914 Highway 49; (209) 532-2386; creative Italian trattoria

SOQUEL

Ranjeet's, 3051 Porter Street; (408) 475-6407; California

The Salmon Poacher Restaurant, 3035 Main Street; (408) 476-1556; seafood

Star of Siam, 3005 Porter Street; (408) 479-0366; Thai cuisine/sushi bar

Theo's, 3101 Main Street; (408) 462-3657; French

Tortilla Flats, 4580 Soquel Drive; (408) 476-1754; Mexican

STINSON BEACH

The Parkside, 43 Arenal Avenue; (415) 868-1272; casual neighborhood cafe/varied menu

Sand Dollar, 3458 Shoreline Highway; (415) 868-0434; simple seaside food

SUTTER CREEK

Pelargonium, #1 Hanford Street (Highway 49 N); (209) 267-5008; California

TAHOE CITY

La Playa, 7046 North Lake Boulevard; (916) 546-5903; creative fresh seafood

River Ranch, Highway 89 at Alpine Meadows Road; (916) 583-4264; Continental/seafood

Rosie's Cafe, 571 North Lake Boulevard; (916) 583-8504; breakfast/lunch/dinner/varied menu/nightly specials

Swiss Lakewood, 5055 West Lake Boulevard; (916) 525-5211; Continental

TEMECULA

Baily Wine Country Cafe, 27644 Ynez Road; (909) 676-9567

Cafe Champagne, 32575 Rancho California Road; (909) 699-0088; California

THREE RIVERS

The Gateway, 45978 Sierra Drive/Highway 198; (209) 561-4133; steaks/seafood/riverside setting

Staff of Life, 41651 Sierra Drive; (209) 561-4937; lunches/homemade soups/salads/sandwiches with vegetarian accent

White Horse Inn, 42975 Sierra Drive; (209) 561-4185; American

TIBURON

The Caprice, 2000 Paradise Drive; (415) 435-3400; Continental

Guaymas, 5 Main Street; (415) 435-6300; upscale Mexican

UKIAH

Sunset Grill, 228 East Perkins Street; (707) 463-0740; eclectic menu for breakfast/lunch/dinner/brunch

VISALIA

The Vintage Press Restaurante, 216 North Willis Street; (209) 733-3033; California

WALNUT CREEK

Calda! Calda!, 1646 North California Boulevard; (510) 939-5555; unusual individual pizzas

The Cantina, 1470 North Broadway; (510) 934-3663; Mexican

Il Pavone, 2291 Olympic Boulevard; (510) 939-9060; cucina Italiana

Mai Thai, 1414 North Main Street; (510) 937-7887

Max's Opera Cafe, 1676 North California Boulevard; (510) 932-3434; American/New York-style deli

Montecatini, 1528 Civic Drive; (510) 943-6608; Italian

Prima Cafe, 1522 North Main Street; (510) 935-7780; California

Ristornate Toscano, 1520 Palos Verdes Mall; (510) 934-3737; Italian

Spiedini, 101 Ygnacio Valley Road; (510) 939-2100; Italian

Takao, 1690 Locust Street; (510) 944-0244; Japanese

Vic Stewart's, 8505 Broadway; (510) 943-5666; steak

Wan Fu, 1375 North Broadway; (510) 938-2288; elegant Szechwan/Mandarin

WATSONVILLE

Amanda's Cafe, 1047 Freedom Boulevard; (408) 763-1448; American/breakfast/lunch

Cilantros, 1934 Main Street in Watsonville Square; (408) 761-2161; Mexican

Jalisco, 618 Main Street, downtown Watsonville; (408) 728-9080; Mexican

YOUNTVILLE

Compadres, 6539 Washington Street; (707) 944-2406; Mexican

The Diner, 6476 Washington Street; (707) 944-2626; American by day, Mexican by night

Mustards Grill, 7399 St. Helena Highway; (707) 944-2424; American grill

OREGON

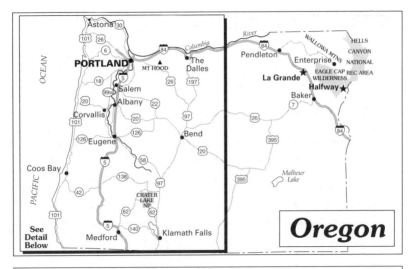

Oregon

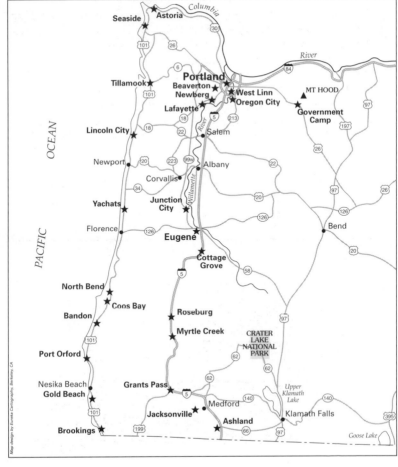

The Woods House Bed & Breakfast Inn   (503) 488-1598
333 North Main Street, Ashland, OR 97520   1(800) 435-8260
(Historic district, four blocks from theaters)   FAX: 482-7912

This beautifully renovated 1908 Craftsman home has a welcoming heart that you feel as soon as you enter the front door. Françoise and Lester Roddy have restored the home's natural charm and added many comforts, services, and aesthetic pleasures that show up in each facet of the inn -- from the inviting common living and dining rooms to the special, individually fashioned bedrooms to the exquisite terraced gardens. Romantic touches include fresh flowers, lovely antiques, lace canopies, and luxurious fabrics. Two accommodations are on the main floor, two on the upper floor, and two in the carriage house. At The Woods House, you'll have plenty of privacy, extravagant breakfasts, and some of the warmest hospitality around.

Dog and cats on premises; no pets, but kennels nearby; smoking outside only; full or Continental breakfast; living room, front porch and garden areas for guests' relaxation; credit cards (V, MC); airport pickup (Ashland). Brochure available.

*Note: Rates vary from $65 to $110 depending on season and day. RESERVE WELL IN ADVANCE DURING SHAKESPEARE FESTIVAL MONTHS, ESPECIALLY MAY - SEPTEMBER!

ROOM	BED	BATH	ENTRANCE	FLOOR	DAILY RATES S - D (EP) +
A	1Q	Pvt	Sep	1	
B	1Q	Pvt	Main	1	
C	1Q & 1T	Pvt	Main	2	*See
D	1Q & 1T	Pvt	Main	2	note.
E	1Q	Pvt	Sep	1G	
F	1K & 1T	Pvt	Sep	1G	

The Inn-Chanted Bed & Breakfast   (503) 325-5223
707 Eighth Street, Astoria, OR 97103
(Historic area near Flavel House)

Dramatically situated where the mighty Columbia meets the Pacific, Astoria has the distinction of being the oldest town west of the Mississippi. Its early importance in the lumber trade prompted the construction of many fine Victorian homes overlooking the river. The Inn-Chanted Bed & Breakfast is one of the loveliest of these "painted ladies," with lots of nooks and crannies, interesting angles, and gingerbread trim. Wood mouldings, medallions, and columns, silk brocade wallcoverings, crystal chandeliers, and other Victorian fancies abound, capturing the formality of a bygone era without sacrificing the comfort of guests. View passing ships from any of the three individually tailored accommodations, including a huge, romantic suite (C) that spans the front of the house. Hosts Richard and Dixie Swart strive to pamper and, yes, enchant you with their special service, food, and accommodations.

No pets, but boarding nearby; smoking outside only; full breakfast from a variety of options; TV in each room; inquire about different types of mattresses; deck/garden area; ample street parking; major credit cards; airport pickup (Astoria/Warrenton); family accommodation over carriage house (B). Brochure available.

ROOM	BED	BATH	ENTRANCE	FLOOR	DAILY RATES S - D	(EP) +
A	1Q	Pvt	Main	2	$70	
B	1Q & 1D	Pvt	Main	2	$75	($10)
C	1Q & 2T	Pvt	Main	2	$95	($10)

The Yankee Tinker Bed & Breakfast   **(503) 649-0932**
5480 SW 183rd Avenue, Beaverton, OR 97007   **1(800) TINKER2**
(Ten miles west of Portland)

In the common surroundings of their quiet suburban neighborhood, Jan and Ralph Wadleigh offer a most uncommon bed and breakfast experience. They meet their guests' needs in a variety of ways, providing comforts, services, and luxuries far exceeding what one might expect. Local wines and cheeses may be enjoyed in the congenial ease of the guest sitting room. Bouquets of fresh flowers are displayed throughout the house, and each of the three guest bedrooms has its own special flair created with New England antiques and collectibles. Lovely quilts, bed linens, and family heirlooms add to the warm ambiance. A great night's sleep is followed by morning fare made up of specialties that the Wadleighs have developed just for their guests. The pleasant surprises and personalized care found at The Yankee Tinker gives Yankee hospitality a whole new meaning.

No pets or smoking; full breakfast; TV, fireplace, and writing desk in sitting room; AC; telephone in each room; rollaway bed available; large deck and lovely gardens; wineries, good restaurants, golf courses, public swimming pool, tennis courts, parks, and hiking trails in vicinity; good public transportation; off-street parking; major credit cards; 10% discount to business travelers. Brochure available.

ROOM	BED	BATH	ENTRANCE	FLOOR	DAILY RATES	
					S - D	(EP) +
A	1Q	Pvt	Main	1G	$65-$70	($10)
B	1Q	Shd*	Main	1G	$55-$60	($10)
C	1T	Shd*	Main	1G	$50	($10)

129

The Chetco River Inn   **(503) 469-8128**
21202 High Prairie Road, Brookings, OR 97415   **1(800) 327-2688**
(Seventeen and one-half miles up North Bank Road)

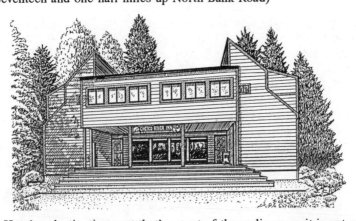

Here's a destination spot that's as out-of-the-ordinary as it is out-of-the-way. Worldly concerns seem to melt away as you drive through pristine countryside following the Chetco River -- sparklingly clear and inviting. In a remote setting on the river bank, Sandra Brugger welcomes guests to her cedar lodge-type inn. It has modern lines, a spacious interior, and a rustic, old-world flavor. Shiny marble floors, Oriental rugs, and fine traditional furnishings grace the large, open living area. On one end, a wood-burning stove is backed by a wall of native stone; on the other end, there's an open kitchen and dining area where country breakfasts and memorable dinners are served. Two of the guest bedrooms have enchanting river views, crisp white walls, elegant brass beds, and delightful memorabilia such as old decoys and photography equipment. Whether you're contemplating the river from a secluded park bench, taking a hike or a swim, angling for steelhead, or just curling up with a good book, an uncommonly relaxing escape awaits you at The Chetco River Inn.

Dog and cat in residence; no pets; older children welcome; smoking outside only (porch); full breakfast; robes provided; dinner with advance notice; picnic lunches available; satellite TV and movies; library; games; fishing packages available; off-street parking; credit cards (V,MC). Brochure available.

ROOM	BED	BATH	ENTRANCE	FLOOR	DAILY RATES S - D (EP)
A	1K or 2T	Pvt	Main	2	$75-$85
B	1Q	Pvt	Main	2	$85
C	1K	Pvt	Main	2	$85

Holmes Sea Cove Bed & Breakfast   **(503) 469-3025**
17350 Holmes Drive, Brookings, OR 97415
(North end of Brookings overlooking Pacific)

Many a guest has been reluctant to leave Holmes Sea Cove Bed & Breakfast. Who would willingly give up the comfort of a private paradise with a heavenly view of the rugged Oregon coast? Each of three guest accommodations has its own entrance, bath, refrigerator, and color TV. One is a large room with a sitting area, another a large suite, and the third a separate cottage. All have excellent views, but the one from the cottage is panoramic. Hosts Jack and Lorene Holmes know how to make you feel welcome and then leave you alone to savor a total escape. They deliver breakfast to your doorstep in the morning and invite you to make full use of the gazebo overlooking the ocean, the benches and picnic tables, and the pathway leading to the beach. Landscaped grounds and gardens round out a truly perfect setting for making memories with that special someone.

No pets; children limited; smoking outside only; sofa bed in each room; off-street parking; credit cards (V,MC); airport pickup (Sierra Pacific). Brochure available.

ROOM	BED	BATH	ENTRANCE	FLOOR	DAILY RATES	
					S - D	(EP) +
A	1Q	Pvt	Sep	LL	$80	($15)
B	1Q	Pvt	Sep	LL	$85	($15)
C	1Q	Pvt	Sep	1	$95	($15)

Upper Room Chalet   (503) 269-5385
306 North Eighth Street, Coos Bay, OR 97420
(Central Coos Bay near Mingus Park)

On a quiet little street near downtown, surrounded by evergreen and rhododendron, is the warm family home of Carl and Barbara Solomon. A piano in the foyer, a living room with cushy places to sit, a fireplace, and country Victorian decor combine to create the essence of hospitality. Family antiques, dolls, mementoes, and photos fill the house. Flanking the stairwell to the second floor is Barbara's extensive doll collection. Three upstairs bedrooms have different focal points: a colorful patchwork quilt, two iron day beds done up in ivory eyelet and mauve, and a king-sized antique brass bed. On the main floor is a cheery bedroom suitable for one. The Solomons' big country kitchen is the heart of the house, a magnet for people who appreciate its old-time ambiance and camaraderie -- not to mention the comfort foods, such as biscuits and gravy, berries and dumplings, or homemade pies, that are served here.

No pets; no alcohol; no children under sixteen; smoking outside only; full country breakfast; candlelight dinners catered by Heavenly Cuisine; clawfoot tub in private bath (C); tennis courts across street; off-street and street parking; airport pickup (North Bend Municipal). Brochure available.

ROOM	BED	BATH	ENTRANCE	FLOOR	DAILY RATES S - D (EP)
A	1D	Shd*	Main	2	$55-$60
B	2T	Shd*	Main	2	$55-$60
C	1K	Pvt	Main	2	$65-$70
D	1T	Shd*	Main	1	$38

Hillcrest Dairy Bed & Breakfast   **(503) 942-0205**
79385 Sears Road, Cottage Grove, OR 97424
(Northeast Cottage Grove, Exit 176 from I-5)

Here's an opportunity to experience genuine Dutch hospitality state-side. Mike and Grace Eisenga bring a bit of the old country to their style of bed and breakfast. Accommodations are immaculate, the breakfasts large and nourishing. The comfortable ranch-style home has common rooms where guests may feel free to play games, read, or use the pool table. Outdoors, it's enjoyable to take a walk and explore the beautiful area surrounding the farm, a great place for viewing wildlife such as deer, elk, and birds. A visit to Hillcrest Dairy will add a pleasant change of pace to your trip.

No pets; infants and children over six welcome; smoking outside only; full breakfast; TV; single cot extra in Room C; off-street parking.

ROOM	BED	BATH	ENTRANCE	FLOOR	DAILY RATES	
					S - D	(EP)
A	1Q	Shd*	Main	1	$30-$45	($10)
B	1D	Shd*	Main	1	$30-$40	
C	2T	Shd*	Main	1	$30-$40	($10)

Aristea's Guest House
(503) 683-2062
1546 Charnelton Street, Eugene, OR 97401
(Downtown area)

As a newcomer to Eugene in 1990, Arie Hupp took to its "little Berkeley" atmosphere right away. She has happily made her home here in the wonderfully restored 1928 bungalow that earlier had been operated as Shelley's Guest House. She carries on the tradition of hospitality whose hallmarks of elegance and personal service continue to bring many repeat visitors. The gardens have been expanded and new breakfast specialties developed. Gleaming woodwork and floors, traditional wallcoverings, brass accents, and selected antiques grace the interior. There's comfortable seating around the living room fireplace and an extensive library to peruse. The upstairs is exclusively for guests. A cozy sitting room with cable television and a telephone connects the Master Bedroom and the Guest Room, both full of charming details. The spacious bathroom has a tub and a separate tiled shower. The delightful character of Aristea's Guest House is matched only by that of Arie herself.

Dog and cat in residence; no pets; smoking outside only; full breakfast; FAX service; ample street parking. Brochure available.

ROOM	BED	BATH	ENTRANCE	FLOOR	DAILY RATES	
					S - D	(EP) +
A	1Q & 1T	Shd*	Main	2	$55-$60	($15)
B	1D	Shd*	Main	2	$45-$50	

B&G's Bed & Breakfast   **(503) 343-5739**
711 West Eleventh Avenue, Eugene, OR 97402
(Downtown area)

To stay at the home of Barbara Koser and her son Gerritt is to feel like a resident of their convenient, tree-shaded neighborhood. Both guest quarters offer a space that is completely one's own. The ambiance of the private cottage (A) overlooking the garden is like a breath of fresh air. A skylight, vaulted windows, crisp white walls, and colorful artwork give the petite abode an open, spring-like feeling. In the main house, the Nobel Room (B) has Scandinavian accents, works by local artists, and a collection of interesting books by Nobel Peace Prize winners in the adjoining sitting area. Full breakfasts featuring organically-grown fruits are served in the Kosers' sunny, plant-filled dining area. Here, with the help of knowledgeable hosts, you can plan your day to best take advantage of Eugene's rich diversity.

Families welcome; smoking outside only; TV/VCR; extensive library; bicycles; walking distance from shops, restaurants, galleries, Rose Garden, and Ridgeline Trail; public transportation; off-street and street parking; credit cards (AE); airport pickup (Mahlon Sweet). Guests invited to join Barbara for daily walks/hikes in and around Eugene. Brochure available.

ROOM	BED	BATH	ENTRANCE	FLOOR	DAILY RATES	
					S - D	(EP) +
A	1Q	Pvt	Sep	1	$55-$59	
B	1D	Shd	Main	1	$45-$49	($10)

135

Duckworth Bed & Breakfast Inn (503) 686-2451

987 East Nineteenth Avenue, Eugene, OR 97403

(South Campus area)

When Fred and Peggy Ward first saw this English Tudor-style home, they could see its potential as a charm-filled haven for guests. With this vision and much loving care, they truly outdid themselves in capturing its heartwarming essence. A duck decoy on the mantelpiece sets the color scheme of evergreen and ivory. The main floor is a study in nostalgia, a comforting blend of English and American antiques, family photos and mementoes, fine old clocks and lamps, a player piano, wallpaper and wainscoting, lace curtains, an intimate hearth, and inviting sofas and chairs. Bouquets of fresh flowers decorate the entire house. Upstairs guest rooms are marked by sloped ceilings, English floral print fabrics, and a variety of homey touches. The endless pampering at Duckworth B&B takes many forms, making a stay here endlessly delightful.

Dog in residence; no pets; children over eleven welcome; shared bath off hallway; full breakfast; round-the-clock coffee, tea, and cookies; TV/VCR in each room; 600-video library; gardens with stone pathways; bicycles; public transportation; off-street parking. Brochure available.

ROOM	BED	BATH	ENTRANCE	FLOOR	DAILY RATES S - D (EP) +
A	1Q	Shd*	Main	2	$75
B	1Q & 1T	Shd*	Main	2	$75
C	1Q	Pvt	Main	2	$85

The House in the Woods   (503) 343-3234
814 Lorane Highway, Eugene, OR 97405
(Southwest Eugene, South Hills area)

The Lorane Highway is a thoroughfare for joggers and cyclists and a convenient route to downtown Eugene, three miles away. The House in the Woods is set back from the road, with a periphery of fir and oak trees, an abundance of azaleas and rhododendrons, and some formally landscaped open areas. Friendly wildlife still abounds on the two acres. Long-time residents Eunice and George Kjaer have restored their 1910 home to its original quiet elegance. There are hardwood floors with Oriental carpets, high ceilings, lots of windows, and three covered porches (one with a swing). A large, comfortable parlor is most pleasant for visiting, listening to music, or reading. Guest rooms are spacious and tastefully decorated. Parks, cultural events, outdoor recreation, and good restaurants can be pointed out by your versatile hosts, but the house and grounds are so peaceful and relaxing that you may be compelled to stay put.

No pets; children over twelve welcome; smoking on outside covered areas; full breakfast (Continental-style for late risers); TV; piano; music library; public transportation; off-street parking; airport pickup (Mahlon Sweet); winter rates. Additional bedroom with twin bed and shared bath at $38 is available as an alternate choice. Brochure available.

ROOM	BED	BATH	ENTRANCE	FLOOR	DAILY RATES	
					S - D	(EP) +
A	1Q	Pvt	Main	1	$40-$65	
B	1D	Shd	Main	2	$38-$55	

Maryellen's Guest House   **(503) 342-7375**
1583 Fircrest Drive, Eugene, OR 97403
(Hendricks Park area)

The natural beauty of rhododendron- and azalea-filled Hendricks
Park extends to the surrounding neighborhood, and on a nearby
fern-covered hillside studded with Douglas fir and Oregon grape is
Maryellen's. The wood home of contemporary lines features a large
rear deck with a swimming pool and Jacuzzi. Inside, the soothing
decor, luxurious private accommodations, and many complimentary
extras make it a special find. Two distinctive suites with decks occupy
the home's lower level, and guests also have use of a spacious living
area with comfortable seating, a wood-burning stove, and a woodland
view. The large Country French Suite is done in Impressionist colors
and has a tiled bath with a Roman soaking tub. The Contemporary
Suite is decorated in neutral and peach tones with accents in black;
modern art enhances the light, airy ambiance. You'll find everything
about Maryellen's Guest House tasteful, serene, and relaxing.

No pets; infants or children over twelve welcome; smoking on
decks only; full or Continental breakfast (special dietary requests
honored); TV; "2T" is a day bed in Room A; guest phone; access to
private health club; hiking trails and bike paths nearby; University and
downtown minutes away by car; major credit cards; public transportation; airport pickup (Mahlon Sweet). Brochure available.

ROOM	BED	BATH	ENTRANCE	FLOOR	DAILY RATES S - D (EP) +
A	1Q & 2T	Pvt	Main	LL	$72-$82
B	1Q	Pvt	Main	LL	$62-$72

138

The Oval Door

(503) 683-3160

988 Lawrence Street at Tenth, Eugene, OR 97401
(Downtown area)

This two-story gray inn, trimmed in violet, has a wide wrap-around porch and an inviting front door with an oval glass. It was built on a corner lot to blend into the quiet older neighborhood. Every detail was planned to maximize the comfort, convenience, and enjoyment of guests. The spacious, traditionally furnished interior is light, airy, and immaculate. Innkeepers Dianne Feist and Judith McLane have brought a 1920s country look to the decor by adding their own special antiques and nostalgic accents. Each guest room is a relaxing haven where it seems one's every need has been anticipated. Just down the hall is the private Tub Room with a whirlpool bath, a lovely spot to unwind after a taxing day. Sumptuous breakfasts are described on posted daily menus; their tantalizing goodness is in perfect keeping with the overall high standards of The Oval Door.

Children welcome; full breakfast; smoking on porch only; TV/VCR; AC; library; robes provided; phone jack and work space in each room; public transportation; off-street parking; credit cards (V,MC); airport pickup (Mahlon Sweet). Brochure available.

ROOM	BED	BATH	ENTRANCE	FLOOR	DAILY RATES S - D	(EP) +
A	1Q	Pvt	Main	2	$70-$75	($10)
B	1Q	Pvt	Main	2	$65-$70	($10)
C	1Q	Pvt	Main	2	$60-$65	
D	2T	Pvt	Main	2	$55-$60	

Pookie's Bed 'n' Breakfast on College Hill   **(503) 343-0383**
2013 Charnelton Street, Eugene, OR 97405
(Near downtown and University campus)

The grace of fine craftsmanship is apparent throughout this beautifully restored 1918 home. It is perfectly maintained, as are the lovely grounds of its elevated corner lot. For guests there are two cozy, sweet rooms upstairs with an art nouveau flavor, period furnishings, and huge closets. Blues, mauves, teal, and cranberry predominate in pleasing combinations. The bathroom, which may be shared or private, features a clawfoot tub and a pedestal sink. The guests' own sitting room is a civilized place to relax with a cup of coffee or tea, read, watch television, or carry on a conversation. The dining room is highlighted by a marvelous collection of Blue Willow china. Pookie Walling is a woman of many talents, not the least of which is providing her guests with first-rate personal service.

Dog and cats on premises; no pets; children over five welcome; smoking outside only; full or Continental breakfast; TV/VCR, stereo, and refrigerator in guest sitting room; good public transportation; off-street parking; either room with private bath, $80. Brochure available.

ROOM	BED	BATH	ENTRANCE	FLOOR	DAILY RATES S - D (EP) +
A	2T	Shd*	Main	2	$55-$65
B	1Q	Shd*	Main	2	$55-$65

Endicott Gardens (503) 247-6513
95768 Jerrys Flat Road, Gold Beach, OR 97444
(Four miles east of U.S. 101)

   Endicott Gardens is the setting for a small nursery and the home of
Mary and Stewart Endicott. Bed and breakfast accommodations have
been constructed in a separate wing of the house. Each of the four
comfortable bedrooms has its own pleasing personality and a private
bath. The back rooms (C and D) open onto a deck that is blessed with
a forest and mountain view. As one might expect, the grounds are
spectacular with flowers and shrubs. Breakfast on the deck is a
delight, but in cool weather Mary presents the morning fare in the
dining room near the crackle and warmth of the fireplace. Guests are
provided with some thoughtful amenities, and the cordial climate is
spiced with humor. Endicott Gardens offers the traveler all this plus
a chance to unwind in a quiet, natural environment.
   No pets; TV available; Rogue River, ocean, and forest recreation
nearby; off-street parking; airport pickup (Gold Beach). Brochure
available.

ROOM	BED	BATH	ENTRANCE	FLOOR	DAILY RATES S - D	(EP)
A	1Q & 1T	Pvt	Sep	1G	$45-$55	($10)
B	1Q	Pvt	Sep	1G	$45-$55	($10)
C	1Q	Pvt	Sep	1G	$45-$55	($10)
D	1Q	Pvt	Sep	1G	$45-$55	($10)

Inn at Nesika Beach   **(503) 247-6434**
33026 Nesika Road, Gold Beach, OR 97444
(North of Gold Beach)

The setting alone won me over: a new Victorian-style home built on a bluff overlooking the Pacific. Inn at Nesika Beach offers deluxe accommodations and the comfort-oriented hospitality of innkeeper Ann Arsenault. All four guest rooms are done in Victorian themes and have down comforters, private baths with whirlpool tubs, and ocean views. Three rooms have feather beds, double bathtubs, and fireplaces; two have seaside private balconies. There is a large recreation room for guests to lounge with TV, fireplace, and a music and card area. From the covered porch, sit and contemplate the mysteries of the Pacific, or use the nearby access to the beach and take a closer look. Inn at Nesika Beach is a place to nourish the senses and kindle some romantic notions.

No pets or children; smoking outside only; full breakfast; bird and animal sanctuaries, salmon and steelhead fishing, golfing, Rogue River jet boat rides, crabbing and clamming nearby; off-street parking; weekly vacation rental also available. Brochure available.

ROOM	BED	BATH	ENTRANCE	FLOOR	DAILY RATES S - D (EP)
A	1K	Pvt	Main	3	$95
B	1K or 2T	Pvt	Main	2	$95
C	1K	Pvt	Main	2	$85
D	1Q	Pvt	Main	2	$85

Falcon's Crest Inn   **(503) 272-3403**
P.O. Box 185, Government Camp, OR 97028   **1(800) 624-7384**
(87287 Government Camp Loop Highway)

See Mount Hood "up close and personal" from Bob and Melody Johnson's Falcon's Crest Inn, a rustic yet luxurious all-wood structure featuring deluxe accommodations and fine dining. The central area of the house is a vast, open space with a vaulted ceiling and several sitting areas geared to comfort and conversation. Savor the magical mountain setting from almost every room. There are guest rooms on each of the inn's three levels, the upper ones opening to the surrounding balcony. Antiques and family heirlooms enhance each room's individual theme. The whole house is chock full of personality -- a reflection of the gregarious hosts, who have as good a time as the guests. Meal preparation is, however, taken seriously, and wonderful candlelight dinners are offered in addition to lavish mountain breakfasts.

No pets; smoking on decks only; older, well-behaved children welcome; full breakfast; afternoon refreshments; candlelight dinners by advance reservation; corporate, private, and mystery parties a specialty; year-round skiing, golf, hiking, and lake activities nearby; Timberline Lodge and Oregon Trail nearby; off-street parking; major credit cards; airport shuttle from Portland International. Brochure available.

ROOM	BED	BATH	ENTRANCE	FLOOR	DAILY RATES S - D (EP) +
A	1Q	Pvt	Main	1G	$110
B	1Q	Pvt	Main	2	$139
C	1Q	Pvt	Main	2	$85
D	1K	Pvt	Main	3	$85
E	2T	Pvt	Main	3	$85

Clemens House   **(503) 476-5564**
612 NW Third Street, Grants Pass, OR 97526
(Central Grants Pass)

The huge corner lot where Clemens House stands is a botanical wonderland, a proper setting for a home of its stature. The 1905 three-story Craftsman was a joyous discovery for owners Gerry and Maureen Clark. All its original charm is intact, and the addition of modern amenities has enhanced its comfort. The interior has considerable aesthetic appeal: lots of gorgeous woodwork, including coffered ceilings and polished floors, combined with soft colors; pretty fabrics, rugs, and wallcoverings; antiques and family heirlooms; lace curtains; and handmade quilts. Upstairs bedrooms are simply beautiful, down to the last elegant detail. Share the joy of the Clarks' discovery as you relax in the warmth of their gracious hospitality.

No pets; smoking outside only; full breakfast; AC; desk and space to set up computer available for business travelers; Rogue River activities five minutes away; off-street parking; credit cards (V,MC); inquire about off-season rates. Room B is a large suite including a sitting room with a fireplace and an adjoining bedroom with extra-long twin beds. Brochure available.

ROOM	BED	BATH	ENTRANCE	FLOOR	DAILY RATES S - D (EP) +	
A	1Q	Pvt	Main	2	$48-$60	
B	1Q & 2T	Pvt	Main	2	$58-$70	($12)
C	1Q & 1D	Pvt	Main	3	$68-$80	($12)

Riverbanks Inn   **(503) 479-1118**
8401 Riverbanks Road, Grants Pass, OR 97527
(Northwest of town on bank of Rogue River)

Riverbanks Inn, situated on twelve acres along the scenic Rogue, is as multifaceted as its owner, Myrtle Franklin. The secluded retreat is a rich tapestry woven from the strands of her life. The completely refurbished main house is endowed with view windows, natural materials, and comfortable seating. Two rooms on the lower level evoke two distinct moods: The Casablanca (A), exotic romance; The Jean Harlow (B), a sort of Floridian art deco glamor with private spa. The three-room Caribbean Dream Suite (C) features a Jacuzzi, a rain forest shower, and a plantation bed with Mombasa netting to add to the mood of a tropical paradise. Two nearby cabins include The Log Cabin (D), with antiques, pine floors, and a covered front porch; and The Zen House (E), a traditional Japanese tea house, with a double futon and a black marble shower. Riverbanks Inn offers a range of options few places can match. Come share in its wealth.

No pets; children welcome; smoking outside only; full country breakfast; TVs; VCRs; fireplace; refrigerators; robes provided; extra long beds; steam room; massage; pond; playhouse; nearby lodge and cottage, with outdoor hot tubs, for families and fishing groups; rafting and birding; off-street parking; credit cards (V,MC). Brochure available.

ROOM	BED	BATH	ENTRANCE	FLOOR	DAILY RATES S - D (EP)
A	1Q	Pvt	Sep	LL	$110
B	1K or 2T	Pvt	Sep	LL	$135
C	1Q	Pvt	Sep	1	$150
D	1Q & 2T	Pvt	Sep	1	$95 ($20)
E	1D	Pvt	Sep	1	$75

Birch Leaf Farm Bed & Breakfast   **(503) 742-2990**
RR#1, Box 91, Halfway, OR 97834
(Foot of Wallowa Mountains in far eastern Oregon)

Fascination with the Hells Canyon and Eagle Cap Wilderness region is fast spreading beyond a few privileged adventurers. Here in beautiful Pine Valley is the forty-two-acre working farm where Dave and Maryellen Olson have refurbished their handsome turn-of-the-century farmhouse with maximum respect for original features such as the wainscoting, the stairway bannister, and the upstairs pine floors. This respect extends to the carefully preserved vintage orchards and the still-used gravity irrigation system. The vividly colored bedrooms feature pretty rugs and stocked bookshelves. The main living area is the picture of civilized comfort: an entire wall of books, a baby grand piano, a cozy woodstove, and inviting places to sit. Genuine country spirit is built into every facet of Birch Leaf Farm.

No pets indoors; farm animals on grounds; smoking outside only; full breakfast; wrap-around veranda; Oregon Trail Interpretive Center, buffalo tours, horse pack trips, fishing, hiking, birding, llama trekking, skiing, and panoramic viewing in area; credit cards (V,MC); airport pickup (Baker City, Halfway). Brochure available.

ROOM	BED	BATH	ENTRANCE	FLOOR	DAILY RATES S - D	(EP)
A	1K	Shd*	Sep	2	$65	($20)
B	2T	Shd*	Main	2	$50	($20)
C	1D & 1T	Shd*	Main	2	$55	($20)
D	1D & 1T	Pvt	Main	1	$65	($20)

Reames House 1868   **(503) 899-1868**
P.O. Box 128, Jacksonville, OR 97530
(540 East California Street)

Reames House 1868 is just four blocks from the center of Jackson-ville, a well preserved gold rush town on the National Register of Historic Places. Encircled by a white picket fence, spacious lawns, and perennial flower gardens, the Queen Anne beauty is also on the Register. It has a fine array of exterior woodwork and an interior enhanced by handsome antiques. Accommodations on the second floor share a lovely sitting room which has a telephone for guests. Exquisite wall stenciling sets the tone for the decor, and period details combined with flair give each bedroom a charm all its own. Reames House 1868 offers superb hospitality to attendees of the celebrated Britt Music Festivals as well as year-round visitors who just want to steep themselves in the history of colorful Jacksonville.

No pets; children by arrangement; smoking outside only; full breakfast; AC; use of bicycles, tennis rackets, and gold pans; Ashland, fifteen miles away; day trips to Crater Lake National Park, Oregon Caves National Monument, and Rogue River rafting; off-street park-ing; Rooms A and B available as a suite at $160. Brochure available.

ROOM	BED	BATH	ENTRANCE	FLOOR	DAILY RATES	
					S - D	(EP) +
A	1Q	Pvt	Main	2	$90	
B	2T	Pvt	Main	2	$90	
C	1Q	Pvt	Main	2	$90	
D	1Q	Pvt	Main	2	$90	

147

Black Bart Bed & Breakfast   **(503) 998-1904**
94125 Love Lake Road, Junction City, OR 97448
(Fifteen minutes north of Eugene)

The heartland of the Willamette Valley is green, flat, and expansive with hills to the east and west. Here the thoroughly renovated 1880s farmhouse of Irma and Don Mode is situated on thirteen acres. The home's namesake is a National Grand Champion mammoth donkey who resides on the property. Guest rooms, like the rest of the home, have personality plus. The Rose Petal features ruffled priscilla curtains, an ornate brass bed, and Early American furnishings. The Canopy Room is done in ivory and blue, with floral carpeting and a fancy maplewood canopy bed. A handcrafted donkey and mule quilt adorns one wall of the twin-bedded Quilt Room. A spirit of whimsy, an appreciation of interesting antiques and collectibles, and a dedication to old-fashioned country comfort abound at Black Bart's.

Dog and cats on property; no pets; no children under twelve; full farm breakfast; TV/VCR; AC; antique shops, fresh fruit stands, and good places to walk, jog, or cycle nearby; off-street parking; major credit cards; airport pickup (in Eugene, Mahlon Sweet). Brochure available.

ROOM	BED	BATH	ENTRANCE	FLOOR	DAILY RATES S - D (EP) +
A	1K	Pvt	Main	2	$60-$70
B	1K	Pvt	Main	2	$60-$70
C	2T	Pvt 1/2	Main	2	$50-$60

Kelty Estate   **(503) 864-3740**
P.O. Box 817, Lafayette, OR 97127
(675 Highway 99 W; central Yamhill County wine region)

Lafayette was an early farming settlement where the James Keltys first built their rural Gothic farmhouse in 1872. In 1934, son Paul Kelty -- then prominent editor of *The Oregonian* in Portland -- bought back his boyhood home, refurbished it in the colonial style, and used it as a summer home. Most recently, Ronald and JoAnn Ross's painstaking restorations have left the interior with a new feeling, while graceful architectural details and selected antiques recall another era. The proud white house with green trim is surrounded by lush lawns, gardens, and trees. Choose one of two lovely corner bedrooms where soft pastels create a soothing ambiance. Guests enjoy gathering around the living room fireplace, on the front porch, or in the beautiful back yard. Kelty Estate is a gracious way station for travelers who appreciate a warm welcome and immaculate accommodations.

No children, pets, or smoking; full breakfast; popular Lafayette Antique Mall diagonally across from B&B; off-street parking.

ROOM	BED	BATH	ENTRANCE	FLOOR	DAILY RATES S - D (EP)
A	1Q	Pvt	Main	2	$55
B	1Q	Pvt	Main	2	$55

Stang Manor Inn (503) 963-2400
1612 Walnut Street, LaGrande, OR 97850
(Near town center)

It was in 1922 that lumber baron August Stang spared no expense to build a home of grand proportion. A huge yard, resplendent with rose gardens, surrounds the Georgian Colonial beauty. In its early days, Stang Manor was the center of the social life in the region, and since then many a notable personality has passed through its doors. In keeping with its standing, the house is finely detailed through and through, with extraordinary woodwork, an imposing staircase, lovely arches, built-in cabinetry, and cedar-lined closets. There is a distinctive variety of guest accommodations, including a two-bedroom suite (D) with a sitting room, a TV, and a fireplace. The private baths offer big, fluffy towels and old-fashioned porcelain bath fixtures and tiles. Breakfast fit for a baron is served ever so elegantly in the dining room. As a guest at Stang Manor Inn, you can relax and feel as pampered as those who visited this magnificent residence in its heyday.

No pets or smoking; full breakfast; late afternoon refreshments; TV/VCR in living room for guests' use; near Wallowa Mountains, artists' colony at Enterprise, and Oregon Trail historic sites; off-street parking; credit cards (V,MC), but cash or checks preferred; airport and Amtrak pickup. Brochure available.

ROOM	BED	BATH	ENTRANCE	FLOOR	DAILY RATES	
					S - D	(EP) +
A	1Q	Pvt	Main	2	$65-$70	($15)
B	1Q & 1T	Pvt	Main	2	$65-$70	($15)
C	1Q & 2T	Pvt	Main	2	$65-$70	($15)
D	1Q & 1D	Pvt	Main	2	$90	($15)

The Brey House Ocean View Bed & Breakfast **(503) 994-7123**
3725 NW Keel, Lincoln City, OR 97367
(North of town center, across street from ocean)

Seeking a casual, relaxing place by the ocean to unwind? A homey respite right across the street from a walk-forever beach is The Brey House, where Milt and Shirley Brey's guests appreciate the do-as-you-please atmosphere, the walking-distance proximity to shops and restaurants, and the unobstructed ocean view from most every room. A nautical theme prevails throughout the house. A new dining room with glass on three sides is the perfect place to enjoy the extravagant breakfasts Milt whips up. The ground-floor accommodation may be used by a family or group; it has two bedrooms, a family room with a pool table, comfy places to sit, a fireplace, and a TV/VCR, as well as a full kitchen, and guests are welcome to use the hot tub. The rooms on the second and third floors have unforgettable ocean views.

No pets; no children; smoking restricted; full breakfast; hot tub; fishing, golf, hiking, antique shopping and more nearby; off-street parking; credit cards (V,MC,D); midweek rates. Brochure available.

ROOM	BED	BATH	ENTRANCE	FLOOR	DAILY RATES
					S - D (EP)
A	1Q	Pvt	Sep	1	$75-$85
B	1Q	Pvt	Sep	1	$55-$65
C	1Q	Pvt	Main	2	$60-$70
D	1Q	Pvt	Main	3	$65-$75

151

Sonka's Sheep Station Inn   **(503) 863-5168**
901 NW Chadwick Lane, Myrtle Creek, OR 97457
(West of I-5 and town of Myrtle Creek)

Sparkling fresh air, vivid green pastures, and the ever-changing beauty of stately trees mark the idyllic setting of the 360-acre working ranch surrounding Sonka's Sheep Station Inn. Outside pressures melt away as one settles into the tempo of ranch life, which can be thoroughly relaxing or busy with activities such as lambing, watching border collies herd flocks of sheep, or walking along the South Umpquah River. Louis and Evelyn Sonka sampled ranch homestays in New Zealand and decided to share similar experiences with guests at their own ranch. Accommodations have a country flavor, with sheepy accents throughout the decor. There are two rooms in the main house and a separate three-bedroom guest house. Hearty breakfasts featuring locally raised products are served. Authentic, rural hospitality just doesn't get any better than this.

No pets; smoking outside only; full breakfast; airport pickup (Tri City). Brochure available. Guest House = Rooms C, D, and E.

ROOM	BED	BATH	ENTRANCE	FLOOR	DAILY RATES S - D (EP)
A	1Q	Shd*	Main	2	$60
B	1D	Shd*	Main	2	$50
C	1Q	Pvt	Sep	1	$60
D	2T				$50
E	1D				$50

Secluded Bed & Breakfast   **(503) 538-2635**
19719 NE Williamson Road, Newberg, OR 97132
(Yamhill County wine region)

Oregon's growing stature as a wine-producing state is enhanced by a visit to its premier grape-growing region in Yamhill County. Whether you're making a quick stop between Portland and the coast or staying long enough to savor the fruits of the vine, Secluded Bed & Breakfast is an ideal stop. It's a woodsy retreat with quiet, natural surroundings and abundant seasonal wildlife. Del and Durell Belanger are long-time residents of the county. Among other things, Durell is a skilled violin maker and Del a fabulous cook. They know some excellent places to send you for dinner, and later you'll have a great sleep in wonderful country silence.

No pets; smoking outside only; full breakfast; living room with fireplace and TV/VCR; AC; off-street parking; airport pickup (Newberg, McMinnville); master suite with queen bed, private bath, and balcony available on request at $50; master suite with shared bath, $45 on request. Brochure available.

ROOM	BED	BATH	ENTRANCE	FLOOR	DAILY RATES S - D (EP)
A	1D	Shd*	Main	2	$40
B	1D	Shd*	Main	2	$40

153

Spring Creek Llama Ranch and Bed & Breakfast   (503) 538-5717
14700 NE Spring Creek Lane, Newberg, OR 97132
(Yamhill County wine region)

Not far off the beaten path but seeming to be worlds away, Spring Creek Llama Ranch is set at the dead end of a private road on twenty-four acres of garden, field, and forest. Bed and breakfast takes place in a spacious contemporary home with cathedral ceilings and huge windows offering a feast of greenery. In this fresh atmosphere, enjoy a morning meal of home-baked treats and seasonal produce from the garden. A restful night is assured in one of two rooms: Spring Meadow, done in cheerful pastels and animal prints, or Red Cloud, a autumn-hued room with a large window overlooking a bank of fern, rhododendron, Douglas fir, and willow. Outside in the barn complex and yard, make friends with some of the Van Bossuyt family's llamas. It's easy to become totally enchanted while taking a guided Llama Walk along winding pathways through evergreen forest. You may even get to meet Red Cloud.

No pets, except other llamas; children welcome; no smoking; full breakfast; TV available; AC; patio; wineries, restaurants, antique shops, George Fox College, Champoeg State Park, and more nearby. Red Cloud Suite has two bedrooms (1Q & 2T) and a bath; 3 adults, $95; 4 adults, $105; inquire about family rates. Brochure available.

ROOM	BED	BATH	ENTRANCE	FLOOR	DAILY RATES S - D (EP)
A	1D	Pvt	Main	1	$50
B	1Q	Pvt	Main	2	$65 ($20)

The Highlands   **(503) 756-0300**
608 Ridge Road, North Bend, OR 97459
(North of Coos Bay; five miles east of U.S. 101)

Here's a stunning, architecturally designed cedar home situated at a high elevation with a dramatic perspective of Haynes Inlet and the Oregon coastal range. But that's just for starters. Guests of Marilyn and Jim Dow are given the entire ground floor which includes a large, fully-equipped kitchen, a spacious family room with a woodstove and a fantastic view, and two bedrooms with private baths (one with a whirlpool tub). Tasteful country furnishings have been well put together to impart a warm, homey, comforting feeling. The view alone might hold your attention, but there's also a TV and VCR for entertainment. Anglers shouldn't miss fishing for steelhead in the inlet below. The huge wrap-around deck is a fine place to sit and enjoy clean, fresh air and absolute serenity. A romantic Hot Springs spa on a secluded private deck makes a perfect ending to a busy day. Consider The Highlands a home base while you explore the area or a retreat to settle into for a while. It's a winner either way.

No pets; no children under ten; smoking outside only; full breakfast; day bed extra in Room A; goldfish pond on property; off-street parking; credit cards (V,MC); wheelchair access. Brochure available.

ROOM	BED	BATH	ENTRANCE	FLOOR	DAILY RATES	
					S - D	(EP)
A	1D	Pvt	Sep	1G	$70-$75	($15)
B	1D	Pvt	Sep	1G	$60-$65	

155

Jagger House Bed & Breakfast   **(503) 657-7820**
512 Sixth Street, Oregon City, OR 97045
(Just southeast of Portland, convenient to I-5 and I-205)

Here at the "official end of the Oregon Trail," you can soak up some history while enjoying the hospitable spirit, beautiful rooms, and extra privacy afforded by Jagger House. Owner Claire Met, who lives next door, is devoted to historic preservation and to making her guests feel at home. The house was built around 1880 in the Vernacular style. Inside, it's a study in American primitive coziness -- muslin or lace window coverings, colonial blues and reds, old pine pieces, stenciling, hand-dipped candles, old quilts, spongeware dishes -- and every detail is perfectly coordinated. The flavor of each guest room is summed up in its name: Garden Delight, Victorian Rose, and Country Charm. In the yard you'll find a romantic little picnic table under an arbor, wooden lawn chairs, and country gardens. Savor a quiet escape in heartwarming surroundings at Jagger House.

Children over twelve welcome; smoking outside only; full breakfast; guest telephone; small gift and book shop on premises; museums, antique shops, historical walking tours nearby; bus transportation nearby; off-street parking; credit cards (V,MC); airport pickup by arrangement (Portland International). Brochure available.

ROOM	BED	BATH	ENTRANCE	FLOOR	DAILY RATES	
					S - D	(EP) +
A	1Q	Pvt	Sep	1	$75	
B	1Q	Shd*	Main	2	$70	
C	1Q & 1T	Shd*	Main	2	$65	($10)

The Clinkerbrick House   **(503) 281-2533**
2311 NE Schuyler, Portland, OR 97212
(Near Lloyd Center, Convention Center, and Coliseum)

In a quiet residential neighborhood just minutes from downtown Portland, discover the warm country comfort of The Clinkerbrick House. The 1908 Dutch Colonial offers all the pleasures of a welcoming, family environment, along with an extra measure of privacy for guests: a separate outside entrance, allowing one to come and go freely. The second-floor accommodations include a full kitchen/TV room and three spacious bedrooms. On the door of each room is a decoration hinting at the perfectly executed theme within. The Garden Room has a private bath, a small deck, and a botanical flavor. The Strawberry Room, with antiques and stenciled walls, shares a bath off the hallway with The Rose Room, a romantic haven done in pink roses and white wicker. Delicious full breakfasts are served in the bright, cheerful dining room. For the traveler who likes feeling independent and pampered at the same time, hosts Bob and Peggie Irvine have created the unique hospitality of The Clinkerbrick House.

No pets or smoking; full breakfast (special dietary needs accommodated); rollaway bed, $15; good area for walking or jogging; good public transportation; off-street and street parking; credit cards (V,MC). Brochure available.

ROOM	BED	BATH	ENTRANCE	FLOOR	DAILY RATES S - D	(EP) +
A	1Q	Pvt	Sep	2	$50-$60	
B	1Q	Shd*	Sep	2	$40-$50	
C	1Q & 1T	Shd*	Sep	2	$40-$50	($15)

Georgian House Bed & Breakfast   **(503) 281-2250**
1828 NE Siskiyou, Portland, OR 97212
(Near Lloyd Center, Convention Center, and Coliseum)

Portland has only three true Georgian Colonial homes; one of them is Georgian House Bed & Breakfast. This authentic beauty, built in 1922, is red brick with white columns and dark blue shutters. It stands on a double corner lot in a fine, old, northeast Portland neighborhood. Host Willie Ackley has expertly restored the home in its every exquisite detail. Her tasteful use of interior colors serves to enhance classic features such as leaded glass windows, built-in china cabinets, heavy mouldings, oak floors, a sun porch, and a fireplace. A graceful stairway leads to the second-floor guest quarters. Each of the antique-furnished bedrooms is a singularly charming creation. The romantic Lovejoy Suite is a light, spacious bed/sitting room with a canopy bed, French windows, a color TV, a ceiling fan, and a view of the lovely grounds. A large room on the lower level (D) can accommodate up to four people. A wide deck and gazebo overlooking the gardens has been added; lingering over breakfast here is indeed a pleasure, one of many you'll experience at Georgian House.

No pets; children welcome; smoking outside only; full breakfast; TV/VCR in common area; robes provided; crib available; extra-long beds in Room B; good public transportation; train and airport connections; off-street and street parking; credit cards (V,MC). One bed in Room D is a futon; accommodations for four, $100. Brochure available.

ROOM	BED	BATH	ENTRANCE	FLOOR	DAILY RATES S - D	(EP) +
A	1Q	Pvt	Main	2	$85	($10)
B	1K or 2T	Shd*	Main	2	$60-$65	
C	1Q	Shd*	Main	2	$60-$65	
D	2Q	Shd	Main	LL	$60-$65	

Portland Guest House
(503) 282-1402

1720 NE Fifteenth Avenue, Portland, OR 97212
(Closest B&B to Lloyd Center, Convention Center, and Coliseum)

An 1890 Victorian renovated with conspicuous care, Portland Guest House accommodates travelers who appreciate the historical sense it conveys, the many conveniences and comforts it offers, and the aesthetic pleasures of its decor. Innkeeper Susan Gisvold welcomes guests to enjoy the parlor, the dining room, and the garden. The interior is fresh, light, and airy, with plenty of white and discreet accents of mauve, gray, rose, and blue. Floral designs and tapestries share space with wonderful, carefully chosen art and antiques. Outfitted with heirloom linens, the guest rooms are especially appealing. There is a spacious family accommodation on the home's lower level, and the two rooms with a shared bath have private balconies. The most recent additions are two air conditioned suites with private baths on the third floor, one with a view of Mt. Hood, the other with a view of downtown Portland.

No pets; children in family room and third floor suites only; smoking outside only; full breakfast; limited kitchen privileges; private phone in each room; FAX service, shopping, dining, and light rail service nearby; bus stop at the corner; off-street parking; major credit cards. Brochure available.

ROOM	BED	BATH	ENTRANCE	FLOOR	DAILY RATES S - D	(EP) +
A	1Q & 2T	Pvt	Main	LL	$75-$85	($10)
B	1D	Pvt	Main	2	$60-$70	
C	1Q	Pvt	Main	2	$60-$70	
D	1Q	Shd*	Main	2	$45-$55	
E	1D	Shd*	Main	2	$45-$55	
F	1Q & 1T	Pvt	Main	3	$75-$85	($10)
G	1Q & 1T	Pvt	Main	3	$75-$85	($10)

Gwendolyn's Bed & Breakfast   **(503) 332-4373**
P.O. Box 913, Port Orford, OR 97465
(735 Oregon Street at coastal Highway 101)

In the quaint little fishing village of Port Orford, Gwendolyn's is a lavender bungalow guest house with four delightful bedrooms and lots of personality. Step inside and you'll be taken back to the magic and color of the twenties. Gwendolyn's is filled with vintage furniture, lace curtains, watercolor paintings, and hand-blown glass vases done by local artists. Restaurants are within walking distance and the beach and dock are only a block away. Port Orford is known for its wild rivers and its rugged, unspoiled ocean beaches. In the evening, sit by a warm fire in the parlor. Next morning, wake up to a country-style breakfast of crab or salmon quiche and fresh, locally-grown berries. Gwendolyn can guide you to the wealth of outdoor wonders and seasonal activities close by. In the springtime, wildflowers cover the hillsides in southern Oregon. Just outside the door, take a leisurely stroll through the garden where sunflowers, roses, lavender, native plants, and herbs grow.

Cable TV; telephone; crab or salmon tasting in season; off-street parking; credit cards (V,MC); airport pickup (Cape Blanco).

ROOM	BED	BATH	ENTRANCE	FLOOR	DAILY RATES S - D	(EP) +
A	1D	Pvt	Main	1	$55-$65	($10)
B	1D	Shd*	Main	2	$45-$55	($10)
C	2T	Shd*	Main	2	$45-$55	($10)
D	1Q	Pvt	Main	1	$65	($10)

HOME by the SEA (503) 332-2855
P.O. Box 606-K, Port Orford, OR 97465
(444 Jackson Street)

Alan and Brenda Mitchell built their contemporary wood home on a spit of land overlooking a stretch of Oregon coast that could take your breath away. The arresting view may be enjoyed from both lovely bedrooms and from the Sunspace where the Mitchells get to know their guests. Queen-sized Oregon Myrtlewood beds and cable TV are featured in both accommodations (Blue Suite and Coral), which make ideal quarters for two couples traveling together. It's a short walk to restaurants, public beaches, historic Battle Rock Park, and the town's harbor -- the home port of Oregon's only crane-launched commercial fishing fleet. Port Orford is a favorite of wind-surfers as well of whale, bird, and storm watchers. It's an enchanting discovery, and so is HOME by the SEA.

No pets, children, or smoking; full breakfast; cable TV; laundry privileges; phone jacks in rooms; off-street parking; Macintosh spoken, CompuServe ID#72672,1072; credit cards (V,MC).

ROOM	BED	BATH	ENTRANCE	FLOOR	DAILY RATES	
					S - D	(EP) +
A	1Q	Pvt	Main	2	$75	($10)
B	1Q	Pvt	Main	2	$70	

House of Hunter   **(503) 672-2335**
813 SE Kane Street, Roseburg, OR 97470
(Bordering downtown Roseburg)

On a quiet residential street in the company of other historic homes, House of Hunter is a classic Italianate built at the turn of the century. In 1990 Walt and Jean Hunter made extensive renovations, preserving the home's essential character while adding modern attributes to enhance its ease and comfort, resulting in a light, airy, expansive atmosphere. The lovely guest rooms, each named for one of the hosts' daughters, feature English wardrobe closets, hand-made quilts, and antique accents. Inspired by their own B&B travels, the Hunters offer their guests such treats as early morning coffee and goodies delivered to the second floor alcove, followed by a full breakfast served in the dining room. The grand room on the main floor is for the use of guests. If you stay two days, the hosts offer free use of their raft on the Umpqua River. A warm welcome is always yours at House of Hunter.

No pets; children over twelve welcome; smoking outside only; AC; full breakfast; TV/VCR; laundry facilities; walk to downtown shops, restaurants, and churches; off-street parking; credit cards (V,MC); airport shuttle (Roseburg). Brochure available.

ROOM	BED	BATH	ENTRANCE	FLOOR	DAILY RATES	
					S - D	(EP) +
A	1Q	Pvt	Main	2	$60-$65	($15)
B	1Q	Pvt	Main	2	$60-$65	($15)
C	2T	Shd*	Main	2	$45-$50	
D	1D	Shd*	Main	2	$45-$50	

Summer House   **(503) 738-5740**
1221 North Franklin, Seaside, OR 97138   **1(800) 745-BEST**
(North end of Seaside, one block from beach)

In bustling Seaside, quiet is a luxury. A tranquil environment is one of the many assets of Summer House, a completely renovated vacation home with a history of beachside hospitality. It has a gray-shingled exterior, ample decking, and latticed and trellised garden areas burgeoning with flowers and vegetables. The interior is clean and modern with plenty of natural light and a subtle Southwest flavor. The Garden Room, a romantic haven on the main level, features a fireplace, a sitting area, a small refrigerator, and a TV. Other lovely rooms express different themes: Sunrise (with mountain view, fire-place, fridge, and TV), Sunset, and Whispering Seas. Host Jerry Newsome's breakfast cuisine is the essence of fresh-from-the-garden goodness. He and his wife, Leslee, provide superb, year-round hospitality at Summer House.

Dog in residence; no pets, children, or teenagers; no smoking; full breakfast; shopping, dining, ocean and river activities, beachcombing, whale and birdwatching, golfing, horseback riding, and more nearby; off-street parking; credit cards (V,MC); weekend and holiday mini-mums. Brochure available.

ROOM	BED	BATH	ENTRANCE	FLOOR	DAILY RATES S - D (EP) +
A	1Q	Pvt	Main	1	$80
B	1Q	Pvt	Main	2	$80
C	1Q	Pvt	Main	2	$60
D	1Q	Pvt	Main	2	$60

Walden House   **(503) 655-4960**
P.O. Box 593, West Linn, OR 97068
(Just southeast of Portland, convenient to I-5 and I-205)

    Located in the historic Willamette Falls area, this Queen Anne Stick Victorian is surrounded by country gardens replete with flowers and shrubs.   In this friendly neighborhood of many beautifully re-stored turn-of-the-century dwellings, the home of Charles and Diane Awalt is a National Register property of utmost authenticity. Furnishings were selected with care to suit the era and scale of the house. Victorian colors predominate in an atmosphere of warm, polished redwood and fir, stained glass, mouldings, and wainscoting with wallpaper. The dining room has a marvelous garden view, a fitting place for breakfast prepared with a gourmet's touch. Vintage table and bed linens are used, and every room displays interesting collectibles. A large bath off the hallway features a long, deep clawfoot tub and a lovely old braided rug. Relax on the wide veranda, in the library, or in your carefully tailored bedroom. Walden House brings the past to life as few places do.

    Cats in residence; no pets; no young children; full breakfast; robes provided; antiquing and river canoeing nearby; ample street parking. Brochure available. *custom mattresses measuring 76" x 40"

ROOM	BED	BATH	ENTRANCE	FLOOR	DAILY RATES	
					S - D	(EP) +
A	2T*	Shd	Main	2	$55-$60	
B	1D	Shd	Main	2	$55-$60	

164

Ziggurat Bed & Breakfast   **(503) 547-3925**
P.O. Box 757, Yachats, OR 97498
(95330 Highway 101; 6.5 miles south of Yachats)

Many coast aficionados would pick this unspoiled stretch of ocean wilderness near Cape Perpetua as an endless source of riches to explore. Here, with immediate beach access just thirty yards away, stands Ziggurat, true to its ancient Sumerian meaning, "terraced pyramid." A dwelling unique in every sense, its ambiance combines supreme comfort, constant communion with nature, fine contemporary art, and most civilized hospitality. Two deluxe accommodations occupy the first floor. The Southeast Suite, facing the mountains, has a queen bed behind French doors, a tiled solarium with comfortable furnishings, a tiled private bath with a sauna, and an alcove with a twin bed. The West Suite, which faces the sea, features a round glass-block shower, a partially mirrored ceiling, hand-made furnishings, and twenty-seven feet of glass! In the expansive second-floor dining area, relish the view along with full breakfasts featuring homemade breads. At the apex of the pyramid with windows on all sides is a superlative guest room one must see to believe. The same could be said of Ziggurat as a whole.

No pets; no children under fourteen; smoking outside only; full breakfast; first floor has west-facing, glass-enclosed deck and a common room with refrigerator and microwave; hiking, fishing, birding, tidepooling, and more nearby; off-street parking. Brochure available.

ROOM	BED	BATH	ENTRANCE	FLOOR	DAILY RATES S - D (EP) +
A	1Q	Pvt	Main	1	$100-$110
B	1Q & 1T	Pvt	Main	1	$85-$95 ($15)
C	1Q	Pvt	Main	4	$85-$95

How each friend represents a world in us, a world possibly not born until they arrive, and it is only by this meeting that a new world is born.

—Anaïs Nin

Do you know that conversation is one of the greatest pleasures in life? But it wants leisure.

—W. Somerset Maugham

Please read "About Dining Highlights" on page *vii*.

ALOHA

Nonna Emilia, 17210 SW Shaw; (503) 649-2232; Italian

ASHLAND

Chateaulin, 50 East Main Street; (503) 482-2264; French

House of Thai, 1667 Siskiyou Boulevard; (503) 488-2583; authentic Thai cuisine

Monet, 36 South Second Street; (503) 482-1339; light French

New Sammy's Cowboy Bistro, 2210 South Pacific Highway, Talent; (503) 535-2779; country French

Plaza Cafe, 47 North Main Street; (503) 488-2233; seafood/pasta/vegetarian specialties

Winchester Country Inn, 35 South Second Street; (503) 488-1113; international fare/historic 1886 home overlooking gardens

ASTORIA

Cafe Uniontown, 218 West Marine Drive; (503) 325-8708; varied menu

Pier 11 Feed Store Restaurant & Lounge, waterfront at foot of Tenth and Eleventh Streets; (503) 325-0279; seafood specialties

Victoria Dahl's, 2921 Marine Drive; (503) 325-7109; salad/sandwich lunches/Italian pasta dinners/espresso drinks

BANDON

Bandon Boatworks, South Jetty; (503) 347-2111; seafood

Lord Bennett's, 1695 Beach Loop Road; (503) 347-3663; Continental/seafood

Sea Star Bistro, Second Street, Old Town; (503) 347-9632; creative house-made dishes

BEAVERTON

McCormick's Fish House & Bar, 9945 SW Beaverton-Hillsdale Highway; (503) 643-1322; extensive seafood menu

BROOKINGS

Caffe Fredde, 1025 Chetco Avenue (U.S. 101); (503) 469-3733

CANNON BEACH

Bistro Restaurant & Bar, 263 North Hemlock Street; (503) 436-2661; Northwest eclectic

Cafe de la Mer, 1287 South Hemlock Street; (503) 436-1179; Northwest/French

CHARLESTON

Portside, 8001 Kingfisher Road at Charleston Boat Basin; (503) 888-5544; fresh seafood/some Chinese dishes

COOS BAY

Blue Heron Bistro, 100 Commercial; (503) 267-3933; Continental

Kum-Yon's, 835 South Broadway; (503) 269-2662; Japanese/Chinese/Korean

COTTAGE GROVE

Casey's Station, 1133 East Main Street; (503) 942-1102; family dining

The Covered Bridge, 401 Main Street; (503) 942-1255; Continental/Italian

Thee Delicatessen Restaurant, 1435 Highway 99; (503) 942-4405; European

DUNDEE

Tina's, 760 SW 99W; (503) 538-8880; Northwest/French/fine dining

EUGENE

Chanterelle, 207 East Fifth Street; (503) 484-4065; fresh fish/pasta

Chez Ray's, Nineteenth Street and Agate; (503) 342-8596; European

The Excelsior Cafe, 754 East Thirteenth Avenue; (503) 342-6963; nouvelle Northwest

The French Horn Cafe & Bakery, in L&L Market at 1591 Willamette, downtown Eugene; (503) 343-7473; soups/breads/takeout items

The Gazebo Restaurant, 1646 East Nineteenth Street; (503) 683-6661; Middle Eastern

Jamie's Great Hamburgers, 2445 Hilyard; (503) 343-8488

L'Auberge, 770 West Sixth Street; (503) 485-8000; French regional

Mediterranean Cafe, 412 Pearl Street; (503) 342-8411; Middle Eastern

West Brothers Bar B Que, 844 Olive Street; (503) 345-8489; regional American

Zenon Cafe, 898 Pearl Street; (503) 343-3005; international/great desserts

FLORENCE

Traveler's Cove, 1362 Bay Street; (503) 997-6845; light meals and snacks

GOLD BEACH

Rod 'n' Reel, on Rogue River at Jot's Resort, Wedderburn; (503) 247-6823; varied menu for breakfast/lunch/dinner

Rogue Landing, 94749 Jerrys Flat Road; (503) 247-6031; seafood and steaks

GRANTS PASS

Bistro, 1214 NW Sixth Street; (503) 479-3412

Buzz's Blue Heron Dinner Theater, 330 Merlin Avenue; (503) 479-6604

Hamilton House, 344 NE Terry Lane; (503) 479-3938; seafood/pasta/fowl/beef

Maria's Mexican Kitchen, 105 NE Mill Street; (503) 474-2429

Matsukaze, 1675 NE Seventh Street; (503) 479-2961; Japanese

Paradise Ranch Inn, 7000 Monument Drive; (503) 479-4333; Continental

Pongsri's, 1571 NE Sixth Street; (503) 479-1345; Thai

R-Haus Restaurant & Bistro, 2140 Rogue River Highway; (503) 476-4287

HILLSBORO

Reedville Cafe, 21935 SW Tualatin Valley Highway; (503) 649-4643; casual, varied menu

JACKSONVILLE

Jacksonville Inn Dinner House, 175 East California Street; (503) 899-1900; Continental/Northwest

McCully House Inn Restaurant, 240 East California Street; (503) 599-1942; creative American/historic home atmosphere

LA GRANDE

Centennial Street, 1606 Sixth Street; (503) 963-6089; modified Continental

Ten Depot Street, 10 Depot Street; (503) 963-8766; steaks/seafood/pasta
LAKE OSWEGO
Amadeus, Second and B Streets; (503) 636-7500; Continental
LINCOLN CITY
Audrey's Restaurant, 1725 SW Highway 101; (503) 994-6210; Continental
Bay House, 5911 SW Highway 101; (503) 996-3222; Continental/seafood
Dory Cove, 5819 Logan Road; (503) 994-5180; clam chowder/seafood
Kernville Steak & Seafood House, 186 Siletz Highway; (503) 994-6200
Kyllo's Seafood & Broiler, 2733 NW Highway 101; (503) 994-3179
Otis Cafe, Highway 18 at Otis Junction; (503) 994-2813; old-fashioned
country cooking
MC MINNVILLE
Augustine's, Highway 18; (503) 843-3225; Continental
Nick's Italian Cafe, 521 East Third Street; (503) 434-4471
Roger's Seafood Restaurant, 2121 East 27th Street; (503) 472-0917
Sir Hinkleman Funnyduffer Cafe, Wine & Antiques, 421 East Third Street;
(503) 472-1309; picnics/lunch/catering
Umberto's, 828 North Adams Street; (503) 472-1717; traditional Italian
MILWAUKIE
Nonna Emilia, 16691 SE McLoughlin Boulevard; (503) 786-1004; Italian
NEWBERG
The Noodle, 2320 Portland Road; (503) 538-0507; exceptional pasta dinners
Ixtapa Restaurant, 307 East First Street; (503) 538-5956; Mexican
Pasquale's Italian Restaurant, 111 West First Street; (503) 538-0910
NEWPORT
Canyon Way Bookstore and Restaurant, 1216 SW Canyon Way; (503) 265-8319;
innovative dishes include fresh fish/salads/desserts/more
OCEANSIDE
Roseanna's Oceanside Cafe, 1490 Pacific NW; (503) 842-7351; seafood/pasta
OREGON CITY
Fellows House, 416 South McLoughlin Boulevard; (503) 650-9322; lunch
PORTLAND
Alexis, 215 West Burnside Street; (503) 224-8577; Greek
Bread & Ink Cafe, 3610 SE Hawthorne Boulevard; (503) 239-4756;
Continental
Cafe des Amis, 1987 NW Kearney Street; (503) 295-6487; lighter
French/Continental
Elizabeth's Cafe, 3135 NE Broadway; (503) 281-8337; Continental
Genoa, 2832 SE Belmont Street; (503) 238-1464; fine Italian cuisine
Heathman Bakery & Pub, 901 SW Salmon; (503) 227-5700; designer
pizza/brewpub
Indigine, 3723 SE Division Street; (503) 238-1470; Asian
Jake's Famous Crawfish, 401 SW Twelfth; (503) 226-1419; Northwest seafood

McCormick & Schmick's Oak Street Restaurant, 235 SW First Avenue; (503) 224-7522; extensive seafood menu

Merchant of Venice Cafe, 1432 NE Broadway; (503) 284-4558; pizza/salads/more

Papa Haydn, 5829 SE Milwaukie; (503) 232-9440; killer desserts

Winterborne, 3520 NE 42nd; (503) 249-8486; intimate dining/fine seafood

PORT ORFORD

CB's Bistro on the Sixes, 93316 Sixes River Road (at The Sixes River Hotel, six miles north of Port Orford); (503) 332-3900; French Continental/seafood

Crazy Norwegian Fish & Chips, U.S. 101 at Sixth and Jackson; (503) 332-8601

The Truculent Oyster, U.S. 101 at Sixth and Jefferson; (503) 332-9461; local seafood/steaks

SANDY

The Ivy Bear, 54735 East Highway 26; (503) 622-3440; Czechoslovakian

SEAL ROCK

Yuzen Japanese, Highway 101; (503) 563-4766

SEASIDE

Emmanuel's Restaurant, 104 Broadway; (503) 738-7038; light Italian plus

WELCHES

Chalet Swiss, Highway 26 on Welches Road; (503) 622-3600; Swiss/Northwest/fresh seafood

The Resort at the Mountain, 68010 East Fairway (at base of Mount Hood); (503) 622-3101; informal dining in The Tartans or elegant dining in The Highlands

WEST LINN

Bugatti's, 18740 Willamette Drive; (503) 636-9555; Italian

YACHATS

La Serre, Second and Beach Streets; (503) 547-3420; breakfast/lunch/dinner; fresh fish/pasta/chicken/small to ample meals

WASHINGTON

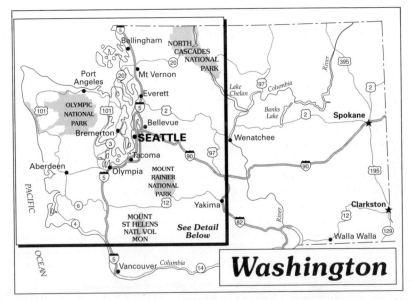

Washington

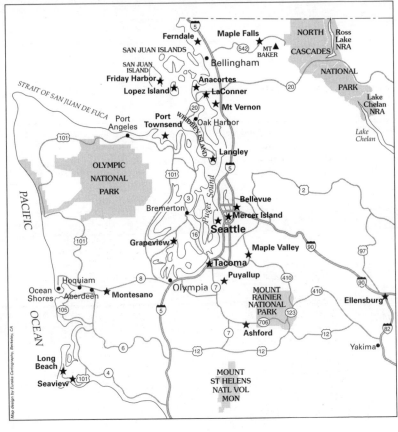

Albatross Bed & Breakfast (206) 293-0677
5708 Kingsway West, Anacortes, WA 98221
(Across from Skyline Marina on Fidalgo Island)

When this home was built in the twenties, almost at water's edge, it was well constructed of solid cedar and survives today as a gracious haven of hospitality. The Albatross Bed & Breakfast provides excellent views of the boat launch area, the sea, and the San Juan Islands. Each comfortable, commodious guest room has a bath, an original painting, a lap blanket, thick carpeting, and a quiet, restful atmosphere. Antiques, fine art, and collectibles are displayed throughout the home. There is a vast selection of books and games, and a spacious living room offers a fireplace, a TV/VCR, and an inspiring panorama. Hosts Ken and Barbie do everything possible to ensure a pleasant stay for their guests, who appreciate especially the made-from-scratch breakfasts featuring local flavors. A sincere welcome and an array of thoughtful extras make staying here a rich experience indeed.

Smoking outside only; full breakfast; recreational opportunities close by, including sailboat cruises aboard hosts' 46-foot "Charisma"; travel information available; transportation to ferries (one mile away); off-street parking; credit cards (V,MC); winter rates. Brochure available.

ROOM	BED	BATH	ENTRANCE	FLOOR	DAILY RATES	
					S - D	(EP) +
A	1Q	Pvt	Main	1	$85	($20)
B	1K	Pvt	Main	1	$85	
C	1K	Pvt	Main	1	$85	
D	1Q	Pvt	Main	1	$75	($20)

Channel House   **(206) 293-9382**
2902 Oakes Avenue, Anacortes, WA 98221   **1(800) 238-4353**
(Overlooking Guemes Channel, five minutes from ferry docks)

Channel House is a joyous discovery for anyone traveling to this corner of the country. It's a home of unusual character; every guest room is uniquely situated for gazing out at the channel and the San Juan Islands. Shiny wood floors with Oriental rugs, fine antique furnishings, a library, and three fireplaces create an atmosphere of classic European elegance. Owners since 1986, Pat and Dennis McIntyre have preserved the flavor of the house while adding their own touches to make it their family home. Hosts are former restaurateurs who take pride in the quality and variety of the breakfasts they serve, usually before a crackling fire. Rooms E and F are in the Rose Cottage, adjacent to main house; the individually decorated quarters feature fireplaces and private baths with whirlpool tubs. A memorable treat for guests is outdoor hot-tubbing with a view of island sunsets. All in all, staying at Channel House is an experience to be savored.

No pets; children over twelve OK; no smoking; full breakfast; evening refreshments; off-street parking; credit cards (V,MC,D); ferry pickup. Brochure available.

ROOM	BED	BATH	ENTRANCE	FLOOR	DAILY RATES	
					S - D	(EP) +
A	1K & 1T	Pvt	Main	2	$79-$89	($20)
B	1Q	Pvt	Main	2	$69-$79	
C	1D	Pvt	Main	1	$69-$79	
D	1D	Pvt	Main	1	$59-$69	
E	1Q	Pvt	Sep	1	$95	
F	1Q	Pvt	Sep	1	$95	

Growly Bear Bed & Breakfast   **(206) 569-2339**
37311 SR 706, Ashford, WA 98304
(One mile from entrance to Mount Rainier National Park)

Just before the park entrance to Mount Rainier National Park, an old wooden homestead house stands hidden by a shield of mammoth cedars. Old-growth cedar was used in the original 1890 building, which has undergone recent renovations. Susan Jenny has made it her home for many years and calls it Growly Bear. As rustic as its surroundings, the house offers three B&B rooms on the second floor, named after the original homesteaders, a nearby mountain peak, and a local river. The first two are cozy and cheery, sharing a bath off the hallway. The third is an expansive space with lots of windows, a sitting area with sofas, a private bath, and Growly Bear slippers in the closet! In each room, stuffed bears form a welcoming committee and a snack basket satisfies the munchies. Be lulled to sleep by the sound of Goat Creek, awake to the aroma of fresh bread from the nearby Sweet Peaks bakery ovens, and then enjoy a hearty mountain breakfast.

No pets; children negotiable; no smoking; full breakfast; off-street parking; major credit cards. Brochure available.

ROOM	BED	BATH	ENTRANCE	FLOOR	DAILY RATES S - D	(EP) +
A	1D	Shd*	Main	2	$60-$70	
B	1D	Shd*	Main	2	$60-$70	
C	1D	Pvt	Main	2	$70-$80	($20)

Jasmer's Guest House at Mount Rainier   **(206) 569-2682**
P.O. Box 347, Ashford, WA 98304
(Five miles from entrance to Mount Rainier National Park)

Tanna and Luke Osterhaus transformed the one-time home of an old logging family, the Jasmers, into a residence for themselves, and have added at the back a very private little guest accommodation they call The Bird's Nest. Ideally suited for one or two people at a time, it is warm, cozy, and romantic. It has the original wood interior, a shower for two, TV/VCR, table and chairs, a small fridge and microwave, and an air of sweet nostalgia. A Continental "Plus" breakfast is provided, to be prepared at your leisure. Tanna is a great source for all the information you could possibly need to make the most of your time at Mount Rainier. Lovely grounds and gardens include a spring-fed goldfish pond, burgeoning foliage and blossoms, and a pasture for Oscar, the llama. Jasmer's offers the perfect balance of pampering and privacy. It's a place to celebrate intimacy, historic surroundings, and nature all at the same time.

No pets; smoking outside only; rate without breakfast, $55; off-street parking; inquire about fully-outfitted cabins and cottages in Ashford (two-night minimum).

ROOM	BED	BATH	ENTRANCE	FLOOR	DAILY RATES S - D (EP) +
A	1Q	Pvt	Sep	1	$65

Mountain Meadows Inn (206) 569-2788
P.O. Box 291, Ashford, WA 98304
(Six miles from entrance to Mount Rainier National Park)

The enchantment of Mountain Meadows Inn starts the minute you turn off the main highway to the clearing where this 1910 Craftsman-style home stands in a meadow encircled by forest and country quiet. It overlooks a stream-fed pond edged with cattails. The sturdy, character-filled house features a kaleidoscope of heartwarming images and artistic touches. Host Chad Darrah, an engineer for "Rail-Link Railroad," displays a life-long collection of railroad paraphernalia. In 1991 he added two guest units (D and E) in a new building next door, and one has a full kitchen. Back at the main house, hearty breakfast fare is prepared on an old, wood-fired cookstove. Other old-fashioned pleasures include gathering 'round the campfire in the evening, visiting on the wide front porch, or reading hearthside in the living room. The property is a magical place to explore, and, of course, the mountain beckons.

Dog, cats, pigs, chickens, and ducks on property; no pets; children over ten welcome; no smoking in bedrooms; full breakfast; VCR in living room; player piano; pond has small dock, trout, and catfish; hiking trail to old National townsite; inquire about Scenic Railroad trips; off-street parking; credit cards (V,MC). Brochure available.

ROOM	BED	BATH	ENTRANCE	FLOOR	DAILY RATES	
					S - D	(EP) +
A	1Q	Pvt	Main	1	$95	
B	1K & 2T	Pvt	Main	1	$85	($15)
C	1Q	Pvt	Main	1	$75	($15)
D	1D & 1T	Pvt	Sep	2	$75	($15)
E	1D	Pvt	Sep	2	$75	($15)

Petersen Bed & Breakfast　　　　　　　**(206) 454-9334**
10228 SE Eighth, Bellevue, WA 98004
(Fifteen minutes east of Seattle)

Though some think of Bellevue simply as part of suburban Seattle, it has come into its own in recent years as a major business and shopping area with its fair share of fine dining establishments and horticultural displays. In a quiet, established neighborhood, Eunice and Carl Petersen open their warm and inviting home to bed and breakfast guests. On the lower (daylight) level of the house you'll find two pretty, relaxing rooms with down comforters, plush carpeting, and tasteful decorator touches. Spend leisure moments on the large deck -- perhaps in the steamy spa -- that overlooks beautifully landscaped grounds. After a wonderful night's rest, enjoy a generous home-style breakfast in the atrium kitchen. Then you should be able to face the day with a smile.

Smoking outside only; full breakfast; TV/VCR; hot tub; waterbed in Room A; one mile from Bellevue Square shopping; good public transportation; off-street parking; one-night stays, $10 extra.

ROOM	BED	BATH	ENTRANCE	FLOOR	DAILY RATES S - D (EP) +
A	1Q	Shd*	Main	LL	$55
B	1K or 2T	Shd*	Main	LL	$55

The Cliff House Bed & Breakfast   (509) 758-1267
2000 Westlake Drive, Clarkston, WA 99403
(Eight miles west of Clarkston, overlooking Snake River)

The Snake River Valley, also known as the Lewis and Clark Valley, is as rich in history as it is in outdoor recreational activities. It is the ancestral home of the Nez Perce Indian tribe, and Chief Timothy State Park is named for one of their most important leaders. The park is located on the Snake River and may be seen from the five-hundred-foot vantage point where The Cliff House is perched. From the house, the river, the canyon, and the vast expanse of sky loom so large that one is constantly astonished at the view from every room. Soaking in the spa on the deck under a starlit sky is unforgettable. Guest accommodations, all on one level, include a large sitting room with a wood-burning stove and comfortable sofas. On either side are The Chief Timothy Room and The Channel Room, both so appealing that it's hard to choose a favorite. If you wish, hosts Doug and Sonia Smith can help you discover the bountiful variety of wildlife, history, and recreation their region has to offer.

No pets; children over ten welcome; smoking outside only; full breakfast; deck; spa; golf privileges available at country club; jogging on trails, cycling on pathways, rafting, birdwatching, and fishing nearby; off-street parking; credit cards (V,MC). Brochure available.

ROOM	BED	BATH	ENTRANCE	FLOOR	DAILY RATES	
					S - D	(EP) +
A	1Q	Pvt	Main	LL	$70-$75	($15)
B	1Q	Pvt	Main	LL	$60-$65	($15)

Murphy's Country Bed & Breakfast   **(509) 925-7986**
Route 1, Box 400, Ellensburg, WA 98926
(Near junction of I-90 and Highway 97)

Ellensburg, situated in a wide, picturesque valley in central Washington, is cattle and horse country. The annual rodeo, western parade, and county fair draw folks from all over. Hiking in state parks, golfing, and cross-country skiing are also popular. Doris Callahan offers some of the area's most pleasant lodging in her stately home, situated on three rural acres. With a foundation of native stone, it is a house with a feeling of substance. From the lovely front porch, enter a commodious living room with high ceilings, an abundance of beautiful woodwork, and an inviting hearth. Also on the main floor is a formal dining room where Doris, a professional baker, serves breakfast. Accommodations on the second floor include two spacious bedrooms attractively decorated in peach and aqua. A large bathroom and a half-bath are shared by guests. Turn-of-the-century style combined with twentieth-century comfort make Murphy's Country Bed & Breakfast an altogether memorable place to stay.

Dog in residence; no pets; limited accommodations for children; no smoking; full breakfast; museums, art galleries, historical buildings, river rafting, cattle drives, berry-picking, and fishing nearby; off-street parking; major credit cards. Brochure available.

ROOM	BED	BATH	ENTRANCE	FLOOR	DAILY RATES S - D (EP) +
A	1Q	Shd*	Main	2	$55-$60
B	1Q	Shd*	Main	2	$55-$60

Anderson House Bed & Breakfast   **(206) 384-3450**
P.O. Box 1547, Ferndale, WA 98248
(2140 Main Street)

David and Kelly Anderson's extensive renovations have brought out
the best in this interesting old house, and the beautifully landscaped
yard with its distinctive lampposts makes a welcoming impression.
Inside, perfectly chosen furnishings strike just the right balance between comfort and aesthetics. Luxurious carpeting, wallcoverings,
and fabrics, plus a stunning Bavarian crystal swan chandelier mark the
decor. With humor and thoughtfulness, the Andersons make guests
feel relaxed and pampered. Accommodations are of the highest quality, as is the cuisine. Each of the bedrooms is charming, but the Tower
Suite (D) is especially unique; the huge space has a sloped ceiling, lots
of angles, touches of wood and brick, an alcove with a day bed, and a
refrigerator. It has one drawback: You may never come out to enjoy
the rest of the Andersons' splendid hospitality.

No pets; children over twelve welcome; smoking outside only;
extensive list of amenities; several restaurants within walking distance; forty-one minutes from downtown Vancouver, BC; thirty minutes from Victoria ferry; off-street parking; all major credit cards;
extra person in room, $10. Brochure available.

ROOM	BED	BATH	ENTRANCE	FLOOR	DAILY RATES	
					S - D	(EP) +
A	1D	Pvt	Main	2	$49	
B	2T	Pvt	Main	2	$49	
C	1Q & 1T	Pvt	Main	2	$59	
D	1K & 2T	Pvt	Main	2	$79	

Llewop Bed & Breakfast   **(206) 275-2287**
Box 97, Grapeview, WA 98546
(Southwest Puget Sound, off Highway 3)

This huge contemporary home rests on a wooded knoll overlooking
an orchard, Case Inlet, and Stretch Island, with the summit of Mount
Rainier showing on clear days. It is endowed with many windows,
skylights, and decks, so it's easy to feel at one with the incredible
beauty of the environment. There are three bedrooms for guests, all
as lovely as can be. Room A has a spacious private deck with full
view. Guests are welcome to sit around the living room fireplace,
explore the property, swim, play pickleball, or unwind in the whirlpool spa (tub in bathroom on main floor). Most of all, Llewop is a
place for restoration and relaxation. Kris Powell wants you to enjoy
her home as much as she enjoys sharing it.

No pets; families welcome; smoking on decks; full breakfast; TV;
extra beds; bathtub spa; pickleball court; golf course and restaurant
four miles away; ample parking; clergy discount.

ROOM	BED	BATH	ENTRANCE	FLOOR	DAILY RATES S - D (EP)	
A	1D	Pvt	Main	2	$45-$65	($20)
B	2T	Pvt	Main	2	$45-$65	($20)
C	2T	Pvt	Main	1	$45-$65	($20)

The White Swan Guest House
(206) 445-6805

1388 Moore Road, Mount Vernon, WA 98273
(Six miles from La Conner, on Skagit River)

Peter Goldfarb made a major shift in life style when he moved from New York City to the quiet countryside of the Pacific Northwest, but adapted to hosting quite easily. He bought a handsome Victorian home, badly in need of attention, and gave it his all. Keeping its charm and character intact, Peter's inspired renovations turned it into the jewel it is today. My favorite aspect of the decor is the bold use of color throughout the house. Vivid hues of a country garden create a cheerful environment, a lift to the spirit on dull days. Comfortable rooms are uniquely decorated, featuring Peter's large collection of antique samplers. Outside, English-style country gardens with seating areas and lots of flowers enhance the grounds. To the rear of the property is a wonderful, private Garden Cottage (D) with its own kitchen, deck, and gorgeous views of the farmlands. Mother Nature has richly endowed the surrounding landscape -- it's great for walking along the river, cycling, and observing wildlife. Any way you look at it, The White Swan is a find.

Dogs in residence; smoking outside only (porch); homemade chocolate chip cookies all day; three rooms share two baths on second floor; double futon sofa bed extra in cottage; off-street parking; credit cards (V,MC).

ROOM	BED	BATH	ENTRANCE	FLOOR	DAILY RATES S - D (EP) +
A	1K	Shd*	Main	2	$65-$75
B	1Q	Shd*	Main	2	$65-$75
C	1Q	Shd*	Main	2	$65-$75
D	1Q	Pvt	Sep	1 & 2	$125($20)

Boreas Bed & Breakfast   **(206) 642-8069**
P.O. Box 1344, Long Beach, WA 98631
(607 North Boulevard)

Where else but on Washington's Long Beach Peninsula can you find twenty-eight miles of uninterrupted beach, a comfy, romantic haven waiting just over the dunes from water's edge, and several top-rated restaurants nearby? Boreas Bed & Breakfast was an early twenties beach house that hosts Sally and Coleman (who live next door) spent years renovating to create a four-room B&B with a rustic, shingled exterior, stone fireplace, and windows that take advantage of coastal views. The interior features high ceilings, exposed wood, brass accents, antiques and collectibles, white walls with well-chosen artwork, fluffy bedcovers in soft prints, and collections of records, games, and books. There are two large common areas, a delightful open kitchen that's available to all, a hot tub room, and a ground-floor suite with a small deck. Upstairs, two of the three wonderful bedrooms were designed with wave-watchers in mind. Boreas Bed & Breakfast is a place to get in touch -- with nature, with the here and now, and with each other.

Dog on premises; no pets; children by prior arrangement; smoking outside only; full breakfast; hot tub; bicycles available; pristine Willapa Bay (kayaking, canoeing, great oysters) nearby; off-street parking; airport pickup with advance notice (Ilwaco, Astoria); inquire about family rates and adjacent three-bedroom beach house for rent. Brochure available.

ROOM	BED	BATH	ENTRANCE	FLOOR	DAILY RATES	
					S - D	(EP) +
A	1Q & 1T	Pvt	Main	1	$75-$85	($10)
B	1Q	Pvt	Main	2	$75-$85	
C	1Q	Shd*	Main	2	$60-$70	
D	1D & 1T	Shd*	Main	2	$50-$60	($10)

Inn at Swifts Bay　　　　　　　　　　**(206) 468-3636**
Route 2, Box 3402, Lopez Island, WA　98261　　FAX: **468-3637**
(Two miles from ferry dock on Port Stanley Road)

A few days on Lopez Island can satisfy many tastes.　It's the
friendliest place in the San Juans (be sure to wave!), so you'll feel
welcome right off.　Cyclists and nature lovers consider it an ideal
getaway.　Those who appreciate luxury and superb cuisine will find
the Inn at Swifts Bay much to their liking.　The Tudor-style inn is
classy, stylish, and oh, so comfortable.　Hosts Christopher and Robert
provide every amenity a guest might need and then some.　An understated elegance marks the decor.　When you're not out exploring the
island, you'll find a choice of areas to relax that are just for guests:
your tastefully appointed bedroom or suite, the living room by the
fireplace, the outdoor hot tub (sign up ahead for complete privacy), or
the sunning area.　Mornings will find you at your very own table
enjoying a breakfast that is nothing short of sensational.　Then take a
stroll down to the private beach across the road and let the day unfold.

No pets, children, or smoking; full breakfast; TV/VCR with good
selection of movies; guest phone; small fridge with complimentary
mineral water and ice; hot tub; bicycles for rent by reservation;
off-street parking; major credit cards; pickup at ferry dock, airstrip,
or seaplane dock.　Brochure available.

ROOM	BED	BATH	ENTRANCE	FLOOR	DAILY RATES S - D　(EP) +
A	1Q	Shd*	Main	1	$75
B	1Q	Shd*	Main	1	$85
C	1Q	Pvt	Main	1	$110
D	1Q	Pvt	Main	2	$125
E	1Q	Pvt	Main	2	$140

Yodeler Inn   **(206) 599-2156**
P.O. Box 222, Maple Falls, WA 98266
(Twenty-six miles east of Bellingham in Mount Baker foothills)

Yodeler Inn seems a natural part of the ambiance in the little alpine village of Maple Falls. With the omnipresence of Mount Baker, the surrounding area is a vacation wonderland with year-round adventures to pursue. Here Jeff and Bethnie Morrison aim to provide "a relaxing environment to sleep, eat, and play in." Their homey inn has one guest room with its own entrance, country decor, and a hot tub just outside the door; a spacious living room with a fireplace may also be used. An intimate private cottage (B) on the property provides additional accommodation. It's a pleasant surprise to find several good restaurants, and one great one, nearby. Some local activities include Alpine and cross-country skiing, river rafting, hiking, mountain climbing, fishing, and photography. Your hosts can suggest many more.

Two cats in residence; smoking outside only; full breakfast; kitchenette in cottage; TV/VCR available; off-street parking; credit cards (V,MC). Brochure available.

ROOM	BED	BATH	ENTRANCE	FLOOR	DAILY RATES	
					S - D	(EP) +
A	1Q	Pvt	Sep	1	$35-$65	
B	1D & 1T	Pvt	Sep	1	$35-$65	

Maple Valley Bed & Breakfast   **(206) 432-1409**
20020 SE 228, Maple Valley, WA 98038
(Nineteen miles due east of Sea-Tac International Airport)

After a demanding week at work or a day of hard traveling, how satisfying to find that perfect haven in the country for a few days of pampered relaxation -- Maple Valley Bed & Breakfast. Jayne and Clarke Hurlbut have fashioned a rustic family home of outstanding warmth and charm. Built by Clarke, it stands in a clearing in the woods, surrounded by a carpet of neat green lawn. The later addition of an "eagles' aerie" lends a fairytale quality. Walls of warm cedar, a huge stone fireplace, open-beamed ceilings, and many interesting angles give the house its singular appeal, and two gabled guest rooms on the second floor couldn't be more endearing. The decor is country Americana, very well done. Each room has lacy curtains, antiques, and nostalgia pieces, as well as French doors that open to a large deck. Featured in Room A are a handhewn four-poster log bed and a pedestal sink; in Room B, beautiful heirloom quilts cover the beds. An upstairs sitting room and adjoining TV area are great for reading, playing games, working puzzles, and viewing the wildlife pond through binoculars. Attention to detail is the essence of what's so special at Maple Valley Bed & Breakfast. Far be it from me to spoil all the surprises.

Outdoor peacocks, chickens, cats, and dog; no pets; smoking outside only; full breakfast; crib available; barbecue area; basketball; hiking; nature walks; available for outdoor weddings; off-street parking.

ROOM	BED	BATH	ENTRANCE	FLOOR	DAILY RATES S - D (EP) +
A	1Q	Shd*	Main	2	$60-$65 ($15)
B	1D & 1T	Shd*	Main	2	$45-$50 ($15)

Duck-In   **(206) 232-2554**
4118 - 100th Avenue, SE, Mercer Island, WA 98040
(East side of island on waterfront)

Removed from urban frenzy, on the bank of Lake Washington, this inviting, cozy cottage makes a great little getaway spot. Take it easy in lounge chairs on the sloping green lawn, grill some fish for dinner, or even send out for pizza -- you'll probably want to stay put for a while. Guests have the cottage to themselves. Full of homey touches, it's comfy as can be. There are two bedrooms separated by a bathroom and an office. Facing the water is the living/dining room. You'll find nice table linens, a well-stocked kitchen, and all kinds of thoughtful amenities (picnic basket, sewing basket, binoculars, books and games, etc.). Hosts Ron and Ruth Mullen encourage snooping in every nook and cranny, really making yourself at home. At the Duck-In, you'll have plenty of privacy in a waterfront setting with all the necessary comforts and many unexpected ones.

No pets; smoking outside only; TV/VCR; desk and private phone; full kitchen with stove, dishwasher, and microwave; off-street parking. Brochure available.

ROOM	BED	BATH	ENTRANCE	FLOOR	DAILY RATES S - D	(EP) +
A	1Q & 2T	Pvt	Main	1	$95	($10)

Mercer Island Hideaway
(206) 232-1092

8820 SE 63rd Street, Mercer Island, WA 98040
(Three miles south of I-90, off Island Crest Way)

It's only a fifteen-minute drive from Seattle or Bellevue, but when you cross a bridge over Lake Washington to Mercer Island, it seems like another world. The Williams' home, Mercer Island Hideaway, is a place of quiet luxury. It is tucked into the lush green landscape that adjoins the wilderness of 120-acre Pioneer Park. No matter which of the attractive accommodations you stay in, it will be like "sleeping in a forest," as one guest put it. The home has been beautifully renovated throughout and is kept in immaculate condition. Anyone with an interest in music will be at home here. The spacious living room has tall windows and a cathedral ceiling. It holds two grand pianos, a reed organ, and a harpsichord, any of which Mary Williams will play on request. She and Bill excel in making every guest feel special. Their personal warmth enhances the outstanding hospitality at Mercer Island Hideaway.

No pets or smoking; full breakfast; TV; room B is a suite with patio entrance; off-street parking; two-night minimum; *open spring, summer, and fall.* Brochure available.

ROOM	BED	BATH	ENTRANCE	FLOOR	DAILY RATES S - D	(EP) +
A	1K or 1Q	Pvt	Main	1	$65-$75	($20)
B	1K or 2T	Pvt	Sep	LL	$65-$75	($20)

Mole House Bed & Breakfast   **(206) 232-1611**
3308 West Mercer Way, Mercer Island, WA 98040
(West shore of island)

It would take an album full of pictures to capture the many facets of Mole House. The rambling contemporary Northwest home overlooks Lake Washington, Seattle, and the Olympic Mountains. It is made up of several distinct sections that are harmoniously linked together by the hosts' collection of art, antiques, and family heirlooms. Don, a native of Seattle, and Petra, who emigrated from West Germany in 1986, extend caring hospitality in a refined atmosphere. Here you can have all the privacy you need, invite friends in for a visit, or enjoy the interesting company of Don and Petra. The three guest accommodations are on different levels of the house. The Eagle has its own sitting room, The Garden Suite has a sitting room and opens onto a brick patio, and The Apartment is a totally self-contained space with a deck and a panoramic view of the lake. Park-like surroundings, soft music, and elegant breakfasts contribute to the sensual delight of staying at Mole House. It is in every respect a rare find.

No pets; well-behaved children welcome; no smoking; full breakfast; sofa bed, telephone, TV, and kitchen with stocked fridge in Room C; patios, decks, and gardens; ten minutes from Seattle, twenty from airport; good public transportation and airport connections; off-street parking; German and Spanish spoken. Brochure available.

ROOM	BED	BATH	ENTRANCE	FLOOR	DAILY RATES	
					S - D	(EP) +
A	1D	Pvt	Main	1	$55	
B	1D	Pvt	Main	LL	$60	
C	1D	Pvt	Main & Sep	2	$70	($5)

190

The Abel House
117 Fleet Street South, Montesano, WA 98563
(Downtown area)

(206) 249-6002
1(800) 235-ABEL

Second only to the imposing Grays Harbor County Courthouse in grandeur, The Abel House was built in 1908 as the home of William H. Abel, who enjoyed a distinguished career as a defense and trial attorney in the nearby courthouse. Among the rooms of the four-floor mansion now owned by Vic Reynolds are eight bedrooms, a game room, a well-stocked library, a formal dining room, and a comfortably appointed living room. Lustrous woodwork, box-beamed ceilings, massive brick fireplaces, and original fixtures enhance the interior. An unusual Tiffany chandelier, commissioned to hang over the dining table, befits the baronial setting. Guests may relax on the wide covered veranda, stroll through the glorious gardens, or set out to cover small, friendly Montesano on foot. To stay at The Abel House is to experience one of the community's best assets first hand.

Dog in residence; no pets; smoking in designated areas; color cable TVs in rooms; ample street parking; credit cards (V,MC). Brochure available.

ROOM	BED	BATH	ENTRANCE	FLOOR	DAILY RATES S - D	(EP) +
A	2T	Shd*	Main	2	$55	($10)
B	1Q	Shd*	Main	2	$55	($10)
C	1Q	Shd*	Main	2	$55	($10)
D	1D	Pvt	Main	2	$75	($10)
E	1K	Shd*	Main	2	$65	($10)

191

The English Inn   **(206) 385-5302**
718 F Street, Port Townsend, WA 98368
(Near Uptown District)

Port Townsend's prominence in the late nineteenth century can be clearly seen today in this Victorian seaport village, a masterpiece of historic preservation. Its commercial district and many of its grandest homes have been restored. One such home is now The English Inn, an 1885 Italianate Victorian situated on a hillside with a view of the Olympic Mountains. Owner Juliette Swenson preserves the spirits of the great English poets by naming the large corner rooms after Wordsworth, Longfellow, Yeats, Rossetti, and Keats. And gorgeous rooms they are! High ceilings, ample windows, and handsome mouldings accentuate the warmth and drama of well-chosen colors. Lovely wallcoverings and English print fabrics, antique photos and furnishings, and unique pieces of artwork give each room its singular character. Juliette, whose roots are in Bath, England, invites you to "The Home of Scones, Shortbread, and Cream Tea." I wouldn't pass it up.

Two cats in residence; no children under twelve; smoking outside only; full breakfast; TV/VCR in guest lounge; rollaway bed upstairs, $25 extra; hot tub with private patio; gazebo; two bicycles available; ten-minute walk to Uptown district; five-minute drive to historic Downtown; off-street parking; credit cards (V,MC); off-season rates. Brochure available.

ROOM	BED	BATH	ENTRANCE	FLOOR	DAILY RATES S - D (EP) +
A	1Q	Pvt	Main	1	$85
B	1Q	Pvt	Main	2	$75
C	1Q	Pvt	Main	2	$85
D	1K	Pvt	Main	2	$95
E	1K	Pvt	Main	2	$85

Holly Hill House

(206) 385-5619

611 Polk Street, Port Townsend, WA 98368
(Historic Uptown District)

This Christmas-card-perfect 1872 Victorian stands on a corner lot with tall holly trees and other plantings from long ago. The lawn is encircled by a white picket fence flanked by roses, and a flower-lined path leads to the front door of Holly Hill House. The second-floor guest rooms are havens of comfort and pleasure, with florals and laces and wonderful views. Overlook the gardens from Lizette's Room, or Admiralty Inlet and the Cascades from the Colonel's Suite or Billie's Room. Equally attractive newer rooms in the Carriage House include the Morning Glory and the Skyview. Sumptuous breakfasts are prepared in the large country kitchen, then served with a gracious air in the formal dining room. Both here and in the living room, notice the original stippled woodwork that was the rage in the house's heyday. Some furnishings are antiques, some reproductions, but the accent is on liveability. Hostesses Lynne Sterling and Phyllis Olson want guests to fully relax and enjoy the whole house and the gardens.

No pets; children over twelve welcome; smoking outside only; full breakfast; queen sofa bed extra in Room A; off-street parking; credit cards (V,MC). Inquire about special off-season packages such as wine-tasting (Ms. Sterling makes an award-winning Merlot) and mystery weekends; intimate weddings and honeymoon packages available. Brochure available.

ROOM	BED	BATH	ENTRANCE	FLOOR	DAILY RATES S - D (EP) +	
A	1K	Pvt	Main	2	$125	($20)
B	1Q	Pvt	Main	2	$86	
C	1Q & 1T	Pvt	Main	2	$78	($12)
D	1Q	Pvt	Sep	1	$78	
E	1Q	Pvt	Sep	1	$72	

Hart's Tayberry House   (206) 848-4594
7406 - 80th Street East, Puyallup, WA 98371
(Puyallup/Tacoma area)

The authenticity of this Victorian charmer is almost palpable, so it's surprising to learn that the home is in fact a reproduction. The original no longer stands, but it was built by a leading pioneer in the area. Unusual care was taken in its re-creation here on a hillside overlooking rich farmlands. Intricately carved exterior woodwork and a wrap-around porch with a gazebo are a perfect prelude to the turn-of-the-century details inside. Upstairs, the front Balcony Room offers fresh air and a view. The smaller but oh-so-sweet Heart Room is just down the hall. A bathroom off the hallway has an old-fashioned chain-pull toilet and a clawfoot tub. A spacious suite spans the back of the house. Lovingly combined wallpapers, rugs, linens, and furnishings give each room a romantic warmth. A friendly, hospitable stay in quiet rural surroundings awaits you at Hart's Tayberry House.

No pets; children over twelve welcome; smoking outside only; small refrigerator in suite; AC; elevator; walk to city park and tennis courts; off-street parking; senior discount. Brochure available.

ROOM	BED	BATH	ENTRANCE	FLOOR	DAILY RATES	
					S - D	(EP) +
A	1Q	Shd*	Main	2	$50	
B	1D	Shd*	Main	2	$40	
C	1Q	Pvt	Main	2	$60	($10)

The Meadows Bed & Breakfast　　　　**(206) 378-4004**
1980 Cattle Point Road, Friday Harbor, WA 98250
(Three miles from ferry landing)

The 1892 farmhouse of Dodie and Burr Henion is surrounded by a pretty yard, oak and fir trees, and open fields that slope gently toward Griffin Bay, with a view of Lopez Island and the Cascade Mountains in the distance. This charmingly renovated home welcomes guests to breakfast by the brick hearth after a restful night in the guest house, which is located just steps away. Accommodations include two large bedrooms connected by an ample bathroom. Dressing room/closets, wall-to-wall carpeting, and very attractive local artwork enhance these relaxing quarters. Spend some time on the deck, explore the four acres, or set out to discover the amazing diversity of San Juan Island in your own way. As a guest at The Meadows, you'll adapt to "island time" before you know it.

No pets or smoking; children by special arrangement; full breakfast; off-street parking; credit cards (V,MC); off-season and weekly rates. Brochure available.

ROOM	BED	BATH	ENTRANCE	FLOOR	DAILY RATES S - D (EP) +
A	1Q & 1T	Shd*	Sep	1	$65-$75 ($15)
B	1Q & 1T	Shd*	Sep	1	$65-$75 ($15)

Tower House Bed & Breakfast   **(206) 378-5464**
1230 Little Road, Friday Harbor, WA 98250
(Three and one-half miles from ferry landing)

On a quiet country road overlooking the San Juan Valley, Tower House rests on ten acres of rural beauty. Hosts Chris and Joe Luma offer a gracious bed and breakfast experience for one or two couples at a time. Luxuries and little surprises grace the vintage home, which manages to be both cozy and elegant. Choose the spacious Sun Room, a light and airy creation in peach and cream; it has its own solarium/library with an antique desk and a marvelous sunrise view. Or choose the mauve and ecru Tower Room, with antique furnishings that complement the spectacular stained glass of the tower windows. A tufted window seat encircles the tower; a sunset view can be savored from here or from the wide veranda. Chris and Joe pride themselves on their breakfast cuisine. Traditional fare (her specialty), as well as low-fat, low-cholesterol meals (his) are available. Caring hospitality and superb accommodations ensure a memorable stay at Tower House.

Cat in residence; no pets, children, or smoking; full breakfast; snacks and beverages always available; great hikes and wildlife viewing from Tower House; off-street parking; credit cards (V,MC). Be the only guests and have a private bath for $125. Brochure available.

ROOM	BED	BATH	ENTRANCE	FLOOR	DAILY RATES S - D (EP) +
A	1Q	Shd*	Main	1	$90
B	1Q	Shd*	Main	1	$90

Tucker House Bed & Breakfast
260 B Street, Friday Harbor, WA 98250
(In town, walking distance fom ferry landing)

(206) 378-2783
1(800) 742-8210
FAX: 378-6437

Friday Harbor is a great walking town on an island that offers the outdoor lover an array of activities: kayaking, fishing, whale and eagle watching, beachcombing, picnicking, hiking, and bicycling. The romantically inclined will be as pleased as families are to find Tucker House, an adorable Victorian farmhouse with a picket fence, a lovely, terraced rock garden, decking, and a hot tub. Two upstairs rooms with sloped ceilings and a shared bath are available to guests. Those who seek extra privacy and amenities will prefer one of the three delightful garden cottages on the property. Each one -- Willow, Rose, and Lilac -- is distinctive and very special. All have wood-burning stoves, and two have kitchen facilities. Deluxe full breakfasts are served in the cheerful solarium of the main house.

Smoking outside only; full breakfast; deck; hot tub; off-street parking; some inside bicycle storage; major credit cards; off-season rates. Owners also operate a larger facility, the San Juan Inn, one-half block from the ferry landing. Brochures available.

ROOM	BED	BATH	ENTRANCE	FLOOR	DAILY RATES S - D (EP) +
A	1D	Shd*	Main	2	$69-$85
B	1Q	Shd*	Main	2	$79-$90
C	1Q	Pvt	Sep	1	$95-$110 ($20)
D	1Q	Pvt	Sep	1	$100-$115 ($20)
E	1Q	Pvt	Sep	1	$105-$125 ($20)

Bacon Mansion/Broadway Guest House
959 Broadway East, Seattle, WA 98102
(Capitol Hill)

(206) 329-1864
1(800) 240-1864

Built in 1909 by Cecil Bacon, this classical home, combining Edwardian and Tudor styling, has been returned to much of its original grandeur and offers refined comfort to all who enter. The Bacon family crest in red and white stained glass enhances the front entrance, and the extensive, carefully preserved woodwork, a 3,000-crystal chandelier, marble fireplaces, handsome library, and magnificent living and dining rooms will delight the connoisseur and casual observer alike. On the floors above are six most pleasant guest rooms offering great variety in decor, size, bed type, and price. The premier accommodation is the Capitol Suite (A), a huge area that features a view of the Space Needle, a sun room with a hide-a-bed, a private bath, a beautiful fireplace, and pine and wicker furnishings. As in the other rooms, a color TV and a telephone are provided. Believe me, the Bacon Mansion is a lot to live up to, but hosts Daryl and Tim pull it off seamlessly.

Smoking outside only; some rooms with fireplaces; near bus route; off-street and street parking; Shuttle Express from airport; major credit cards; off-season rates; also available are a Garden Suite (below the main floor) and a Carriage House (across patio), a two-story retreat with full kitchen, living room with hide-a-bed, bedroom, and bath. Brochure available.

ROOM	BED	BATH	ENTRANCE	FLOOR	DAILY RATES S - D (EP) +
A	1Q	Pvt	Main	2	$99-$109 ($15)
B	1D	Pvt	Main	2	$89-$99
C	1Q	Pvt	Main	2	$79-$89
D	1D	Pvt	Main	2	$79-$89
E	1Q	Shd*	Main	3	$74-$79
F	1D	Shd*	Main	3	$69-$74

198

Bellevue Place   **(206) 325-9253**
1111 Bellevue Place East, Seattle, WA 98102
(Capitol Hill)

One is immediately impressed by the majestic columns and edifice of the home known as Bellevue Place. It is a rare Oriental Victorian, as evidenced by a slight curve of the roofline, and it is a storybook home inside and out. Elaborate mouldings, leaded glass windows, and Oriental rugs set the stage for strikingly beautiful furnishings, tableware, and decorative accents. In the three lovely upstairs bedrooms, beds are made with cotton sheets and down comforters. The eight o'clock breakfasts are always a hit with guests, who may feel free to come down in the robes provided. It is the goal of hosts Gunner and Joe to guarantee each guest cleanliness, consistency, and hospitality. What a treat it is to be pamperd and waited on in this elegant Capitol Hill home.

Two standard poodles in residence; no pets; smoking outside only; full breakfast; grand piano; formal gardens with patios; solarium; two full baths, one on each floor; private baths to be completed during 1994; near bus route; Shuttle Express from airport; major credit cards. Brochure available.

ROOM	BED	BATH	ENTRANCE	FLOOR	DAILY RATES S - D	(EP) +
A	1Q	Shd*	Main	2	$75-$85	
B	1Q	Shd*	Main	2	$75-$85	
C	1Q	Shd*	Main	2	$75-$85	

Continental Inn
(206) 324-9511
955 Tenth Avenue East, Seattle, WA 98102
(Capitol Hill)

The Continental Inn is a handsome two-story brick home with classical mouldings topped by a red tile roof. Each of the large corner rooms is decorated to recall one of hosts' Martha and Jean Dunn's favorite cities: Madrid, Casablanca, Copenhagen, and Paris. Guest quarters are enhanced by commodious bathrooms with old ceramic tiles and porcelain tubs, large closets with shelves and ample hanging space, and a color TV and a telephone in each room. The Dunns' extensive art collection is on display throughout the tastefully furnished house. The spacious living room has an elegant dining area at one end, an information table at the other, and plenty of spots to relax in between. There is a lovely private yard in back with tables and chaises and a deck where summer breakfasts and afternoon snacks may be served.

Dog in residence; no pets; smoking confined to library and deck; full breakfast; Madrid (A) offered with private bath (Jacuzzi tub) at $94; bus stop at front door; off-street and street parking; Shuttle Express from airport; credit cards (V,MC,D). Brochure available.

ROOM	BED	BATH	ENTRANCE	FLOOR	DAILY RATES S - D (EP) +	
A	1Q	Shd*	Main	2	$74-$84	
B	1Q	Shd*	Main	2	$74-$84	
C	1Q	Shd*	Main	2	$67-$74	
D	2T	Shd*	Main	2	$74-$84	

Green Gables Guesthouse

(206) 282-6863

1503 Second Avenue West, Seattle, WA 98119
(Queen Anne Hill)

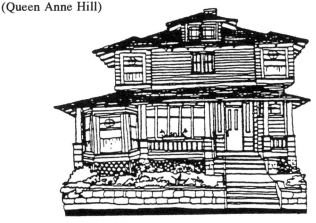

Queen Anne Hill boasts some particularly striking Victorian homes, and one stands out as a haven of graceful hospitality. At Green Gables Guesthouse, antiques and collectibles steeped in the hosts' family history are joined by intriguing works of art and costumes on display. Lila and David Chapman are professional costumers (their work outfits many city productions) who bring a sense of fun and drama to the ambiance. A bay-windowed solarium at the side of the main floor provides a great setting for tea, reading, conversation, or eyeing small gift items. Upstairs there are three bedrooms, two of which share a full bath; Chestnut Bower (A) has a wrap-around corner window, creating a treehouse effect. The Queen Anne's Lace Room (C) includes its own bath, sitting room, and kitchenette. Downstairs at the back of the house is a spacious, self-contained unit (D) that is lovely and extra quiet. For casual comfort, warm personal service, and a terrific Seattle location, Green Gables is a find.

Dog in residence; smoking on veranda only; full breakfast; TV/VCR in two rooms; rollaway bed available for Room C; private bath for Room C ready by 5/1/94; excellent walks in historic neighborhood; near Kerry Park viewpoint, with quintessential Seattle view; near bus route; off-street and street parking; Shuttle Express from airport; longer term stays in house next door. Brochure available.

ROOM	BED	BATH	ENTRANCE	FLOOR	DAILY RATES S - D (EP) +
A	1K or 2T	Shd*	Main	2	$69-$79
B	1D	Shd*	Main	2	$59-$75
C	1Q	Pvt	Main	2	$85-$95 ($15)
D	1K & 2T	Pvt	Sep	1	$95-$110 ($15)

Hill House Bed & Breakfast   (206) 720-7161
1113 East John Street, Seattle, WA 98102
(Capitol Hill, two and one-half blocks off Broadway)

It is only a short distance from bustling Broadway to the quiet sophistication of Hill House, but it is worlds away. The 1903 Victorian has been expertly restored and decorated with a sure eye for color and a marvelous sense of design. Smart, handsome hues of celadon, gold, rose, palomino, and Bordeaux grace the guest rooms. The judicious use of brass, lace, botanical prints, and fine woods and fabrics brings the stylish interior together, contributing to the atmosphere of serene comfort that extends throughout the house. Savor some romantic luxuries in one of three upstairs bedrooms or one of the garden suites, which include sitting rooms, full baths, TVs, and telephones. Common rooms, as well as the backyard deck, are most appealing places to relax. Hosts Ken and Eric are rightfully proud of Hill House and offer suitably splendid hospitality.

No pets, children, or smoking; full breakfast; many shops and restaurants in walking distance; bus stop just outside door; Shuttle Express from airport; off-street parking; credit cards (V,MC). Brochure available.

ROOM	BED	BATH	ENTRANCE	FLOOR	DAILY RATES S - D	(EP) +
A	1Q	Shd*	Main	2	$75	
B	1Q	Shd*	Main	2	$65	
C	1Q	Pvt	Main	2	$85	
D	1Q	Pvt	Sep	1G	$95	
E	1Q	Pvt	Sep	1G	$85	

Mildred's Bed & Breakfast   **(206) 325-6072**
1202 Fifteenth Avenue East, Seattle, WA 98112
(Capitol Hill, facing east side of Volunteer Park)

If ever a place could tug at your heartstrings, Mildred's would do it. It's the ultimate trip-to-Grandmother's fantasy come true. A large, double-turreted, white Victorian possessed of a friendly charm, it's the perfect setting for Mildred Sarver's caring hospitality. Three guest rooms on the upper floor couldn't be prettier. Lace curtains, stained glass, and antiques add to the ambiance of warmth and security. An alcove adjacent to the guest rooms offers the convenience of a drop-down ironing board with full-length mirrored door, a refrigerator, makings for tea and coffee, a sink, and a telephone. Mildred's special touches and lavish breakfasts make her guests feel truly pampered.

No pets; smoking in restricted areas; full breakfast; TV available; fireplace and grand piano in living room; 40-acre park across street, good for walking or jogging; ample street parking; good public transportation; Shuttle Express from airport; major credit cards.

ROOM	BED	BATH	ENTRANCE	FLOOR	DAILY RATES	
					S - D	(EP) +
A	1Q	Pvt	Main	2	$75-$85	($15)
B	1Q	Pvt	Main	2	$75-$85	($15)
C	1Q	Pvt	Main	2	$75-$85	($15)

203

Prince of Wales   **(206) 325-9692**
133 Thirteenth Avenue East, Seattle, WA 98102   **1(800) 327-9692**
(Capitol Hill)

From this handsome turn-of-the-century home you can easily reach the city's conference sites and all the downtown attractions you'll want to visit. Equally well-suited for business or vacation travelers, Prince of Wales has home-like comfort with hints of royalty throughout. Enjoy a relaxing stay in the Princess Suite, the King's Room, the Queen's Room, or the top-floor Prince's Retreat, which features a clawfoot tub, a city and mountain view, and a private deck. On the second floor you'll find such conveniences as a private telephone line and a laundry room. The cheerful, friendly atmosphere of the home is enhanced by interesting collections, handcrafted collages, and touches of whimsy. A delicious full breakfast rounds out the generous hospitality offered by hosts Carol and Chuck. But most impressive of all is the view -- a stunning panorama of the city skyline, Olympic Mountains, and Puget Sound, with the Space Needle in the fore-ground. Three of the four guest rooms feature this ever-present reminder that you couldn't be anywhere but Seattle.

Cat and dog in residence; no pets or smoking; full breakfast; fireplace in living room; private garden; good public transportation; Shuttle Express from airport; off-street and street parking; major credit cards; two-night minimum *May 15-October 15*. Brochure available.

ROOM	BED	BATH	ENTRANCE	FLOOR	DAILY RATES S - D	(EP)+
A	1D	Shd*	Main	2	$60	
B	2T	Shd*	Main	2	$65	
C	1Q	Pvt	Main	2	$75	($10)
D	1Q	Pvt	Sep	3	$85	($10)

Roberta's Bed & Breakfast   **(206) 329-3326**
1147 Sixteenth Avenue East, Seattle, WA 98112
(Capitol Hill)

The friendly appeal of Roberta Barry's classic turn-of-the-century home is obvious at first glance. It fits comfortably into this quiet Capitol Hill neighborhood near the University of Washington and Volunteer Park and is convenient to downtown, and you'll fit comfortably into one of the lovely guest rooms on the upper floors. Choose the romantic Peach Room (C) with its bay window and love seat, or perhaps the Madrona (B), a cheery corner room that gets the morning sun. The gable-windowed Hideaway (E) takes the uppermost floor and has a window seat, a sitting area, a full bath, and a delicious feeling of escape. Every room is special at Roberta's. Her home is full of beautiful Oriental rugs, antiques, and good books. Add to these attributes the spice of her humor, and you've got a combination that's hard to top.

No pets; older children by prior arrangement; smoking on porch only; full breakfast; ample street parking; public transportation; Shuttle Express from airport; major credit cards. Brochure available.

ROOM	BED	BATH	ENTRANCE	FLOOR	DAILY RATES S - D (EP) +
A	1Q	Pvt	Main	2	$72-$78
B	1Q	Pvt	Main	2	$78-$85
C	1Q	Pvt	Main	2	$84-$90
D	1Q	Pvt	Main	2	$78-$85
E	1Q	Pvt	Main	2	$90-$97

Villa Heidelberg   **(206) 938-3658**
4845 - 45th Avenue, Seattle, WA 98116
(West Seattle)

The splendid skyline of downtown Seattle can be seen from many spots in West Seattle, and Villa Heidelberg is oriented toward Puget Sound and the Olympic Mountains. John and Barbara Thompson's 1909 Mission-style home retains many of its original light fixtures, leaded glass windows, and built-in cabinets. Wallcoverings have subdued patterns, and walls and ceilings are bordered by original dark wood; vintage furnishings (some from Germany) are augmented by additional pieces chosen for comfort. Braided rugs on wood floors look just right throughout the house. The overall feeling is homey, old-fashioned, and unpretentious. Four bedrooms that vary in size and share two full baths comprise the second floor. Of the two larger rooms, one has a view and a deck, and the other has a fireplace. Different breakfast entrees presented on different dishes each day are served in the formal dining room or on the wide, wrap-around porch overlooking beautifully landscaped grounds.

Cat in residence; children over ten welcome; smoking on porch only; full breakfast; fireplace, TV/VCR in living room; robes provided; public transportation; Alki Beach, two miles away, has restaurants, picnic spots, and a great view; street parking; major credit cards; Spanish spoken; public transportation; Shuttle Express from airport. Brochure available.

ROOM	BED	BATH	ENTRANCE	FLOOR	DAILY RATES S - D (EP) +
A	1K	Shd*	Main	2	$65-$75
B	1K	Shd*	Main	2	$75-$85
C	1D	Shd*	Main	2	$45-$55
D	2T	Shd*	Main	2	$55-$65

Gumm's Bed & Breakfast Inn   **(206) 642-8887**
P.O. Box 447, Seaview, WA 98644
(3310 Highway 101 & 33rd)

This fine 1911 Northwest Craftsman house is endowed with extensive original woodwork throughout, and the superb restoration job has only highlighted its warmth and character. It's the kind of house that needs a "Grandma in Residence," and Mickey Slack couldn't be a more qualified candidate. A living room with a great stone fireplace, a delightful sun porch, a beauty of a yard and garden, and a hot tub inside a gazebo are all equally inviting spots to enjoy at your leisure. Lace curtains and lovely furnishings throughout the house combine comfort with turn-of-the century charm. Mickey has created some fabulous breakfast specialties to please a variety of palates, and her welcoming presence makes people feel thoroughly at home in no time at all.

No pets or smoking; full breakfast; TV in each room; hot tub; off-street parking; credit cards; (V,MC); inquire about special family, senior, and winter rates. Brochure available.

ROOM	BED	BATH	ENTRANCE	FLOOR	DAILY RATES S - D	(EP) +
A	1D & 1T	Pvt	Main	2	$70-$75	($5)
B	1Q	Pvt	Main	2	$70-$75	
C	2D	Shd*	Main	2	$65-$70	
D	1D	Shd*	Main	2	$60-$65	

Marianna Stoltz House   (509) 483-4316
East 427 Indiana, Spokane, WA 99207
(Central Spokane, historic Gonzaga University area)

Phyllis and Jim Maguire have the good fortune to live in the 1908 American foursquare classic home in which Phyllis grew up. She named it Marianna Stoltz in honor of her mother. Now one of Spokane's historic landmarks, it has the feel of a big, old-fashioned family home that's comfortable through and through. Period furnishings, handsome woodwork, leaded glass cabinets, and a lovely tile fireplace enhance the gracious interior. Accommodations are all on the second floor, and guests are welcome to come and go as they please; the front entrance is theirs alone. Beds are covered with the wonderful collection of old quilts that Phyllis so generously shares. Fond memories of Marianna Stoltz House might include visiting or reading on the wide, wrap-around porch or breakfasting on Stoltz House strada, peach Melba parfaits, or Dutch babies. These and other pleasures await you at this popular intown B&B.

No pets; no children under twelve; smoking outside only; full breakfast; TV in each room; AC; choice of shower or clawfoot tub; good public transportation and airport connections; off-street parking; all major credit cards. Brochure available.

ROOM	BED	BATH	ENTRANCE	FLOOR	DAILY RATES S - D (EP) +
A	1K & 1T	Shd*	Main	2	$50-$60 ($15)
B	1Q	Shd*	Main	2	$50-$60
C	1Q	Pvt	Main	2	$55-$65
D	1Q	Pvt	Main	2	$55-$65

Commencement Bay Bed & Breakfast   **(206) 752-8175**
3312 North Union Avenue, Tacoma, WA 98407
(Historic North Tacoma, near Point Defiance Park and waterfront)

From its elevated position, this stately white Colonial home affords a breathtaking view of Commencement Bay and Mount Rainier beyond. Hosts Bill and Sharon Kaufmann keep the velvety lawn green, the gardens tended, their home immaculate, and the welcome mat always out for guests. Upon arrival, you'll make one pleasant discovery after another: elegantly appointed guest rooms; a variety of common areas for relaxing, socializing, dining, even conducting business; a deck with a hot tub; a game room; and hospitality that makes you feel your every need has been anticipated. The Kaufmanns' generosity extends to helping visitors discover the wealth of historical, cultural, and natural assets that make the Tacoma-Pierce County area an increasingly attractive and interesting destination. A stay at Commencement Bay Bed & Breakfast couldn't be a better introduction.

Dog in residence; no pets; children over twelve OK; outdoor smoking area; full breakfast; robes provided; cable TV/VCR in each room; office for business use; public transportation; historic districts, nature trails, parks, zoo, aquarium, universities, boating marinas, antique shops, restaurants, theaters and more nearby; ample street parking; major credit cards; Shuttle Express from Sea-Tac; airport (Pierce County), ferry, and Amtrak pickup; rate for single weekend night slightly higher at peak periods. Brochure available.

ROOM	BED	BATH	ENTRANCE	FLOOR	DAILY RATES S - D (EP) +
A	1Q	Pvt	Main	2	$90
B	1Q	Shd*	Main	2	$70
C	1Q	Shd*	Main	2	$80

Eagles Nest Inn   **(206) 221-5331**
3236 East Saratoga Road, Langley, WA 98260
(One and one-half miles from village, overlooking Saratoga Passage)

Nancy and Dale Bowman's ingeniously designed home is set amidst fir and cedar with commanding vistas of Saratoga Passage, Camano Island, and Mount Baker. A pleasing contrast of contemporary and traditional gives the interior an ambiance that is refined, comfortable, and aesthetically satisfying. Abundant windows and open space help to bring the outside in; you feel secluded and close to nature while being pampered beyond expectation. Each of the four spacious guest rooms has a sitting area and a TV/VCR. The Saratoga Room has majestic views and triple French doors leading to a private balcony; The Forest Room has a large bay window with a view through the trees, plus a skylight; The Eagles Nest is perched at the top of the house with a private balcony and a dramatic 360-degree panorama. The newest accommodation is the delightful Garden Room on the ground floor. Breakfast selections from Nancy's wide-ranging repertoire start the day off right. Stroll about the grounds, soak in the spa under the stars, savor the privacy of your romantic room -- beautiful memories are yours for the making at Eagles Nest Inn.

No pets or children; smoking outside only; full breakfast; guest lounge/library; 400 video selections; robes provided; decks; spa; "bottomless" cookie jar; off-street parking; major credit cards.

ROOM	BED	BATH	ENTRANCE	FLOOR	DAILY RATES S - D (EP) +
A	1K	Pvt	Main	3	$105-$115
B	1K	Pvt	Sep	3	$95-$105
C	1Q	Pvt	Main	4	$105-$115
D	1Q	Pvt	Sep	1G	$85-$95 ($45)

Please read "About Dining Highlights" on page *vii*.

ABERDEEN
Bridges Restaurant, 112 North G Street; (206) 532-6563; seafood/prime rib/pasta

ANACORTES
Boomer's Landing, 209 T Avenue; (206) 293-5109; seafood

Charlie's, 5407 Ferry Terminal Road; (206) 293-7377; prime rib/steaks/seafood

The Compass Rose, 5320 Ferry Terminal Drive; (206) 293-6600; varied lunch menu

GERE-A-DELI, 502 Commercial Avenue; (206) 293-7383; deli/pasta/pastries

La Petite, 3401 Commercial Avenue; (206) 293-4644; European/fine dining

Slocum's Restaurant, 2201 Skyline Way; (206) 293-0644; innovative seafood

ASHFORD
Alexander's Country Inn, Highway 706 E; (206) 569-2300; Continental

BELLEVUE
Eques, NE Eighth and Bellevue Way, Hyatt Regency Hotel; (206) 451-3012; West Coast/fine dining

The New Jake O'Shaughnessey's, 401 Bellevue Square, NE Sixth and Bellevue Way; (206) 455-5559; peachwood broiled poultry/meats/seafood

BELLINGHAM
Cafe Toulouse, 114 West Magnolia, #102; (206) 733-8996; artfully prepared breakfasts/lunches/desserts

il Fiasco, 1308 Railroad Avenue; (206) 676-9136; Italian

La Belle Rose, 1801 Roeder Avenue; Harbor Center; (206) 647-0833; French

Le Chat Noir, 1200 Harris, The Marketplace; (206) 733-6136; French

Pacific Cafe, 100 North Commercial; (206) 647-0800; Asian/Northwest

Pepper Sisters Restaurant, 1222 North Garden; (206) 671-3414; Southwest

BOW
The Oyster Bar, 240 Chuckanut Drive; (206) 766-6185; Northwest seafood

Oyster Creek Inn, 190 Chuckanut Drive; (206) 766-6179; oysters/seafood

CHINOOK
The Sanctuary, Highway 101 and Hazel Street; (206) 777-8380; seafood/meat/poultry/fine dining in historic former church

CLARKSTON
Fazzari's, 1281 Bridge Street; (509) 758-3386; Italian/pizza

Jonathan's, 301 D Street, Lewiston, Idaho; (208) 746-3438; varied menu

ELLENSBURG
The Blue Grouse, 1401 Dollar Way (Exit 106 off I-90); (509) 925-4808; American

Giovanni's on Pearl, 402 North Pearl; (509) 962-2260; Italian/seafood/Ellensburg lamb/steaks

The Grill House, Eighth and Chestnut; (509) 962-5050; steaks/seafood/chicken/vegetarian

Valley Cafe, 105 West Third; (509) 925-3050; seafood/pasta/Ellensburg lamb/espresso drinks

FERNDALE

Douglas House, 2254 Douglas Drive; (206) 384-5262; seafood/steak/chicken/lobster bisque/daily specials

FRIDAY HARBOR

Roberto's, First and A Street; (206) 378-6333; Italian

Springtree Eating Establishment and Farm, 310 Spring Street; (206) 378-4848; varied, imaginative menu featuring organic and local products

GLACIER

InnisFree Restaurant, 9393 Mount Baker Highway; (206) 599-2373; seasonal fresh/innovative Northwest dishes

Milano's, 9990 Mount Baker Highway; (206) 599-2863; Italian

HOQUIAM

Levee Street Restaurant, 709 Levee Street; (206) 532-1959; imaginative seafood plus

KIRKLAND

Cafe Juanita, 9702 NE 120th Place; (206) 823-1505; Italian

LA CONNER

Palmer's, Second and Washington Streets; (206) 466-4261; European

China Pearl, 505 South First Street; (206) 466-1000; Oriental

Calico Cupboard, 720 South First Street; (206) 466-4451; bakery items/sandwiches/soups/desserts/all from scratch

LANGLEY

Cafe Langley, 113 First Street; (206) 221-3090; Greek/Continental

Star Bistro, 201-1/2 First Street; (206) 221-2627; salads/burgers/pasta/seafood

LONG BEACH PENINSULA

The Ark Restaurant, Nahcotta (at Willapa Bay); (206) 665-4133; creative Northwest cuisine with seasonal local specialties

The Lightship Restaurant, 409 SW Tenth, Long Beach (at Nendel's Edgewater Inn); (206) 642-3252; family dining/varied menu

The Shoalwater Restaurant, Highway 103 and 45th Street, Shelburne Inn; (206) 642-4142; nationally renowned Northwest regional cuisine/fine dining

LOPEZ ISLAND

Bay Cafe, Lopez Village; (206) 468-3700; eclectic menu

MERCER ISLAND

Thai on Mercer, 7691 - 27th Street SE; (206) 236-9990

MONTESANO

Savory Faire, 135 South Main Street; (206) 249-3701; breakfast/lunch/occasional dinner

MOUNT VERNON

Wildflowers, 2001 East College Way; (206) 424-9724; Skagit Valley/Northwest

PORT TOWNSEND

Silverwater Cafe, 126 Quincy; (206) 385-6448; Continental

SEATTLE

Cafe Flora, 2901 East Madison; (206) 325-9100; vegetarian

Campagne, 86 Pine Street, Inn at the Market; (206) 728-2800; Country French/Italian/Northwest

Chandler's Crabhouse & Fresh Fish Market, 901 Fairview Avenue North; (206) 223-2722; extensive seafood menu/view dining

Chinook's at Salmon Bay, Fishermen's Terminal; (206) 283-HOOK; seafood

Coastal Kitchen, 429 Fifteenth Avenue East; (206) 322-1145; fresh, creative dishes with Cajun/Creole accent

Dahlia Lounge, 1904 Fourth Avenue; (206) 682-4142; Northwest/comfort food/fine dining

Fuller's, 1400 Sixth Avenue, Sheraton Seattle Hotel; (206) 447-5544; Northwest/seafood/fine dining

Hiram's-At-The Locks Restaurant, 5300 - 34th NW; (206) 784-1733; seafood

Il Bistro, 93-A Pike Street, Pike Place Market; (206) 682-3049; Country French/Italian/seafood

Ivar's Fish Bar, Pier 54, 1000 Alaskan Way between Madison and Spring; (206) 624-6852; casual seafood

Jack's Bistro, 405 Fifteenth Avenue East; (206) 324-9625

Kamon on Lake Union, 1177 Fairview Avenue North; (206) 622-4665; Asian

Le Gourmand, 425 NW Market Street; (206) 784-3463; upscale Northwest

Pailin, 2223 California Avenue SW, West Seattle; (206) 937-8807; Thai

Pasta Bella, 1530 Queen Anne Avenue North; (206) 284-9827

Phoenecia at Alki, 2716 Alki Avenue, West Seattle; (206) 935-6550; Mediterranean

Rain City Grill, 2359 Tenth Avenue East; (206) 325-5003; Northwest/American with Asian influence

Ray's Boathouse, 6049 Seaview Avenue NW; (206) 447-5544; seafood

Rover's, 2808 East Madison Street; (206) 325-7442; French/Northwest

Salty's on Alki, 1936 Harbor Avenue SW, West Seattle; (206) 937-1600; casual seafood

Santa Fe Cafe, 5910 Phinney Avenue North; (206) 783-9755; Southwest

Shuckers, Fourth Avenue at Seneca; (206) 621-1984; seafood/oysters

Siam on Broadway, 616 Broadway East; (206) 324-0892; Thai

Wild Ginger, 1400 Western Avenue; (206) 623-4450; Asian/Satay Bar

Zula, 916 East John; (206) 322-0852; East African

SNOQUALMIE

Old Honey Farm Inn Restaurant, 8910 - 384th Avenue SE; (206) 888-9399; Northwest

SPOKANE

C.I. Shenanigan's, 322 North Spokane Falls Court; (509) 455-5072; seafood/steak

Clinkerdagger, West 621 Mallon (Flour Mill); (509) 328-5965; seafood/steak/chicken

Milford's Fish House and Oyster Bar, North 719 Monroe Street; (509) 326-7251

The Onion, West 302 Riverside; (509) 747-3852, and North 7522 Division, (509) 482-6100; soups/salads/burgers/dinners

Patsy Clark's, West 2208 Second Street; (509) 838-8300; Continental

TACOMA

C.I. Shenanigan's, 3017 Ruston Way; (206) 752-8811; seafood/steak

El Toro, 5723 North 26th and Pearl; (206) 759-7889; Mexican

Harbor Lights, 2761 Ruston Way; (206) 752-8600; seafood/steak

The Lobster Shop, 4013 Ruston Way; (206) 759-2165; lobster/seafood/fine waterfront dining

The Old House Cafe, 2717 North Proctor; (206) 759-7336; versatile menu for lunch/tea/dinner served in elegant yet homey setting

Stanley and Seaforts Steak, Chop, and Fish House, 115 East 34th Street; (206) 473-7300

Zeppo, 100 South Ninth Street; (206) 627-1009; Italian

BRITISH COLUMBIA

British Columbia

TWEEDSMUIR PROVINCIAL PARK

COAST MOUNTAINS

Prince George

WELLS GRAY PROV PARK

Kinbasket Lake

YOHO NATL PARK

STRAIT

Port Hardy ★

VANCOUVER

PACIFIC OCEAN

STRATHCONA PROV PARK

Pemberton ★ ★ Mt Currie

GARIBALDI PROVINCIAL PARK

VANCOUVER

Nanaimo

ISLAND

OF GEORGIA

Victoria

Revelstoke ★

Monashee Pass

KOOTENAY MOUNTAINS

Kamloops

Vernon ★

Summerland ★ ★ Kelowna

Hope

Penticton

Nelson

Oliver ★
Osoyoos ★

See Detail Below

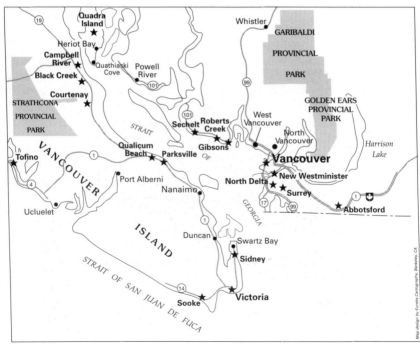

Quadra Island ★

Heriot Bay

Campbell River ★

Black Creek ★

Courtenay ★

STRATHCONA PROVINCIAL PARK

VANCOUVER

Tofino ★

Ucluelet

Quathiaski Cove

Powell River

STRAIT

Sechelt ★ Roberts Creek

Qualicum Beach ★ Gibsons

Parksville ★

OF

Port Alberni

Nanaimo

Duncan

ISLAND

Swartz Bay

Sidney ★

STRAIT OF SAN JUAN DE FUCA

Sooke ★

Victoria ★

Whistler ●

GARIBALDI PROVINCIAL PARK

West Vancouver

North Vancouver

Vancouver ★

New Westminister ★

North Delta ★ ★
Surrey ★

Abbotsford ★

GOLDEN EARS PROVINCIAL PARK

Harrison Lake

GEORGIA

Map design by Eureka Cartography, Berkeley, CA

The Cliff House Bed & Breakfast   **(604) 852-5787**
36050 Southridge Place, Abbotsford, BC V3G 1E2
(One hour east of Vancouver via Trans-Canada Highway -- Route 3)

The Cliff House couldn't be easier to reach from the freeway, yet its location in the Mountain Village community gives it a wonderful view across valley farmlands to Mount Baker. A newer home with architectural touches of Victoriana, it has traditional decor and tasteful, immaculate accommodations. The Lace Room, done in ecru, offers a Baker-view; The Country Room is handsomely outfitted in dark green with an iron and brass bed. A luxurious full bathroom off the second-floor landing is shared by the two rooms. If required, hosts Walter and Ina Friesen also offer the Master Suite with private bath (two-night minimum). Guests are most welcome to use the living room or the cozy family room. This comfortable stop along a well-traveled route offers far more than convenience.

Two small poodles in residence; children welcome if both rooms are booked; smoking outside only; full breakfast; llama farms, Wonderland Amusement Park, and interesting shopping stops nearby; off-street parking; Dutch spoken; inquire about rate for Master Suite. Brochure available.

ROOM	BED	BATH	ENTRANCE	FLOOR	DAILY RATES S - D (EP)
A	1Q	Shd*	Main	2	$50-$55
B	1Q	Shd*	Main	2	$50-$55

Rates stated in Canadian funds

217

Country Comfort
(604) 337-5273

8214 Island Highway, Black Creek, BC V9J 1H6
(Between Courtenay and Campbell River)

If you like a rural atmosphere but appreciate modern conveniences and handy access to the highway, Ron and Elaine Bohn's Country Comfort has it all -- on fifty beautiful acres! It is equally satisfying for overnighters or for those who make it home base while exploring parks and beaches, fishing waters, Mount Washington, and Forbidden Plateau. The three neat guest rooms are done in pastel shades, and each has a different quilt theme. Elaine's handcrafted items enhance the cheerful decor, and her variety of breakfasts include farm fresh eggs, homemade bread, jams, and muffins. Guests are welcome in the main living areas but may enjoy the exclusive use of a downstairs family room for watching TV, reading, or visiting. An all-around generous spirit marks the hospitality found at Country Comfort.

No smoking in bedrooms; beach, golf course, boat marina, stores, restaurants, tennis court, petting zoo, and mini-golf nearby; off-street parking; EP rates for children aged six to twelve; no charge for younger children. Brochure available.

ROOM	BED	BATH	ENTRANCE	FLOOR	DAILY RATES S - D	(EP)
A	1Q	Shd*	Main	1	$30-$45	($10)
B	1D	Shd*	Main	1	$30-$45	($10)
C	1D	Shd*	Main	1	$30-$45	($10)

Rates stated in Canadian funds

Miracle Beach Bed & Breakfast   **(604) 337-5310**
2161 Miracle Beach Drive, Black Creek, BC V9J 1K3
(East of Island Highway, about a mile from Miracle Beach Provincial Park)

Soon after turning off the main highway and heading toward delightful Miracle Beach Provincial Park, one comes upon a new house on the right, set well back from the road. A vast lawn and lovingly planted gardens lead up to the home, which is constructed in traditional style with gray wood siding, a pitched roof, and five dormers across the front. Proud owner-builders, Rita, Willi, and family have included over the garage a comfortable guest apartment with two bedrooms, a bath, a sitting room with a TV/VCR, and a full kitchen with a dining table. It is especially suitable for two couples or a family and brings the pleasures of Miracle Beach and sandy Saratoga Beach within easy reach.

Kennel across road for pets; families welcome; no smoking; full breakfast; washer/dryer available; walk to beaches; excellent salmon fishing nearby; Mt. Washington, forty minutes away; off-street parking; credit cards (V,MC); EP rate for guests over age eight.

ROOM	BED	BATH	ENTRANCE	FLOOR	DAILY RATES	
					S - D	(EP)
A	1K	Shd*	Sep	2	$30-$45	($10)
B	1D	Shd*	Sep	2	$30-$45	($10)

Rates stated in Canadian funds

Bright's Willow Point Guest House   **(604) 923-1086**
2460 South Island Highway, Campbell River, BC V9W 1C6
(On left when heading north, south of town center)

This contemporary home offers a good stopover point enroute to or from Port Hardy and easy access to the fishing activities of the "Salmon Capital of the World," plus shipshape accommodations and top-notch hosts. Valerie and George Bright extend a style of hospitality that is friendly, courteous, and tailored to each guest's requirements. If you need to make a fishing charter, there will be a 4:00 a.m. breakfast and a packed lunch waiting (if required). Return later to a warm, clean place for some civilized comfort. You'll sleep in one of three impeccably furnished bedrooms on the home's upper level. All front windows face a breathtaking view of mountains and Discovery Passage. A full English breakfast -- or, if you choose, a lighter breakfast -- is served in a manner perfectly suited to the refined ambiance of Bright's Willow Point Guest House.

Cat in residence; no pets or smoking; no children under twelve; full or light breakfast; refreshments offered on arrival; extra charge for packed lunch; TV and fireplace available to guests; fishing charters arranged; off-street parking; credit cards (V); airport pickup (Campbell River); AAA/CAA triple-diamond rated. Brochure available.

ROOM	BED	BATH	ENTRANCE	FLOOR	DAILY RATES S - D (EP)
A	1D	Shd*	Main	2	$40-$60
B	1K or 2T	Shd*	Main	2	$40-$60
C	1K or 2T	Pvt	Main	2	$50-$60

Rates stated in Canadian funds

Pier House Bed & Breakfast   **(604) 287-2943**
670 Island Highway, Campbell River, BC V9W 2C3
(Heart of Campbell River facing ocean and harbor)

Pier House, circa 1924, is distinguished as the oldest house in town and the home of its first provincial policeman. Furnished with antiques of the period, it is an utterly charming combination of old curiosity shop, museum, and "Grandma's house." The allure of the library is most immediate: There are floor-to-ceiling bookshelves packed with vintage hardbacks, a dictionary on a stand, a globe, an old short-wave radio, and myriad other relics that beg to be examined. It's a place to settle in for a good read or a visit. Guest rooms, too, are long on character. Mementoes, art, and reading matter create the sense that the residents of yesteryear have just stepped out for a bit. Tunes from the old Victrola may accompany breakfast set with bone china and unique serving pieces now found mostly in antique shops. Pleasant surprises and touches of whimsy abound in the easygoing warmth of the Pier House.

No pets or children; smoking outside only; full breakfast; restaurants, pubs, shops, harbor, fishing pier, and Quadra Island ferry nearby; off-street parking; credit cards (V,MC).

ROOM	BED	BATH	ENTRANCE	FLOOR	DAILY RATES	
					S - D	(EP) +
A	1Q	Pvt 1/2	Main	1	$60-$70	
B	1D	Shd*	Main	2	$60-$70	
C	1D	Shd*	Main	2	$50-$60	
D	2T	Pvt 1/2	Main	2	$65-$75	($20)

Rates stated in Canadian funds

221

Greystone Manor   **(604) 338-1422**
RR#6, S-684, C-2, Courtenay, BC V9N 8H9
(On Comox Bay, across from mainland Powell River)

You can reach this outdoor recreation mecca, the Comox Valley, via the Sunshine Coast or the highway from Nanaimo or Port Hardy. One of the oldest homes in the Comox Valley, Greystone Manor is set in one and a half acres of waterfront with views across Comox Bay to the mainland coast mountains. This is a perfect place to relax and use as a base for sampling the region's many activities. Hosts Mike and Mo Shipton moved to Canada from England in 1991. Both are keen gardeners, which is reflected in their colorful flower beds, hanging baskets, and window boxes. Mo enjoys cooking and serves a full breakfast including freshly baked muffins and scones. Watch the seals, herons, and bald eagles from the deck or take a stroll through the gardens down to the beach. Winter skiing at two resorts, summer salmon fishing, and hiking are among the area's most popular attractions. When you're not busy outdoors, you'll appreciate all the homey comforts of Greystone Manor.

No pets or smoking; no children under twelve; full breakfast; guest sitting room with fireplace; off-street parking.

ROOM	BED	BATH	ENTRANCE	FLOOR	DAILY RATES S - D (EP)	
A	2T	Shd*	Main	2	$49-$63	($20)
B	1D	Shd*	Main	2	$49-$63	
C	1D	Shd*	Main	2	$49-$63	
D	1Q	Shd*	Main	2	$49-$63	($20)

Rates stated in Canadian funds

Bonniebrook Lodge   **(604) 886-2887**
RR#4, S-10, C-34, Gibsons, BC V0N 1V0
(1532 Ocean Beach Esplanade, Gower Point)

This 1920s oceanside lodge has been brought up to present-day standards and redecorated throughout by Karen and Philippe Lacoste. The upper floor is comprised of four guest rooms; one has a private bath and the others share two baths. Bedrooms are beautifully appointed with bordered wallcoverings, floral valances and bedspreads, velvety carpeting, soothing artwork, fresh flowers, and plants. A large front sun deck is a relaxing vantage point from which to watch crashing waves and passing ships. For breakfast or dinner, simply descend the stairs into Chez Philippe, a dining room with considerable charm, excellent service, and divine French/West Coast cuisine. Take an after-dinner moonlit walk along the shore or retire to your comfortable room on the floor above. Bonniebrook Lodge is a romantic seaside getaway where you'll find everything you need right where you are.

Cat in residence; no pets; no smoking in bedrooms; full breakfast in Chez Philippe; sofa bed extra in Room B; extra-long bed in Room D; beach, salmon spawning creek, Chaster Park, and Molly's Lane Craft Market nearby; off-street parking; French spoken; credit cards (V,MC); outside staircase to second-floor rooms. Brochure and information sheet available.

ROOM	BED	BATH	ENTRANCE	FLOOR	DAILY RATES S - D	(EP) +
A	1D	Shd*	Main	2	$70	
B	1D	Shd*	Main	2	$80	($10)
C	1Q	Shd*	Main	2	$80	
D	1D	Pvt	Main	2	$80	

Rates stated in Canadian funds

223

Ocean View Cottage   **(604) 886-7943**
RR#2, S-46, C-10, Gibsons, BC V0N 1V0
(On Sunshine Coast, west of Highway 101 just north of Gibsons)

When Bert and Dianne Verzyl designed their home and guest cottage on three rural acres, the view took top priority -- and rightfully so. The cliffside setting looks out across the Strait of Georgia with Vancouver Island in the background. There are two neat quest rooms with private baths in the main house; they're at the opposite end from the hosts' quarters, and one has a great view. Set well away from the main house, the contemporary wood cottage is generously proportioned and completely self-contained. It has a full kitchen, a bedroom, a sofa bed, a futon, cable television, skylights, plenty of comfortable seating, a deck with table and chairs, and expansive windows to bring in the mesmerizing panorama. A few days at Ocean View Cottage should prove peaceful, restful, and utterly undemanding.

No pets or smoking; full breakfast; shopping, dining, golfing, hiking, fishing, scenic cruises, and sandy beaches nearby; off-street parking; Dutch and French spoken; airport pickup (Tyee at Sechelt). Brochure available.

ROOM	BED	BATH	ENTRANCE	FLOOR	DAILY RATES S - D (EP)
A	1Q	Pvt	Main	1	$55-$60
B	2T	Pvt	Main	1	$45-$55
C	1D	Pvt	Sep	1	$80 ($20)

Rates stated in Canadian funds

224

Sonora View Bed & Breakfast
(604) 763-0969
998 Augusta Court, Kelowna, BC V1Y 7T9
(Central Kelowna)

The established, well-kept neighborhood in which you'll find Sonora View Bed & Breakfast is near the hub of Okanagan Valley activity. Even so, it's quiet here, and the mountains and woods in the background lend a countrified air. Kurt and Edith Grube's two-story home offers a clean, comfortable, friendly environment. A large guest room on the first floor is tastefully decorated in soft, elegant peach tones with a crown canopy over the bed. The other two bedrooms are done in soft blues. Antique furnishings enrich the decor, and Edith's artistic touches adorn a wall here or a door there throughout the house. Her sumptuous breakfasts are often served on the garden sun deck with a beautiful panoramic view of city, lake, mountains, and golf course.

No pets; smoking outside only; full breakfast; TV/VCR and library available in guest sitting room; AC; sofa bed also in Room C; tennis courts and major golf course nearby; off-street parking; German spoken; airport and bus depot pickup; off-season rates. Brochure available.

ROOM	BED	BATH	ENTRANCE	FLOOR	DAILY RATES S - D	(EP)
A	2T	Pvt	Main	2	$40-$60	($20)
B	1Q	Pvt	Main	1G	$40-$60	($20)
C	1Q & 1T	Pvt	Main	1G	$40-$70	

Rates stated in Canadian funds

Mt. Currie Bed & Breakfast   **(604) 894-6864**
P.O. Box 192, Mt. Currie, BC V0N 2K0
(In Pemberton Valley, north of Whistler)

Mount Currie can be reached by continuing north from famous Mount Whistler or by traversing the scenic, unpopulated mountain route southwest from Lillooet. Either way, you're in pretty spectacular territory, and Mt. Currie Bed & Breakfast comes as a welcome stop. Here you can catch your breath, plan your explorations, walk up the road for a bistro dinner, and get a good night's rest. Hosts Bob and Jolene Green offer the entire lower floor of their home for guests. It has a cozy fireside TV lounge, two bedrooms, and a bath. Upstairs there is one guest room with a private bath. Here also is the dining area where tasty full breakfasts are savored in the quiet country atmosphere.

No pets or smoking; full breakfast; horseback riding, raft and jet boat trips, hot springs, skiing and snowmobiling, hiking, Nairn Falls, Joffre Glacier, and more in vicinity; off-street parking; credit cards (V). Brochure available.

ROOM	BED	BATH	ENTRANCE	FLOOR	DAILY RATES S - D (EP)
A	1Q	Shd*	Main	1	$45-$60
B	2T	Shd*	Main	1	$45-$60
C	1D	Pvt	Main	2	$50-$65

Rates stated in Canadian funds

Gilgan's Bed & Breakfast   **(604) 521-8592**
333 Third Street, New Westminster, BC V3L 2R8
(Just southeast of Vancouver)

The municipality of New Westminster has many heritage homes from the turn of the century when it was, for a time, the capital of British Columbia. Some of the most notable architects of the day left their mark here along streets where the homes seem to be maturing as gracefully as the trees. One such home in the Queen's Park area is Gilgan's Bed & Breakfast; it's been fully refurbished and updated with modern conveniences. A spacious suite on the lower level has high ceilings, plenty of light, and a sitting area with a fireplace. There is another smaller room off the hallway and a separate guest entrance for easy access to the backyard sun deck, heated pool, and hot tub. The hospitality offered by the Gilgans is as gracious as one might expect in this distinctive neighborhood; the extra privacy is quite nice, too.

No pets or smoking; full breakfast; extra beds available; great area for walking; good selection of restaurants close by; ten-minute walk to Skytrain, then thirty minutes to downtown Vancouver; off-street parking; airport pickup (Vancouver).

ROOM	BED	BATH	ENTRANCE	FLOOR	DAILY RATES S - D (EP)
A	1Q	Pvt	Sep	LL	$70 ($10)
B	1D				$50

Rates stated in Canadian funds

227

Sunshine Hills Bed & Breakfast　　　　　**(604) 596-6496**
11200 Bond Boulevard, North Delta, BC V4E 1M7　　FAX: **596-6496**
(Twenty minutes north of U.S.-Canadian border)

Putzi and Wim Honing are seasoned travelers and experienced tourguides who are especially attuned to the individual needs of their guests. They are also knowledgeable about the area's unique attractions and the logistics of getting to them. In the quiet surroundings of a well-established neighborhood, the Honings' Sunshine Hills Bed & Breakfast has a welcoming spirit and the extra privacy of guest quarters with a separate entrance on the ground floor. There are two comfortable bedrooms, a bath, a kitchenette, and an enclosed backyard garden. Full European-style breakfasts are served in the main floor dining room. People desiring reasonably priced lodgings in a location that is central to the border, the airport, ferries, the beach at White Rock, and the Skytrain to Vancouver will find Sunshine Hills just the ticket.

Cat in residence; no pets; smoking outside only; full breakfast; TV, radio, and fireplace on guest floor; park with tennis courts across street; off-street parking; German, Dutch, some French spoken; two-night minimum. Brochure available.

ROOM	BED	BATH	ENTRANCE	FLOOR	DAILY RATES	
					S - D	(EP)
A	2T	Shd*	Sep	1G	$45-$50	($15)
B	1D	Shd*	Sep	1G	$45-$50	($15)

Rates stated in Canadian funds

Mirror Lake Guest House   Phone/FAX: **(604) 495-7959**
Box 425, Oliver, BC V0H 1T0
(Southeast corner of Highway 97 and Road 20)

The grounds surrounding this stately, seven-gabled heritage home
are comprised of a wide front lawn studded with old shade trees, a
thirteen-acre organic fruit orchard, and the tranquility of beautiful
Mirror Lake. Hosts Gwen and Joseph Rundle put their hearts into
every aspect of the home and property: carefully tended orchards,
thoughtfully decorated country Victorian rooms, breakfasts featuring
organic breads and eggs from free range chickens, and the caring
hospitality that warms every guest. The Gazebo is a suite with a view
that is favored by honeymooners, though each of the other rooms has
its own array of charms. A stroll down to privately owned Mirror
Lake might just end with a swim; a short drive can lead to wine-tasting rooms, golf courses, hiking trails, water recreation, and much
more -- provided you can tear yourself away from Mirror Lake Guest
House, a hard place to leave.

No pets; no children under eleven; smoking on veranda only; full
breakfast; robes provided; guest sitting room with TV/VCR and fireplace; AC; phones in rooms; off-street parking; Japanese spoken;
credit cards (V,MC); airport pickup (Oliver); off-season rates. Brochure available.

ROOM	BED	BATH	ENTRANCE	FLOOR	DAILY RATES S - D (EP) +
A	1Q	Pvt	Main	1	$70-$90
B	1Q	Shd	Main	1	$50-$60
C	2T	Shd*	Main	2	$45-$65
D	1Q	Shd*	Main	2	$50-$70
E	1Q	Shd*	Main	2	$50-$70

Rates stated in Canadian funds

229

Haynes Point Lakeside Guest House (604) 495-7443
RR#1, S-93, C-2, Osoyoos, BC V0H 1V0
(3619 - 87th Street, near Haynes Point Provincial Park)

The quiet end of the Okanagan Valley is a perfect home base for sampling local wineries, golfing, and participating in all manner of water recreation, and it is just minutes from the U.S.-Canadian border. Haynes Point Lakeside Guest House is a comfortable, modern home set on a hillside that slopes down to beautiful Lake Osoyoos. Taking full advantage of this relaxing garden setting might include enjoying an outdoor barbecue, reclining in the shaded hammock, or sipping a beverage on the sun deck. Outdoors or in, prepare to be spoiled by hosts John and June Wallace. Their warmth and openness make it easy to settle in and feel at home. At one end of the house is the Honeymoon Suite; at the other are the Antique Room and the Oriental Room, which share a bath with a Jacuzzi tub. Handcrafted decorator touches evoke nostalgia and whimsy. The Wallaces' personalized hospitality is their hallmark.

No pets or children; smoking outside only; full breakfast; TV/VCR and Grandpa Fisher stove in downstairs family room; AC; off-street parking; airport pickup (Penticton); off-season rates. Brochure available.

ROOM	BED	BATH	ENTRANCE	FLOOR	DAILY RATES S - D (EP)
A	1Q	Pvt	Main	1	$50-$75
B	1D	Shd*	Main	1	$50-$60
C	1Q	Shd*	Main	1	$50-$65

Rates stated in Canadian funds

Loon Watch Bed & Breakfast   **(604) 752-9698**
1513 Admiral Tryon Boulevard, Parksville, BC   V9P 1Y3
(At water's edge overlooking Columbia Beach)

Yes, at Loon Watch you can really watch loons -- from October through April -- along with herons, killer whales, seals, and bald eagles, and you can do so from your own private balcony. There are two spacious water-view bedrooms on the upper floor. One is done in white, blue, pink, and yellow and has a lovely writing desk. The other, in a pink and white floral motif, has an alcove with a dressing table. Both are stocked with all kinds of amenities. Early coffee or tea awaits you outside your door in the morning, something to get you started before indulging in a scrumptious breakfast by candlelight with hosts John and Dorothy Gourlay. If necessary, a fire in the nearby hearth can keep off the slightest chill in the air. At day's end, catch the soothing glow of a sunset from your balcony as the cruise ships sparkle by on their way up the Inland Passage.

Cat in residence; no pets; smoking on balconies only; TV in each room; cot available; king-sized headboard on twin beds in Room A; sitting room with fireplace always available to guests; hot tub overlooking Strait of Georgia; beachcombing from property; fishing charters arranged; off-street parking; credit cards (MC); airport pickup (Qualicum Beach). Brochure available.

ROOM	BED	BATH	ENTRANCE	FLOOR	DAILY RATES S - D (EP)
A	2T	Pvt	Main	2	$55-$75
B	1Q	Pvt	Main	2	$55-$75

Rates stated in Canadian funds

231

Marina View Bed & Breakfast   **(604) 248-9308**
895 Glenhale Crescent, Parksville, BC V9P 1Z7
(Between Parksville and Qualicum Beach)

In a spectacular setting overlooking the Strait of Georgia, the islands, and the mountains beyond is Marina View Bed & Breakfast. It's a home full of modern luxuries where the main floor is almost entirely turned over to guests. From one guest room, from the large deck, and from the expansive solarium, you might catch the unforgettable sight of Alaskan cruise ships sailing past the marina into showy sunsets. Use the handy binoculars to spot eagles, shorebirds, seals, otters, and the occasional whale. A comfortable guest lounge offers TV, games, and bumper pool. Bedrooms feature bay windows with cushioned window seats. There is handy access to the shoreline where serious beachcombing might ensue, and host Dea Kern has worked out many intriguing day trips for people keen to explore. She can even charter you a fishing expedition and send you off with a delicious breakfast to enjoy on the boat. At Marina View, the setting and the personalized service stand out.

No pets or small children; smoking outside only; full breakfast; rollaway bed available; off-street parking; credit cards (V); airport pickup (Qualicum); *closed mid-November to mid-March.* Brochure available.

ROOM	BED	BATH	ENTRANCE	FLOOR	DAILY RATES	
					S - D	(EP)
A	2T	Shd*	Main	1	$50-$65	($20)
B	1D	Shd*	Main	1	$50-$60	($20)
C	1Q	Pvt	Main	1	$70	($20)

Rates stated in Canadian funds

Pemberton Creekside Bed & Breakfast   **(604) 894-6520**
Box 639, Pemberton, BC V0N 2L0   FAX: **894-5350**
(In Pemberton Valley, north of Whistler)

The tiny village of Pemberton lies in a peaceful valley of the same name surrounded by snow-capped mountains. Here Freda and Clyde Bostrom offer old-fashioned warmth year round in a home full of modern-day comforts. Guest quarters are all on the ground floor. Two of the rooms share a bath and one has an ensuite bath with a Jacuzzi tub. There is also a fireside guest lounge with TV/VCR and books. Wall paintings, stenciling, and other thoughtful decorator touches give each room strong individual appeal. Fans of *Anne of Green Gables* will be especially delighted with the Avonlea Room. While breakfasting in the upper floor dining room, spy feathered friends at their feeding station just outside the window. Everyone gets a warm welcome at Pemberton Creekside B&B.

No pets or smoking; full breakfast; robes furnished; skiing one-half hour away at Whistler; cross-country skiing, snowmobiling, horseback riding, river rafting, hiking, cycling, and golf in vicinity; bus service to Whistler and Vancouver three times a day; daily BC rail to Vancouver; off-street parking; some German spoken; wheelchair access (Room C); credit cards (V). Brochure available.

ROOM	BED	BATH	ENTRANCE	FLOOR	DAILY RATES S - D (EP)
A	2T	Shd*	Main	1G	$45-$60
B	1Q	Shd*	Main	1G	$45-$60
C	1Q	Pvt	Main	1G	$45-$60

Rates stated in Canadian funds

Hamilton Bed & Breakfast   **(604) 949-6638**
Box 1926, Port Hardy, BC V0N 2P0
(9415 Mayor's Way, northwest section of town)

The uninformed traveler tends to think of Port Hardy merely as a jumping-off point for the trip up the Inside Passage to Prince Rupert. But many outdoor enthusiasts are aware of Port Hardy's unique attributes. The area boasts excellent diving conditions; great waters for catching hefty halibut, salmon, and cod; and access to the wild, open ocean, raging surf, and white beaches of the island's West Coast (a day trip to San Josef Bay is a *must*). Touring the local copper mine and the Port Hardy Museum with its impressive collection of native artifacts is also popular. Lorne and Betty Hamilton offer clean and tidy accommodations in their quiet residential area, about a fifteen-minute walk from the waterfront. Both helpful and accommodating, the Hamiltons have hosted backpackers, business travelers, vacationers, outdoor lovers, sportsmen, and international students. Their home is a welcoming place for a good night's sleep at the remote tip of Vancouver Island.

No pets; children by arrangement; smoking outside only; TV available; transportation to ferry dock or airport; off-street parking; inquire about off-season rates for business travelers.

ROOM	BED	BATH	ENTRANCE	FLOOR	DAILY RATES S - D (EP)
A	1Q	Shd	Main	LL	$35-$50
B	2T	Shd*	Main	1	$35-$50
C	1D	Shd*	Main	1	$35-$45

Rates stated in Canadian funds

Bonnie Belle Bed & Breakfast　　　　　　**(604) 285-3578**
Box 331, Campbell River, BC V9W 5B6
(On West Road, two and one-half miles from ferry dock)

When John and Trudy Parkyn designed the country home of their dreams, respect for the natural setting was their prime concern. Situated on seven acres, this B&B is set in the leafy privacy of alder and fir overlooking Gowlland Harbour, where loons and seals may be sighted. In every aspect, the ambiance is simple and pure, clean and uncluttered. The traditionally-styled home combines country freshness with handcrafted construction. The living and dining area has an open-beamed ceiling and high windows all around. White walls, a brick hearth, and an array of fine woodwork are enhanced by a few well-chosen antiques and heirlooms. Second-floor guest quarters with tree and water views consist of two wonderful bedrooms, a large, old-fashioned bathroom, a reading nook, and an enclosed porch. If you choose, you may charter the Heritage West Coast Vessel Bonnie Belle, skippered by John, a Master Mariner and lifelong resident. After a tranquil night's sleep, arise to an ample breakfast prepared by Trudy on the wood-fired cookstove; it can be plain or fancy, depending on your appetite. I suggest you let Trudy use her imagination -- you won't be sorry.

Dog in residence; smoking on porch; full breakfast.   Brochure available.

ROOM	BED	BATH	ENTRANCE	FLOOR	DAILY RATES S - D (EP)
A	2T	Shd*	Main	2	$35-$50
B	1D	Shd*	Main	2	$35-$50

Rates stated in Canadian funds

235

Hyacinthe Bay Bed & Breakfast   **(604) 285-2126**
Box 343, Heriot Bay, BC V0P 1H0
(East coast of island, seven miles from ferry dock)

The contemporary home of Janice Kenyon and Ross Henry features dramatic open-beamed cedar construction, a wide, wrap-around deck with a hot tub, and huge windows that frame a spectacular view of Hyacinthe Bay. Light bathes the interior, where traditional furnishings, family heirlooms, and Oriental rugs on polished wood floors create a most appealing contrast of old and new. A guest bedroom and bath on the main floor have been outfitted for maximum comfort and ease; there's extra sleeping space for children in the loft. The deck is a great place for sunbathing, stargazing from the hot tub, or enjoying a leisurely breakfast. Janice, a cookbook author, prepares a delectable specialty each morning and can provide a thermos of coffee to take to the beach. You may wish to share the good company of Janice and Ross, a retired physician; bask in the serene beauty of Hyacinthe Bay; take a hike up Chinese Mountain; spend time in quiet repose; or all of the above. A time of relaxation and renewal awaits you at this Quadra Island retreat.

No pets; children welcome; no smoking; full breakfast; TV and VCR for movies (rentals nearby); barbecue; hot tub; fishing charters arranged; off-street parking; French and German spoken. Brochure available.

ROOM	BED	BATH	ENTRANCE	FLOOR	DAILY RATES S - D (EP)
A	1K or 2T	Pvt	Main	1	$50-$60 ($10)

Rates stated in Canadian funds

Joha House   **(604) 285-2247**
Box 668, Quathiaski Cove, Quadra Island, BC V0P 1N0
(Less than one mile from ferry dock)

Beautiful coastal holidays on Quadra Island inspired Joyce and Harold Johnson's early retirement, and B&B hosting became a way of sharing the joy of island living. Their unbridled enthusiasm is justi-fied, as any visitor quickly learns. The contemporary wood home is oriented toward a breathtaking view of Quathiaski Cove, tiny Grouse Island, and the Inside Passage. Watch occasional cruise ships and regular ferries, or spot eagles and herons. Accommodations at Joha House include a self-contained, private garden suite and two B&B rooms on the upper level. Bedrooms are full of country charm with attractive quilts providing the color schemes. The living/dining area features custom-designed stained-glass windows and a fireplace of smooth local stones with hand-hewn yellow cedar trim. It's a splendid setting for enjoying a tasty breakfast in full view of nature's glory. With the Johnsons' help, discover the many joys of Quadra Island.

No pets; children welcome in suite; smoking permitted on deck; full breakfast; robes provided; woodstove and sofa bed in suite; dock for guest boats; good collection of literature on hiking, whale-watch-ing trips (July-September), and other local activities; fishing charters arranged; off-street parking; ferry pickup for walkers; three-night minimum in suite; weekly rates available. Brochure available.

ROOM	BED	BATH	ENTRANCE	FLOOR	DAILY RATES	
					S - D	(EP)
A	1D	Shd*	Main	2	$45-$55	
B	1Q	Shd*	Main	2	$50-$60	
C	1Q	Pvt	Sep	LL	$75	($12)

Rates stated in Canadian funds

237

Blue Willow Bed & Breakfast (604) 752-9052
524 Quatna Road, Qualicum Beach, BC V9K 1B4   FAX: 752-9039
(South end of town, just before golf course)

The fame of the Blue Willow's breakfasts -- bountiful English fare packed with homemade goodness -- is well deserved, but its other assets are equally notable. A world of country luxury resides at the the Tudor-style home nestled in a cottage garden bursting with foliage and blossoms. The interior has a hint of French country flavor, with dark ceiling beams against white, accented by brass, copper, and lace. There is a guest lounge with a clubby atmosphere, beautifully tailored guest rooms with various bed and bath choices, and a dining room that is a vision of old pine and Blue Willow china. As often as possible, breakfast is served at white wicker tables on the garden patio. Separate accommodation for a family or two couples is available in the lovely Garden Suite, consisting of a bed/sitting room, a full bath, and a bedroom. Arlene and John England are the superb hosts of this truly exceptional B&B.

Dog in residence; children welcome in Garden Suite; smoking outside only; English or Continental breakfast; robes provided; TV/VCR in guest lounge/library; village, golf courses, beaches, bird sanctuaries, and waterfalls nearby; off-street parking; French and German spoken; credit cards; airport (Qualicum Beach) and train pickup; off-season rates; Rooms D and E *sometimes* available. Brochure available.

ROOM	BED	BATH	ENTRANCE	FLOOR	DAILY RATES S - D	(EP)
A	1K or 2T	Pvt	Main	1G	$55-$75	
B	1Q	Pvt	Main	1G	$55-$75	
C	1Q & 3T	Pvt	Sep	2	$80	($20)
D	1D	Shd*	Main	2	$50-$65	
E	1D	Shd*	Main	2	$50-$65	

Rates stated in Canadian funds

Grauer's Getaway, Destination Bed & Breakfast   **(604) 752-5851**
395 Burnham Road, Qualicum Beach, BC V9K 1G5   FAX: **752-5860**
(Overlooking Strait of Georgia)

A rare discovery indeed is this English-style cottage built in the twenties on a bluff overlooking the sea with a pathway down to the beach. Grauer's Getaway has evolved into a bed and breakfast resort, boasting a tennis court with a ball machine, a swimming pool with a sliding board, and a spa -- all with a knockout view of water and distant mountains of the mainland. There are rose gardens and patios where guests may linger or picnic. Rooms are particularly spacious, including the breakfast room where couples can savor the view at their own table for two. B&B rooms offer the extra privacy of ensuite baths and a separate entrance. Both romantic creations are light and airy, with pretty wallcoverings and linens, luxurious carpeting, and tastefully chosen antiques and artwork. Steven and Brenda Grauer go to great lengths to make theirs the perfect getaway -- and it is.

Dog and cat in residence; no pets; smoking outside only; tennis court with ball machine; pool; spa; five-minute walk to golf course; off-street parking; weekly, off-season, and family rates; two-night minimum for long holiday weekends. Also available by the week in summer is a self-contained, one-bedroom cottage on property with loft, kitchen, and cots and cribs (as needed). Brochure available.

ROOM	BED	BATH	ENTRANCE	FLOOR	DAILY RATES S - D	(EP)
A	2T	Pvt	Sep	1	$80-$85	($15)
B	1Q	Pvt	Sep	1	$80-$85	($15)

Rates stated in Canadian funds

239

Pathways Bed & Breakfast   **(604) 752-2434**
323 Hoy Lake Road West, Qualicum Beach, BC V9K 1K5
(Inland side of Island Highway, central to golf course, village, and
beach)

The Schmidts' home, set on a quiet residential street, has a conventional outward appearance that belies the world of colorful folk art and
country scenarios within. At every turn there is a new visual treat, a
pleasing collection of one sort or another. Carol likes reminders of
the early days on the prairies of Manitoba (the origin of most pieces),
where furnishings, while functional, brought color and warmth to a
hard way of life. The comfortable bedrooms are as artfully decorated
as the rest of the house. The lively interior is complemented by
wonderful vistas across the Strait of Georgia and cheerful, generous
hospitality. The name is derived from pathways that lead from the
house to the golf course, the delighful village, and the beach. It's also
a place to cross paths with interesting folks, not the least of whom are
hosts Carol and Ray Schmidt.

Two small dogs in residence; no pets or smoking; children over
twelve welcome; full or Continental breakfast; nature trail from property; off-street parking; credit cards (V,MC). Brochure available.

ROOM	BED	BATH	ENTRANCE	FLOOR	DAILY RATES S - D (EP)
A	1Q	Pvt	Main	1	$60
B	1D	Shd*	Main	1	$40-$50
C	2T	Shd*	Main	1	$40-$55

Rates stated in Canadian funds

Quatna Manor   (604) 752-6685
512 Quatna Road, Qualicum Beach, BC V9K 1B4
(South end of town, just before golf course)

    Set on one gorgeous acre, the English Tudor-style home of Bill and Betty Ross is surrounded by lush grounds with a fish pond, a patio, a grape arbor, flower gardens, and benches. Quatna Manor's multiple dormers and bay windows enhance the home's considerable character, and the interior has an elegant, old-world ambiance. Crystal chandeliers collected abroad, beautiful wallcoverings, borders, and linens blend well with a marvelous array of antiques -- Betty rescues wonderful old pieces of furniture and revives them to their original glory. Second-floor accommodations include a guest lounge and four bedrooms, offering a variety of bed sizes, private and shared baths, and the option of a two-bedroom suite. Breakfast in the dining room amid antiques and fine silver is a civilized affair; pretty mornings find guests enjoying a meal on the patio under the arbor. For luxurious lodgings, fine hospitality, and great value, Quatna Manor is a find.

    Cat in residence; no pets; no small children; smoking outside only; English or Continental breakfast; TV and fireplace in guest lounge; village, golf courses, beaches, bird sanctuaries, and waterfalls nearby; off-street parking; credit cards (V); airport (Qualicum Beach), train, and bus pickup; off-season and family rates. Brochure available.

ROOM	BED	BATH	ENTRANCE	FLOOR	DAILY RATES S - D	(EP)
A	1K	Pvt	Main	2	$60-$75	($15)
B	1Q	Shd*	Main	2	$50-$60	($15)
C	2T	Shd*	Main	2	$50-$60	($15)
D	1Q	Shd*	Main	2	$50-$60	($15)

Rates stated in Canadian funds

L&R Nelles Ranch (604) 837-3800
P.O. Box 430, Revelstoke, BC V0E 2S0
(Highway 23 South)

Set amid the majesty of the Selkirk Mountains is L&R Nelles Ranch, located just a few miles out of delightfully refurbished downtown Revelstoke. Just being in this spectacular area affords a sense of wonder and exhilaration, and no one could love it more than Larry and Rosalyne Nelles. B&B guests are greeted with a warm, open, down-to-earth reception that makes them feel like members of the family. You'll find no urban cowboys here, but a realistic picture of life on a working horse ranch. For those so inclined, Larry offers wilderness trail rides of varying lengths at reasonable prices. Many photos and trophies displayed in the house attest to his expertise as a horseman. An expert skier as well, he knows intimately the area's variety of skiing opportunities. Rosalyne's full ranch breakfasts are sure to satisfy the most powerful of appetites. An enjoyable family atmosphere, comfortable accommodations, and breathtaking natural beauty are in store for you at L&R Nelles Ranch.

Small dog in residence; overnight horse accommodation; no smoking; full breakfast; TV/VCR; crib and rollaway bed; doll museum with over 300 dolls and treasures on premises; numerous outdoor activities nearby; EP rate for adults in same room, $15. Brochure available.

ROOM	BED	BATH	ENTRANCE	FLOOR	DAILY RATES S - D	(EP) +
A	1D & 1T	Shd*	Main	2	$35-$50	($10)
B	1D	Shd*	Main	1G	$35-$45	($10)
C	2D	Pvt	Main	1G	$35-$50	($10)
D	1Q	Shd*	Main	1G	$35-$45	($10)
E	1Q	Shd*	Main	2	$35-$45	($10)
F	1Q, 1D, 1T	Pvt	Main	1G	$55	($10)

Rates stated in Canadian funds

Bed & Breakfast at Roberts Creek   **(604) 885-5444**
RR#2, S-18, C-7, Gibsons, BC V0N 1V0
(Off Highway 101 at 1756 Hanbury Road in Roberts Creek)

Walls of huge logs imbue the interior of the Cattanachs' home on five wooded acres with golden warmth. Trees on the property were felled to build this rustic dwelling where the feeling of domestic security is almost tangible. On the main floor, there's an antique wood cookstove, a floor-to-ceiling natural stone hearth and woodburning stove, and a view of grazing horses from the dining room. Upstairs, guests have their own sitting room, a bathroom off the hallway, and two bedrooms full of cozy charm. A crib can be provided, and there are books, games, and a television. Families find the arrangement particularly comfortable, but most anyone would take pleasure in the snug country ambiance of Bed & Breakfast at Roberts Creek.

No pets or smoking; full breakfast; golfing, dining, horseback riding, picnicking, and good beaches nearby; off-street parking.

ROOM	BED	BATH	ENTRANCE	FLOOR	DAILY RATES S - D (EP)
A	1D	Shd*	Main	2	$40-$50 ($10)
B	2T	Shd*	Main	2	$40-$50 ($10)

Rates stated in Canadian funds

Country Cottage Bed & Breakfast   **(604) 885-7448**
General Delivery, Roberts Creek, BC V0N 2W0
(On Sunshine Coast, off Highway 101 just north of Gibsons)

In the tiny hamlet of Roberts Creek, Loragene and Philip Gaulin's Country Cottage is a small, butterscotch-colored farmhouse with flower gardens flanking the walkway. The interior is a vision of rich woodwork, handloomed rugs, nostalgic collectibles, and family heirlooms, recalling the simple pleasures of an earlier time. Upstairs, the Rose Room evokes in every detail a Victorian rose garden, and a delightful solarium/half-bath is attached. Loragene's legendary breakfasts, prepared on a wood-burning cookstove, are served with care in the old-fashioned country kitchen. Incurable romantics like to escape to their own sweet little cottage, just to the right of the farmhouse. It has an iron bed, a pull-out sofa, a full kitchen, cable TV, a woodstove, colorful rugs, and decor in blues and reds. The newest accommodation, Cedar Lodge, is set on its own forested acre overlooking the sheep pasture. It sleeps up to six, has a full kitchen, and resembles an Adirondack trout fishing lodge, with lots of fly fishing memorabilia, wooden skis, Arts and Crafts furniture, Navajo rugs, and rich Indian colors.

Dog and cat in main house; no pets or smoking; children over thirteen welcome; full breakfast; afternoon tea and scones; for bathing, Rose Room shares full bath on main floor; short walk to beach and restaurant; credit cards (V,MC); French spoken.

ROOM	BED	BATH	ENTRANCE	FLOOR	DAILY RATES S - D (EP)
A	1D	Pvt 1/2	Main	2	$55-$65
B	1D	Pvt	Sep	1	$75-$85 ($25)
C	3Q	Pvt	Sep	1 & 2	$99-$105 ($25)

Rates stated in Canadian funds

The Willows Inn   **(604) 885-2452**
Box 1036, Sechelt, BC V0N 3A0
(On Beach Avenue, off Highway 101 at Roberts Creek)

Imagine getting away to a meticulously handcrafted little cottage in the woods with its own yard enclosed by a rose-clad split-rail fence. The 500-square-foot dollhouse has beautiful hardwood floors and cabinetry, skylights, ceiling fans, a full tiled bath with a host of little luxuries, a table for two by a picture window, a glass-front woodstove, and a small kitchen area where coffee, tea, and goodies are kept. Peachy-pink walls cast a warm glow on an interior accented by evergreen, white, and brass. After a restful night in a bed of exceptional comfort, a home-cooked breakfast is delivered to your doorstep at the time of your choosing. John and Donna Gibson, whose luxurious log home is at the front of the property, have created this heart-warming haven in the forest where their guests are pampered in countless ways. The Willows Inn is a place to make some romantic dreams come true.

No pets; no smoking; country Continental breakfast; color TV; sink and small fridge; fine dining, salmon fishing (information available), beaches, shops, and galleries nearby; guest parking beside cottage; golf holiday packages available; airport pickup (Tyee at Sechelt).

ROOM	BED	BATH	ENTRANCE	FLOOR	DAILY RATES	
					S - D	(EP)
A	1Q	Pvt	Sep	1	$65-$75	($15)

Rates stated in Canadian funds

245

Mason Road Bed & Breakfast   **(604) 885-3506**
RR#1, TLC Site, C-73, Sechelt, BC V0N 3A0
(North of town center at 5873 Mason Road)

Just minutes from the seashore, enjoy a sojourn at a forty-acre farm specializing in organic strawberries, sheep's wool products, and down-home hospitality. The comfortable, attractive post-and-beam home of Joyce Rigaux and John Rayment was built of cedar milled from the property. Guest quarters at the back of the house are quiet and private; each room has a full ensuite bath and a separate entrance. Wool from the farm's friendly sheep fills a duvet on each bed. Breakfast may include eggs from the free-range chickens, strawberries in season, and fresh bread baked in the woodstove. A huge hot tub on the deck offers an ideal way to relax under the stars after an active day. Mason Road Bed & Breakfast can provide a romantic, rural experience for a couple; a family farmstay vacation; or an outdoor adventurer's dream: a pre-arranged sequence of activities that might include boat explorations of Sechelt Inlet, salmon fishing, hiking, biking, kayaking, diving, swimming, or horseback riding. All-inclusive packages can be tailored to suit individual guests.

Sheep, border collies, and chickens on property; no pets or smoking; full breakfast; guest sitting/dining room; off-street parking. Inquire about weekly, full-board, farmstay rates and adventure package rates. Brochure available.

ROOM	BED	BATH	ENTRANCE	FLOOR	DAILY RATES S - D (EP)
A	1Q	Pvt	Sep	1	$50-$75 ($25)
B	2T	Pvt	Sep	1	$50-$75 ($25)

Rates stated in Canadian funds

Borthwick Country Manor   **(604) 656-9498**
RR#2, 9750 Ardmore Drive, Sidney, BC V8L 5H5
(Near Saanich Inlet)

Scenes of English fox hunts spring to mind at your first glimpse of the authentic country Tudor home of Ann and Brian Reid. It is half timbered with black wood on white plaster and is set on beautifully landscaped grounds edged by ancient oak trees. The huge back lawn is studded with flower beds, trellises, a rockery, pathways, park benches, and a gazebo with a hot tub. Guests at Borthwick Country Manor relish the ample breakfasts served in the formal dining room and are welcome to use the large guest lounge/library as their own. On the second floor of the house are a commodious suite and a large bedroom, both with ensuite baths, and three other rooms with shared baths. Most are done in soft pastels with attractive decorator touches. A sojourn at the Manor promises peaceful comfort and good-spirited hospitality.

Cat in residence; no pets; children over ten welcome; smoking outside only; full breakfast; TV in lounge/library; hot tub; short drive from Butchart Gardens, golf courses, beaches, pubs and restaurants, ferries, and airport; under half an hour from Victoria; off-street parking; credit cards (V,MC); rollaway bed ($15EP); off-season, weekly, and monthly rates. Brochure available.

ROOM	BED	BATH	ENTRANCE	FLOOR	DAILY RATES S - D (EP)
A	1Q & 1D	Pvt	Main	2	$130
B	1Q	Pvt	Main	2	$120
C	1Q	Shd*	Main	2	$85
D	1Q	Shd*	Main	2	$85
E	1Q	Shd*	Main	2	$65

Rates stated in Canadian funds

247

Orchard House Bed & Breakfast   **(604) 656-9194**
9646 Sixth Street, Sidney, BC V8L 2W2
(Central Sidney)

Lovely gardens and old trees punctuate this orchard land of yester-year that once extended to water's edge. The Craftsman-style heritage home was built in 1914 by the son of the town's founder. Its friendly appearance hints at the welcoming spirit within. Handsome interior features include ample woodwork, leaded and stained glass, built-in cabinetry, and a quaint fireplace of small beach stones and shells. On the main floor are the spacious Rose Room and the Duck Room, which has its own sink and toilet, so it shares only the shower of the bathroom down the hall. Charming upstairs quarters are all wood, angles, and sloped ceilings. The Lace Room and the Tree Room share a hallway bath and a cozy woodstove in the common area. Breakfasts are large, healthy, and homemade. Hosts Joan and Gerry enjoy their lovingly preserved home -- and so will you.

No pets; no children under twelve; smoking outside only; full breakfast; walk to parks, tennis courts, shops, restaurants, and Anacortes ferry terminal; short drive to Swartz Bay ferries, airport, and Butchart Gardens; under half an hour from Victoria; off-street parking; credit cards (MC). Brochure available.

ROOM	BED	BATH	ENTRANCE	FLOOR	DAILY RATES S - D	(EP)
A	1Q	Shd*	Main	1	$59-$69	($15)
B	1Q	Shd*	Main	1	$59-$69	($15)
C	1D	Shd*	Main	2	$49-$59	($15)
D	1D	Shd*	Main	2	$49-$59	($15)

Rates stated in Canadian funds

Bed & Breakfast by the Sea   **(604) 642-5136**
RR#1, 6007 Sooke Road, Sooke, BC V0S 1N0
(Twenty-five minutes west of Victoria on Highway 14)

The sheer physical beauty of the setting is overwhelming. Facing Sooke Basin (part of the Pacific), the land is heavily forested with Douglas fir and western red cedar and bordered by a creek to the west and an inlet and private beach to the east. Here Marjorie and Dalton Schrank offer the quiet, gentle environment of their home where guest accommodations, located well away from the hosts' sleeping quarters, consist of two bedrooms sharing a bath off the hallway. One is prettily done in white and lilac; navy blue prevails in the other. Guests also have exclusive use of a large, luxurious living room with a brick fireplace and an expansive ocean view. Or, for total privacy, choose the sunny, secluded cottage just steps from the water with its own beach. It has a full kitchen, a bed with a view, and extra sleeping space for up to six people. Sighting herons, swans, otters, deer, and rabbits is common at Bed & Breakfast by the Sea. So is the joy of pure relaxation.

Dog in residence; no pets in main house; no smoking; full breakfast; cable TV and rollaway beds in cottage; VCR available; barbecue and picnic area; off-street parking.

ROOM	BED	BATH	ENTRANCE	FLOOR	DAILY RATES S - D (EP)	
A	1D	Shd*	Main	1	$75-$85	
B	1Q	Shd*	Main	1	$75-$85	
C	1Q & 1D	Pvt	Sep	1	$95	($15)

Rates stated in Canadian funds

Cove By The Lighthouse   **(604) 646-2063** *or* **480-9236**
RR#2, Seaside Drive, Sooke, BC V0S 1N0
(Thirteen miles west of Sooke off Highway 14)

As you wend your way out of Sooke up the west coast of Vancouver Island, the landscape begins to take on a rugged wildness. A quick glimpse of a distant lighthouse hints of things to come. Just beyond this beacon, nestled into a rocky cove with a panoramic view across the Juan de Fuca Strait to the majestic Olympics, is a choice destination. Watch passing pods of killer whales or a variety of marine birds from the sanctuary of this multi-windowed-and-decked retreat, Cove By The Lighthouse. Hosts Paul and Eleanor Kolada offer accommodation from late June to early September in two spacious second-floor bedrooms, each with a deck and an awesome view, opening into a large common room with a TV/VCR for guests. Breakfast is served on the main floor in either of two separate dining areas. Year-round, up to four guests are welcome in a separate, self-contained cottage with balcony and view. Ocean kayaking, beachcombing, and endless explorations await the wanderer to this neck of the woods. And a stay at Cove By The Lighthouse is a true escape.

No pets; children limited; smoking outside only; full breakfast; Jacuzzi tub in Room A; hide-a-bed and kitchen in cottage; salmon fishing charters easily arranged; ample parking. Brochure available.

ROOM	BED	BATH	ENTRANCE	FLOOR	DAILY RATES S - D	(EP)
A	1Q	Pvt	Main	2	$60-$80	
B	1Q	Pvt	Main	2	$60-$80	
C	1Q	Pvt	Sep	2	$80	($10)

Rates stated in Canadian funds

Malahat Farm   **(604) 642-6868**
RR#2, Anderson Road, Sooke, BC V0S 1N0
(Eight miles west of Sooke)

A genuine Canadian farm vacation awaits you at a fully restored heritage house near Sooke. Surrounded by acres of bucolic farmland, the wonderful vintage home has two accommodations of the highest caliber on each floor. Upstairs there is a guest lounge and two of the most inviting bedrooms imaginable, outfitted with antiques, down comforters, ruffled curtains, and bathrooms with whiter-than-white clawfoot tubs. The same is true of the bath in the main-floor bed/sitting room that has a fireplace and a four-poster bed. Another bedroom with a big snowball tree at the window has a brass bed, a bay window, a corner fireplace, and a bath with a shower. Host Diana Clare's abundant breakfasts are the quintessence of farm-fresh, home-made goodness and feature her own organic produce. In the gazebo-covered hot tub overlooking the pastures, one may take private soaks by reservation. Visitors love the silence and tranquility of the farm. They thrill to see how bright stars can be in an ink-black sky. But most of all, they're touched by the caring hospitality at the very heart of Malahat Farm.

Dogs, cat, and farm animals on property; no pets; no children under thirteen; full country breakfast; claw foot tubs have hand-held showers; fridge, beverage-brewing center, and sitting area in guest lounge; bicycles available; beachcombing, bird and whale-watching, hiking, and picnicking in nearby parks; salmon charters arranged.

ROOM	BED	BATH	ENTRANCE	FLOOR	DAILY RATES	
					S - D	(EP) +
A	1Q	Pvt	Main	2	$90	($20)
B	1Q	Pvt	Main	2	$90	($20)
C	1Q	Pvt	Main	1	$105	($20)
D	1Q	Pvt	Main	1	$115	($20)

Rates stated in Canadian funds

251

Heritage House   **(604) 494-0039**
Box 326, Summerland, BC V0H 1Z0
(Walking distance from town center at 11919 Jubilee Road)

   Marsha Clark's heritage home was built in 1907, around the time
Summerland was founded. The sparkling white frame house with a
blue door stands on a hill surrounded by stately old trees, with
mountains in the background and a view out over the town. Ever so
inviting is the wrap-around veranda, ideally suited for sitting, visiting,
reading, or enjoying Marsha's wonderful, home-cooked breakfasts.
Guests have a choice of three bright, spacious, second-floor rooms
that share two large bathrooms (with a choice of shower or tub). The
front room, done in pale yellow with antiques, can sleep three people
or a family. The overall feeling of the house combines a sense of
dignity, admirable simplicity, and informal comfort. The hospitality
is easygoing and accommodating. From this secure home base, all the
wonders of the Okanagan are yours to explore year-round.
   No pets; smoking outside only; full breakfast; robes provided;
laundry privileges; off-street parking. Brochure available.

ROOM	BED	BATH	ENTRANCE	FLOOR	DAILY RATES S - D	(EP)
A	1Q & 1T	Shd*	Main	2	$40-$50	($15)
B	1Q	Shd*	Main	2	$40-$50	
C	2T	Shd*	Main	2	$40-$50	

Rates stated in Canadian funds

Bed & Breakfast on the Ridge   **(604) 591-6065**
5741 - 146 Street, Surrey, BC V3S 2Z8
(Off Highway 10, south Surrey)

Panorama Ridge is home to Dale and Mary Fennell, who appreciate its quiet, rural flavor along with its good access to the U.S.-Canadian border crossing, ferries, the airport, shopping centers, the Skytrain to Vancouver, and major freeways. Their large contemporary home is set on a wooded half acre, where the country ambiance is ever-present whether you're going for a walk, relaxing on the wide sun deck that encircles the house, or enjoying the hospitality indoors. Cathedral ceilings and lots of skylighting give the whole interior a bright, airy feeling. On the upper level, guests may read or watch TV in their own sitting area. Furnishings lean toward modern comfort, with a sprinkling of antiques for counterpoint. Bed & Breakfast on the Ridge is an easygoing place where a family could feel as much at home as a business traveler or a vacationing couple.

No smoking in bedrooms; TV/VCR available in recreation room; crib, folding cot, sofa bed, and playpen available; off-street parking; airport pickup (Vancouver). Brochure available.

ROOM	BED	BATH	ENTRANCE	FLOOR	DAILY RATES S - D	(EP)
A	1Q	Pvt	Main	1	$55	
B	1Q	Shd*	Main	2	$45-$50	
C	2T	Shd*	Main	2	$45-$50	
D	1Q	Shd*	Main	2	$45-$50	($15)

Rates stated in Canadian funds

253

White Heather Guest House   **(604) 581-9797**
12571 - 98 Avenue, Surrey, BC V3V 2K6
(Twenty minutes from U.S.-Canada border at Blaine)

A sincere welcome awaits you at White Heather Guest House, home of Glad and Chuck Bury. The quiet southeast suburb of Vancouver offers good bus service, as well as a fun and easy trip downtown by Skytrain. At afternoon tea time, you may wish to enlist the help of your seasoned hosts in planning your stay. They consistently search out cream-of-the-crop experiences to share with guests. Whether you're looking for the perfect restaurant -- ethnic, family, or special occasion -- or for attractions that are most worth visiting, the Burys offer sound advice. Full English breakfasts, cooked to perfection by Chuck, are served in a sunny, garden-like room with a dramatic view of snow-capped mountains. Spend leisure moments relaxing or visiting on the patio overlooking the back garden. All this, plus a good night's sleep, makes White Heather Guest House a most hospitable place to stay.

No pets; family accommodation by arrangement; no smoking; no RV parking; full breakfast; fireplace and TV available; game room with toys and piano; licensed chauffeur available; off-street parking; pickup from airport or cruise ships; inquire about EP rates.

ROOM	BED	BATH	ENTRANCE	FLOOR	DAILY RATES S - D (EP) +
A	1Q	Pvt 1/2	Main	1	$45-$50
B	1D	Shd*	Main	1	$40-$45

Rates stated in Canadian funds

Duffin Cove Bed & Breakfast   **(604) 725-3765**
P.O. Box 325, Tofino, BC V0R 2Z0
(160 Arnet Road, steps from shore of Duffin Cove)

The tranquil beauty of Duffin Cove is ever-present from the ground-floor guest quarters of Val and James Sloman's comfortable home. Savor the dramatic, close-up view from the spacious guest lounge, one of the bedrooms, the deck, the hot tub, or from the shoreline itself. Explore the tidepools or take a short stroll to sandy Tonquin Beach. Indoors, relax in homey surroundings as you read, visit, or watch television or a movie; an entire level of the house with a separate entrance is devoted to guests. The two bedrooms with a shared bath are perfect for a family or for two couples traveling together, but even people who have just met can share the good fortune of spending a holiday at Duffin Cove Bed & Breakfast.

No pets or smoking; no young children unless both rooms booked at full rate; full homemade breakfast delivered to guest quarters; robes provided; TV/VCR; deck; hot tub; off-street parking; Pacific Rim National Park, year-round golf course, fishing, boating, kayaking, whale watching, and beachcombing nearby; open year round; off-season rates. Brochure available.

ROOM	BED	BATH	ENTRANCE	FLOOR	DAILY RATES S - D (EP)
A	2T	Shd*	Sep	1G	$55-$65
B	1Q	Shd*	Sep	1G	$55-$65

Rates stated in Canadian funds

255

Wilp Gybuu   **(604) 725-2330**
P.O. Box 396, Tofino, BC V0R 2Z0
(311 Leighton Way, overlooking Duffin Inlet)

Wilp Gybuu, meaning Wolf House, derives from Ralph Burgess's native heritage. Since he and Wendy moved to Tofino, he has honed his skills as a fine craftsman in silver and gold, and his work is found in better BC galleries. Their natural wood home is exceptionally quiet and immaculate, with a mesmerizing view of water, mountains, mist, and sky from the main floor. Flattering peachy pink walls add to the warm atmosphere. Guests are accommodated on the entry level of the house in a pleasant bedroom with ensuite bath. Relax in comfort among Emily Carr prints and peruse the wealth of information provided on the wonders of the wild yet fragile environment that makes Tofino so special. Join your hosts upstairs for breakfast and engaging conversation. They appreciate having guests from a variety of life styles.

Cat in residence; no pets or children; smoking outside only; early coffee/tea delivered; full breakfast; TV/VCR in living room; deck; Pacific Rim National Park, year-round golf course, fishing, boating, kayaking, whale watching, and beachcombing nearby; off-street parking; open year round; off-season rates October-April. Brochure available.

ROOM	BED	BATH	ENTRANCE	FLOOR	DAILY RATES S - D (EP)
A	1Q	Pvt	Main	1G	$65-$70

Rates stated in Canadian funds

Beachside Bed & Breakfast   **(604) 922-7773**
4208 Evergreen Avenue, West Vancouver, BC   V7V 1H1
(West of Lion's Gate Bridge, just south of Marine Drive)

It would be difficult to top this Vancouver location: Just steps from the door you're on a sandy beach sniffing the salt air, watching gulls circle overhead, and feeling buoyant. The contemporary waterfront home offers fantastic views from the dining room where breakfast is served, from the outdoor whirlpool spa and deck, and from the deluxe suite at the rear of the ground-level guest floor. Soothing pastel colors blend with the seaside setting, and fresh fruit and flowers, delightful artwork, and comfortable furnishings enhance the accommodations. Hosts Gordon and Joan Gibbs want you to enjoy the quiet, relaxing ambiance of their home as well as the interesting local activities and day trips that they thoughtfully describe in the literature placed in each room. Gordon and Joan promise "a warm, friendly Canadian welcome." Believe me, that's only the beginning.

Dog in residence; no pets; no children under eight; no smoking; TV available; full breakfast; off-street parking; credit cards (V,MC); off-season rates. Brochure available.

ROOM	BED	BATH	ENTRANCE	FLOOR	DAILY RATES S - D (EP) +
A	1Q & 1T	Pvt	Sep	1G	$90-$100 ($20)
B	1Q	Pvt	Sep	1G	$105-$115
C	1Q	Pvt	Sep	1G	$125-$160

Rates stated in Canadian funds

Brighton House   **(604) 253-7175**
2826 Trinity Street, Vancouver, BC V5K 1E9
(East Vancouver, near Second Narrows Bridge)

A 1906 character home renovated as a B&B with great care and vision, Brighton House offers extraordinary accommodations. There are two very private, quiet, and romantic suites, individually designed with richly detailed motifs, French Country and Folk Art. Each features a down duvet, a luxurious ensuite bath, a sitting area, and a private balcony with harbor and mountain views. Breakfast is served in the dining room using beautiful bone china and linen napkins. June Bennett caters to honeymooners, business travelers, and vacationers with equal ease. History buffs will want to ask her about the neighborhood's importance in the early history of Vancouver, and she'll also point out how to get quickly from Brighton House to key attractions in and around Vancouver.

Cat in residence; no pets; no children under twelve; smoking outside only; full breakfast; near bus stop; off-street parking; credit cards (V); off-season rates. Brochure available.

ROOM	BED	BATH	ENTRANCE	FLOOR	DAILY RATES S - D (EP)
A	1Q	Pvt	Main	2	$95
B	1Q	Pvt	Main	2	$95

Rates stated in Canadian funds

258

Jane's Gourmet Bed & Breakfast   **(604) 929-6083**
4187 Fairway Place, North Vancouver, BC   V7G 1Y8
(Deep Cove, twenty-five minutes from downtown Vancouver)

Jane Rae's culinary skills figure heavily in the rave reviews from her B&B guests, but they also appreciate having an entire ground-floor apartment all to themselves. Fresh flowers and family heirlooms add to the luxurious warmth of the guest quarters, consisting of a beautiful bedroom that includes a kitchenette behind folding doors, a bathroom with a wonderful spa bathtub, a utility area with washer and dryer, a commodious living room with a large stone fireplace and a dining area, and a garden patio with table and chairs. From Jane's, a fascinating day of exploration might include a circular route to the major attractions of Vancouver, hiking at nearby Mount Seymour, or strolling around the seaside village of Deep Cove. Theater, golf, tennis, cycling, swimming, diving, canoeing, and kayaking are all within minutes of Jane's. At her place, you'll find the best aspects of a quiet, posh, country resort and home sweet home, all rolled into one!

No pets; smoking outside only; full breakfast; TV/VCR; bicycle, diving gear, canoe, and kayak rentals nearby; express bus to downtown; off-street parking; wheelchair access; EP rates vary according to age; double sofa bed in living room; *open March 1 to October 31.* Brochure available.

ROOM	BED	BATH	ENTRANCE	FLOOR	DAILY RATES	
					S - D	(EP)
A	1Q	Pvt	Sep	1G	$85	($20)

Rates stated in Canadian funds

The Johnson House   (604) 266-4175
2278 West 34th Avenue, Vancouver, BC V6M 1G6
(Central to UBC, Van Duesen Gardens and Queen Elizabeth Park)

Rock-solid is an apt description of The Johnson House, from the neighborhood, to the front stone and flower garden, to the home's construction. A lovingly thorough restoration has left this 1920s Craftsman-style beauty standing tall, proud, and oh, so welcoming. Very large rooms with wood floors and extensive mouldings are full of homey charm and comfort. Unique brass and iron beds are joined by Canadian wooden antiques and the hosts' impressive collection of carousel animals, coffee grinders, Victrolas, and more. Nostalgia reigns in every aspect of this marvelous home. The two guest rooms and the deluxe suite have distinct personalities of their own, and a couple have mountain views. Everywhere there is something to make you smile. Indeed, staying at The Johnson House is a joy through and through.

No pets; children over ten welcome; smoking outside only; full breakfast; TV/VCR and fireplace in living room; front covered porch; back sun porch; handy to downtown and many attractions; quiet neighborhood, good for walking; near bus line; off-street and street parking; off-season rates. Brochure available.

ROOM	BED	BATH	ENTRANCE	FLOOR	DAILY RATES S - D (EP)	
A	1Q & 1T	Shd*	Main	2	$75	($20)
B	1Q	Shd*	Main	2	$65	
C	1Q & 1T	Pvt	Main	2	$95	($20)

Rates stated in Canadian funds

Laburnum Cottage   (604) 988-4877
1388 Terrace Avenue, North Vancouver, BC V7R 1B4
(Off Capilano Road, enroute to Grouse Mountain)

    The home of Delphine Masterton is tucked away in a quiet corner of a gracious older neighborhood that is wonderful for walking. Despite its feeling of seclusion, it's convenient to downtown Vancouver, Horseshoe Bay, Grouse Mountain, and other attractions. Laburnum Cottage is set in a half-acre English garden so breathtaking that one feels privileged to experience its serene beauty. A meandering stream crossed by three little bridges, an exquisite array of pampered plants, and three ponds -- one with a rippling fountain -- delight the senses and the soul. The enchantment of the garden permeates the guest quarters. A refined English charm marks the interior of the main house, where lovely bedrooms on the second floor overlook the garden. Set in its midst is the Summerhouse Cottage (pictured), a self-contained haven with a romantic brass bed and a fresh, light atmosphere. There is another, larger cottage (E) that sleeps up to six. It's all here: lodging for most any occasion and first-rate hospitality to match the magnificent setting.

    Cat in residence; no pets; smoking outside only; full breakfast; good public transportation; nine-hole golf course and public tennis courts nearby; off-street parking; French and German spoken; credit cards (V,MC).

ROOM	BED	BATH	ENTRANCE	FLOOR	DAILY RATES S - D (EP) +
A	1Q	Pvt	Main	2	$115 ($30)
B	1Q	Pvt	Main	2	$115 ($30)
C	1Q	Pvt	Main	2	$115 ($30)
D	1D	Pvt	Sep	1	$135 ($30)
E	1Q	Pvt	Sep	1	$135 ($30)

Rates stated in Canadian funds

Locarno Beach Bed & Breakfast   **(604) 224-2177**
4550 NW Marine Drive, Vancouver, BC V6R 1B8
(Overlooking Locarno Beach, on scenic route to UBC)

Billy Wittman's cedar and glass home of contemporary design has a spectacular view, handy beach access, and a casual, intriguing ambiance that not only puts guests at ease but gives them the sense of discovery. Her collection of Asian art and artifacts fills the house, engaging the eye as well as the imagination. On the second floor, four delightfully furnished bedrooms share two full baths. From the front rooms (A and B), the marine activities of English Bay are in full view. There is also a kitchen for guests, which many find a welcome convenience. Billy's hospitality is helpful, easygoing, and touched with humor. Locarno Beach B&B is a singular creation guaranteed to provide a memorable stay in Vancouver.

No pets or smoking; full breakfast; guest kitchen; park and beach across street; near bus stop; off-street and street parking; German spoken; off-season and weekly rates. Brochure available.

ROOM	BED	BATH	ENTRANCE	FLOOR	DAILY RATES S - D (EP)
A	1Q	Shd*	Main	2	$50-$75
B	1Q	Shd*	Main	2	$50-$75
C	1Q	Shd*	Main	2	$45-$70
D	2T	Shd*	Main	2	$45-$70

Rates stated in Canadian funds

The Penny Farthing Inn   (604) 739-9002
2855 West Sixth Avenue, Vancouver, BC V6K 1X2   FAX: 739-9004
(Six blocks from Kitsilano Beach)

It's cheering just to look at this 1912 character home painted in vivid colors and surrounded by an English country garden. The warmth of the welcome matches that of the bright, bold shades used tastefully throughout the house. Hostess Lyn Hainstock has combined lovely antiques brought from England with Victorian lace. The home's stained glass windows and inlaid oak floors add to an ambiance rich in warmth and comfort. Among the choice accommodations is Bettina's Boudoir (A), with a queen-sized pine four-poster bed, en-suite bath, a porch facing the rear garden with partial mountain views, and a sitting room with TV and sofa bed. Abigail's Attic (D) is a deluxe suite with a queen brass bed; ensuite bath with skylight; and a sitting room with mountain and water views, TV, and sofa bed. Breakfast in the rear garden among flowers and herbs is a sensory delight. But then, everything about Penny Farthing is a delight, including its super location.

Cats in residence; no pets; teens welcome; smoking on porches only; full breakfast; guest sitting room with TV/VCR; easy walk to beach, shops, and restaurants; 8 to 10 minutes downtown; near bus stop; ample street parking; some French spoken; off-season and long-term rates. Brochure available.

ROOM	BED	BATH	ENTRANCE	FLOOR	DAILY RATES S - D (EP)
A	1Q & 1D	Pvt	Main	2	$115-$135 ($20)
B	1D	Shd*	Main	2	$65-$75
C	1K or 2T	Shd*	Main	2	$65-$75
D	1Q & 1D	Pvt	Main	3	$135-$155 ($20)

Rates stated in Canadian funds

263

Pillow 'n Porridge   (604) 879-8977
2859 Manitoba Street, Vancouver, BC V5Y 3B3
(City Hall heritage area, near Cambie Street Bridge)

Dianne Reader Haag is realizing a vision for her little corner of the neighborhood by renovating three adjacent buildings from the turn of the century where she offers an array of B&B accommodations. The central structure (pictured) has a carriage house ambiance, a dining room where all the breakfasts are served, two living rooms, and three distinctive guest rooms. Next door is a corner building that was once a general store where Dianne now makes her art studio. Its side entrance leads to a spacious ground-floor apartment where B&B guests may have private, self-contained quarters decorated in the general store theme. The last building, a home, has a living room with a clever hunting and fishing motif and two sweet, lovely rooms that share a bath. On the top floor is a suite with a TV, fireplace, bath, and deck. Antiques and collectibles from around the globe add to the warm, interesting ambiance of Pillow 'n Porridge. Dianne's casual graciousness puts people at ease, so that they blend right into her comfortable home and neighborhood.

No pets or smoking; full breakfast; apartment has kitchen and sitting room with hide-a-bed; last building has two bedrooms at $70 and a suite at $100; location convenient to downtown and many points of interest; bus and Skytrain routes nearby; street parking. Brochure available.

ROOM	BED	BATH	ENTRANCE	FLOOR	DAILY RATES S - D (EP) +
A	2T	Pvt	Main	1	$70-$85
B	2T	Shd*	Sep	1G	$65-$75
C	1D	Shd*	Sep	1G	$65-$70
D	1Q	Pvt	Sep	1G	$85-$100($15)

Rates stated in Canadian funds

Castle on the Mountain   **(604) 542-4593**
RR#8, S-10, C-12, Vernon, BC V1T 8L6
(Upper Okanagan Valley at 8227 Silver Star Road)

This large Tudor-style home is located on the southern exposure of Silver Star Mountain, seven miles from city center. The elevation not only allows a sweeping view of valley, lakes, and the lights of Vernon, but gives you a head start in getting to the ski slopes at Silver Star (seven miles away). In this choice setting, Castle on the Mountain offers a unique lodging experience. Hosts Sharon and Eskil Larson are artists/craftspeople; they have an ever-changing collection in their in-home gallery studio where people enjoy browsing. The entire ground floor is for guests. There's a living room with places to relax by the fire; a kitchen area for light meals; two bedrooms that share a bathroom with a shower; and one bedroom with a private or shared bath -- views are phenomenal from this huge turret-shaped and multi-windowed room (C). The third floor has one comfortable guest room, a bath with a large shower, and a private "crow's nest" balcony. All in all, Castle on the Mountain is spectacular.

Smoking outside only; allergy-free environment; full breakfast; TV; phone; outdoor spa; picnic area; summer hiking, beaches, and fruit-picking; winter skiing (Alpine and Nordic) and snowmobiling; off-street parking; wheelchair access; major credit cards; inquire about separate, two-story family apartment with outdoor hot tub.

ROOM	BED	BATH	ENTRANCE	FLOOR	DAILY RATES	
					S - D	(EP) +
A	1D	Shd*	Sep	1G	$50-$65	
B	1Q	Shd*	Sep	1G	$50-$65	
C	1Q & 1T	Pvt	Sep	1G	$65-$75	($30)
D	1K & 1T	Pvt	Main	3	$65-$75	($30)

Rates stated in Canadian funds

265

Harbourlight Bed & Breakfast   **(604) 549-5117**
RR#4, S-11, C-50, 135 Joharon Road, Vernon, BC V1T 6L7
(Near downtown Vernon, overlooking Okanagan Lake)

Harbourlight Bed & Breakfast, convenient to downtown Vernon and Silver Star Resort, is situated on two quiet acres with panoramic lake and mountain views. The newer modern home of Helga and Peter Neckel has spacious, immaculate rooms offering great comfort and privacy. Plenty of windows, shiny wood floors covered with beautiful rugs, and the three-piece ensuite baths add to the luxurious ambiance of the Neckels' home. Featured in their generous full breakfasts are homemade jams and breads. Just moments away are beaches, public boat launching, fishing, golf courses, and hiking trails. Each season brings its own pleasures in the Okanagan, and Harbourlight beckons guests to discover them all year round.

No pets, children, or smoking; full breakfast; AC; deck; wineries and varied outdoor recreation nearby; German spoken. Brochure available.

ROOM	BED	BATH	ENTRANCE	FLOOR	DAILY RATES S - D (EP)
A	1Q	Pvt	Main	1	$45-$55
B	1Q	Pvt	Main	1G	$45-$55
C	1Q	Pvt	Main	1G	$45-$55

Rates stated in Canadian funds

Ambleside Bed & Breakfast   **(604) 383-9948**
1121 Faithful Street, Victoria, BC V8V 2R5   FAX: **383-3647**
(Just east of Beacon Hill Park and a block from waterfront)

Ambleside is an inviting home located on a quiet street in Fairfield, one of Victoria's friendliest and most walkable neighborhoods. A fine Craftsman home built in 1920, it is decorated with assured restraint that's in perfect keeping with the style and scale of the house. Walls and vintage woodwork in shades of white set off the gleaming hardwood floors and the dark, handsome colors of the furnishings. On the main floor, guests feel right at home in the comfortable, attractive living room, the office with writing desk and phone, and the dining room where sumptuous multi-course breakfasts are beautifully served. There's a fresh, clean feeling throughout the house. Antiques, floral and botanical motifs, Oriental and braided rugs, and custom bedcoverings and valances enhance the guest rooms. The wonderful location of this gracious home and the relaxed, helpful hospitality of hosts Marilyn and Gordon make staying at Ambleside the perfect treat while visiting Victoria.

No pets or smoking; children over fifteen welcome; full breakfast; robes provided; fireplace and piano in living room; 20-25-minute stroll downtown through Beacon Hill Park, or 8 minutes by bus; near public tennis courts, popular neighborhood eateries, and oceanside pathways; off-street and street parking; French and some German spoken; credit cards (V,MC); off-season rates. Brochure available.

ROOM	BED	BATH	ENTRANCE	FLOOR	DAILY RATES	
					S - D	(EP) +
A	1Q	Pvt	Main	1	$75-$85	
B	1K or 2T	Shd*	Main	2	$70-$80	($25)
C	1D	Shd*	Main	2	$60-$70	

Rates stated in Canadian funds

267

Arundel Manor   **(604) 385-5442**
980 Arundel Drive, Victoria, BC V9A 2C3
(Near Gorge Waterway, minutes from downtown)

June Earl's character-laden heritage home is situated among majestic old trees and gardens, and the front yard slopes down to picturesque Portage Inlet. This peaceful, secluded haven affords sunset and wildlife views from the waterfront, yard, or veranda, or from one of the front bedroom balconies. Inside, gorgeous woodwork abounds, and the homey furnishings include antiques, collectibles, and family heirlooms. The warmth and comfort of the house are an extension of June herself. She makes her guests feel infinitely pampered, yet honors their need for relaxing privacy. On the second floor are four generously proportioned corner guest rooms with ensuite baths; a fifth guest room is at the apex of the house. Each luxuriously appointed room has a special theme, with every detail attended to, every amenity provided. At Arundel Manor you'll find a refuge of gentility for the romantic at heart.

No pets, children, or smoking; full breakfast; guest lounge with fireplace; near bus route; off-street parking; inquire about off-season rates. Brochure available.

ROOM	BED	BATH	ENTRANCE	FLOOR	DAILY RATES S - D	(EP)
A	1K	Pvt	Main	2	$95	
B	1K	Pvt	Main	2	$95	
C	1Q	Pvt	Main	2	$85	
D	1Q & 1T	Pvt	Main	2	$85	($20)
E	2T	Pvt	Main	3	$75	

Rates stated in Canadian funds

Bender's Bed & Breakfast   **(604) 477-6804**
4254 Thornhill Crescent, Victoria, BC   V8N 3G7
(One mile from University, five miles from downtown)

Bender's suburban location is near University of Victoria, Mount Douglas Park, Cordova Bay, and shopping centers, yet only five miles from the heart of town. The clean, comfortable accommodations here are easy on the budget and offer variety and flexibility -- very helpful for families or larger groups. Guests in the bedrooms on the lower level of the house may enjoy a large sitting room with a stone fireplace and a TV. Upstairs, guests tend to gather in the living room. The neighborhood is safe, quiet, and good for walking. Mrs. Bender has a lot of regular guests who appreciate her easy, come-and-go-as-you-please manner and the all-around good value she offers.

No pets or smoking; full breakfast; TV in Rooms A and E; off-street and street parking. Brochure available.

ROOM	BED	BATH	ENTRANCE	FLOOR	DAILY RATES S - D	(EP)
A	1D	Pvt	Main	1	$50	
B	1D	Shd*	Main	1	$40	
C	1D	Shd*	Main	1	$40	
D	1D & 1T	Shd*	Main	LL	$45	($20)
E	1D & 1T	Pvt	Main	LL	$55	($20)
F	1Q	Shd*	Main	LL	$50	

Rates stated in Canadian funds

Carriage Stop Bed & Breakfast   **(604) 383-6240**
117 Menzies Street, Victoria, BC V8V 2G4
(Short walk from beach and downtown)

   Close proximity to the heart of Victoria is just one of the assets of
Carriage Stop Bed & Breakfast. Jane McAllister's blue heritage home
has a gabled roof, interesting angles, and lots of character. The charm
of its age comes through, while renovations have given the interior a
clean, new feeling of light and openness. With this background, the
well-chosen artwork shows up to good advantage. One of the guest
rooms is on the first floor; two rooms and a bath on the second floor
make ideal quarters for several people traveling together. Besides the
convenient location and agreeable atmosphere, you'll get expert advice
on picking that special restaurant to suit your mood, your palate, and
your purse. At Carriage Stop, the best of old and new come together
in an ambiance of casual comfort.

   Two cats in residence; no pets; no children under twelve; smoking
outside only; full breakfast; robes provided; common room with
fireplace and TV; patio in summer; credit cards (V); good public
transportation and airport connections.

ROOM	BED	BATH	ENTRANCE	FLOOR	DAILY RATES	
					S - D	(EP)
A	1D & 1T	Pvt	Main	1	$50-$60	($15)
B	1D	Shd*	Main	2	$50-$60	
C	1D & 1T	Shd*	Main	2	$50-$60	($15)

Rates stated in Canadian funds

270

The Crow's Nest **(604) 383-4492**
71 Linden Avenue, Victoria, BC V8V 4C9 FAX: **383-3140**
(Just east of Beacon Hill Park and a half-block from waterfront)

This 1911 heritage home was designed by Samuel Maclure, a leading architect of the time, in his American Chalet style. It has large, sunny rooms, an abundance of impressive woodwork, beveled and stained glass, and polished fir floors covered with Oriental rugs. Original light fixtures lend an Arthurian charm. Furnishings are largely English and Flemish antiques. A second-floor guest room at the front of the house uses the original bathroom off the hallway, and another at the back has an ensuite shower. Kit and Dene Mainguy are superb hosts. Kit has honed his skills as a former hotelier down to a smaller, more personal scale. He serves a most savory English breakfast in the formal dining room. He and Dene intuit guests' needs very well and accommodate them in every way possible.

Dog and cat in residence; no pets; infants and children over eight welcome; no smoking; full breakfast; special diets accommodated; robes provided; rollaway beds available; Dallas Road waterfront, shops, bistros, and tearooms nearby; 25-minute walk to town, or 10 minutes by bus; ample street parking; French spoken; off-season rates. Brochure available.

ROOM	BED	BATH	ENTRANCE	FLOOR	DAILY RATES S - D (EP)
A	1Q	Pvt	Main	2	$75-$90 ($15)
B	1K or 2T	Pvt	Main	2	$75-$90 ($15)

Rates stated in Canadian funds

Eagles Rest Bed & Breakfast   **(604) 478-5996**
3307 B Metchosin Road, Victoria, BC V9C 2A4
(On Highway 1A between Victoria and Sooke)

When Marg Mercer decided to turn her neat and clean contemporary home into a B&B, she chose a name that reflects her fondness for eagles. Many are on display throughout the house. The upper floor is just for guests, and the names of the comfortable bedrooms -- Lilac, Rose, and Fern -- indicate their color schemes. Lilac has an ensuite bath, while the other two share a bath off the hallway. Marg invites guests to enjoy her friendly kitchen, where she serves full country breakfasts. She also shares the kitchen with those who prefer eating in (a deli, bakery, and market are within walking distance). Hiking is superb in nearby East Sooke Park, while some may prefer golfing or salmon fishing. At Eagles Rest, you'll be well-situated to explore the fascinating Sooke region and enjoy the charming city of Victoria as well.

No pets; children over eight welcome; smoking outside only; full breakfast; TV in some rooms; bus stop nearby; off-street parking. Brochure available.

ROOM	BED	BATH	ENTRANCE	FLOOR	DAILY RATES	
					S - D	(EP)
A	1D	Pvt	Main	2	$65	($5)
B	2T	Shd*	Main	2	$55	
C	1T	Shd*	Main	2	$45	

Rates stated in Canadian funds

272

Heritage House Bed & Breakfast   (604) 479-0892
3808 Heritage Lane, Victoria, BC V8Z 7A7
(Between Highway 17 and Trans-Canada Highway)

Just minutes from downtown Victoria in a setting of country seclusion, Heritage House stands tall and proud at the end of a quiet lane. Old gardens, trees, and landscaping beautifully complement this quintessential character home overlooking Portage Inlet. Built in 1910, the home exemplifies the finest craftsmanship of the day, and it has aged exceedingly well. Endowed with ten-foot ceilings, leaded glass windows, and rich woodwork, the interior glows with warmth and comfort. Guests may gather around the parlor fireplace, in the handsome library/den, or at the elegant dining room table. Upstairs, the five guest rooms share three full baths. Varying in size, decor, and view, the attractive bedrooms feature charming combinations of antiques, wicker pieces, linens and laces, wallcoverings, and area rugs on gleaming wood floors. Three of the rooms are augmented by cozy annexes for extra sleeping. Hosts Larry and Sandra Gray found an architectural treasure in Heritage House and serve up sterling hospitality to match.

No pets or smoking; well-behaved children over thirteen welcome; full breakfast; lounging veranda; off-street parking; near bus route; credit cards (V,MC); two-night minimum. Brochure available.

ROOM	BED	BATH	ENTRANCE	FLOOR	DAILY RATES S - D	(EP)
A	1Q & 1T	Shd*	Main	2	$95	($35)
B	1Q & 1D	Shd*	Main	2	$95	($35)
C	1Q & 1D	Shd*	Main	2	$95	($35)
D	1K or 2T	Shd*	Main	2	$75	
E	1D	Shd*	Main	2	$60	

Rates stated in Canadian funds

Hibernia Bed & Breakfast   **(604) 658-5519**
747 Helvetia Crescent, Victoria, BC V8Y 1M1
(Near Cordova Bay)

Aideen Lydon, who hails from Galway Bay, is Irish through and through -- and so is her home. As it is in the old country, hospitality here is lively, warm, and generous. The two-story brick home, set at the end of a cul-de-sac, is surrounded by extensive grounds with lovely old trees, vines and flowers, and country quiet. Inside, its ample character is enhanced by lots of wood paneling, Oriental rugs, antiques, artwork, and family memorabilia. The guest lounge downstairs, offering television, a grand piano, books, and games, is especially cozy and inviting. Relax here or in the garden -- and you're welcome in the main living area as well. Aideen's many repeat guests come back for the comfortable beds, the huge, delicious breakfasts, and (most of all) a visit with their quintessential Irish hostess.

No pets; smoking outside only; full breakfast; location central to ferries, airport, Butchart Gardens, and city; lakes, parks, golf, tennis, dining, and country walks nearby; off-street parking. Brochure available.

ROOM	BED	BATH	ENTRANCE	FLOOR	DAILY RATES S - D (EP)
A	1Q	Pvt	Main	1	$50-$70
B	1D	Pvt	Main	1	$50-$70
C	2T	Pvt	Main	2	$50-$70

Rates stated in Canadian funds

274

The Inn on St. Andrews   **(604) 384-8613**
231 St. Andrews Street, Victoria, BC V8V 2N1 **1(800) 668-5993**
(James Bay area, near Beacon Hill Park)

The glorious gardens surrounding this heritage property do justice to its stature and grace. Built in 1913 by Edith Carr, eldest sister of the famous Canadian artist and author Emily Carr, the grand home is lovingly tended by proud owner Joan Peggs. Starting with its innate fine craftsmanship, elegant woodwork, stained and beveled glass, and gracious proportions, she has used ivory, pale green, peach, and pink in fashioning an interior that is at once light, welcoming, and soothing. Common areas -- living room, delightful sun room, formal dining room, and TV room -- seem truly meant to be enjoyed as one's own. Large, bright bedrooms are located off the central second-floor landing. At Joan's beautifully preserved inn, guests usually reach such a level of at-homeness that they return whenever possible to its familiar embrace.

Smoking outside only; full breakfast; walk to heart of town, ocean front, and Beacon Hill Park; near bus route; ample street parking; credit cards (MC, en route); off-season rates. Brochure available.

ROOM	BED	BATH	ENTRANCE	FLOOR	DAILY RATES	
					S - D	(EP) +
A	1D	Shd*	Main	2	$55-$70	($15)
B	1Q	Shd*	Main	2	$55-$70	
C	2T	Shd*	Main	2	$55-$70	($15)

Rates stated in Canadian funds

Laird House   **(604) 384-3177**
134 St. Andrews Street, Victoria, BC V8V 2M5
(James Bay area, near Beacon Hill Park)

An exceptional place to stay in the quiet and lovely James Bay section of Victoria is the inviting 1912 heritage-style home of Ruth Laird. It has been restored and decorated with the utmost attention to detail. In fact, one gets the feeling that every square inch of Laird House was fashioned to offer visual delight and comfort to its inhabitants. On the main floor, a guest living room and parlor exude quality; coffered ceilings and impressive woodwork are enhanced by beautiful floral motifs in rose, green, and cream. Tea and sherry are available to sip by the fireplace as soft music soothes the senses. On the second floor, three most attractive bedrooms (one with a fireplace and balcony) are full of special touches including fresh flowers and fruit. Two shared bathrooms are stocked with amenities while another room contains a guest refrigerator, sink, coffee, tea, and cookies. Elegant three-course breakfasts are served in the prettiest dining room imaginable -- a sterling way to start your glorious day in Victoria!

Two cats in residence; no pets, children, or smoking; full breakfast (Heart Smart menu on request); robes and hair dryers provided; walk to heart of town, ocean front, and Beacon Hill Park; near bus route; off-street parking; credit cards (V,MC).

ROOM	BED	BATH	ENTRANCE	FLOOR	DAILY RATES S - D (EP) +
A	1D	Shd*	Main	2	$60-$75
B	1Q	Shd*	Main	2	$60-$75
C	2T	Shd*	Main	2	$60-$75

Rates stated in Canadian funds

Maridou House (604) 360-0747
116 Eberts Street, Victoria, BC V8S 3H7 FAX: 383-3550
(East of Beacon Hill Park, one-half block from waterfront)

Few houses have had a more dramatic transition than this charmingly refurbished gem of Edwardian architecture. Its recent history has been well-documented by hosts Marilyn and Douglas Allison, to the delight of their guests. (Get ready for a good story!) A congenial tone is set by the Allisons, who offer friendly, personal service and lovely guest rooms named after Scottish clans. Each room has its own delights. One at the front has a sea view and a dressing table nook; another, the honeymoon suite, has a lace-canopied bed and an ensuite bath with Jacuzzi tub. Common areas include a sitting/dining room where wholesome full breakfasts are accompanied by spirited conversation. After all the pampering and individual attention, you will have a hard time leaving Maridou House. It stays with you in spirit for a long, long time.

No pets; children over twelve welcome; no smoking; full breakfast; robes provided; laundry facilities; piano and fireplace in guest parlor; quiet area; good walking; park across street; on bus route; off-street parking; credit cards (V,MC). Brochure available.

ROOM	BED	BATH	ENTRANCE	FLOOR	DAILY RATES S - D (EP)
A	1Q	Pvt	Main	2	$95
B	1Q	Shd*	Main	2	$75
C	2T	Shd*	Main	2	$55-$75

Rates stated in Canadian funds

Mulberry Manor   **(604) 370-1918**
611 Foul Bay Road, Victoria, BC V8S 1H2
(Between Crescent Road waterfront and Oak Bay)

Mulberry Manor, a stately heritage home designed by Samuel
Maclure, has the understated style and elegance of an exclusive country estate. It is surrounded by park-like gardens and is almost completely hidden behind tall trees, affording utmost privacy and
tranquility. Connoisseurs of the good life will appreciate the level of
perfection that hosts Susan and Tony Temple have achieved. Rooms of
grand proportion have elaborately carved ceilings and mouldings,
custom wallcoverings, window treatments, and linens, and exquisite
antiques, carpets, and works of art, yet possess the warmth and
comfort of a family residence. On the second floor are the four guest
accommodations. Each is decorated in a beautifully executed motif
with romantic accoutrements and charming details. Garden views
enhance each lovely bedroom and the deluxe Jasmin Suite. Fine
sterling, china, and crystal sparkle each morning in the vibrant red
dining room -- entirely fitting for the pampered guests at Mulberry
Manor.

Small dog in residence; no pets or smoking; children by arrangement; full breakfast; guest lounge; fireplace in sitting room of Jasmin
Suite (A); balconies (A and B); near bus route; off-street parking;
credit cards (V,MC); off-season rates. Brochure available.

ROOM	BED	BATH	ENTRANCE	FLOOR	DAILY RATES S - D	(EP)
A	1K	Pvt	Main	2	$145	($20)
B	1Q	Pvt	Main	2	$125	
C	1Q	Pvt	Main	2	$105	
D	2T	Pvt	Main	2	$95	

Rates stated in Canadian funds

Raventree Iris Gardens Bed & Breakfast   **(604) 642-5248**
RR#2, 1853 Connie Road, Victoria, BC V9B 5B4
(Twenty-five minutes from Victoria, ten from Sooke)

Shortly after you turn off the main highway, space opens up and you soon find the driveway to Raventree Iris Gardens. What a thrill it is to see the beautiful Tudor-style home on acres of idyllically land-scaped grounds featuring iris fields worthy of van Gogh. Inside, there's an artistic, comforting environment with luscious views from every window -- a trout pond, abundant wildlife, and an amazing variety of flora with a look of well-tended wildness. Shells, fresh and dried flowers, wood carvings, and stained glass accent the interior in a tasteful array. Each of the well-separated second-floor guest accom-modations is a special creation, a haven unto itself. Relax in the lounge or on the terrace, or stroll through ten acres of gardens and woodland paths. Hosts can suggest numerous excursions and activi-ties that make the Sooke region an outdoor lovers' paradise.

No pets; no children under twelve; smoking on terrace only; full breakfast; early coffee and conversation with a look at the enticing menu of homemade, home-grown specialties; afternoon tea service; ensuite baths (Rooms A and C); off-street parking; credit cards (V,MC); *open Easter to mid-October*. Brochure available.

ROOM	BED	BATH	ENTRANCE	FLOOR	DAILY RATES S - D	(EP)
A	1K	Pvt	Main	2	$90	
B	1Q	Pvt	Main	2	$75	
C	1D & 1T	Pvt	Main	2	$85	($20)

Rates stated in Canadian funds

279

Scholefield House   **(604) 385-2025**
731 Vancouver Street, Victoria, BC V8V 3V4   **1(800) 661-1623**
(Four blocks behind the Empress Hotel)

Enjoy the privilege of staying in a designated heritage Victorian home, built in 1892 for Ethelbert Olaf Stuart Scholefield, provincial librarian and archivist. Randy and Janet Thompson offer the refinement and splendor of a bygone age in their handsome home. Guest rooms are individually decorated in antiques, beautiful old quilts, and fine linens and lace. The bathrooms offer a choice of clawfoot tub or shower. Upon awakening in the morning, catch the aroma of fresh coffee and a luscious breakfast that includes fresh herbs, homemade jams, and fruit butters. Then take off to explore Victoria, knowing that when you return you'll be greeted with a calming cuppa tea or evening sherry in the Library Room. Gracious comfort in historical surroundings awaits you at Scholefield House.

Two cats in residence; no pets or smoking; no children under twelve; full breakfast; ensuite bath in Room A; on bus route; off-street and street parking; credit cards (V,MC). Brochure available.

ROOM	BED	BATH	ENTRANCE	FLOOR	DAILY RATES	
					S - D	(EP)
A	1K	Pvt	Main	2	$80-$90	($15)
B	1Q	Shd*	Main	2	$60-$70	
C	1Q	Shd*	Main	2	$60-$70	

Rates stated in Canadian funds

The Sea Rose   **(604) 381-7932**
1250 Dallas Road, Victoria, BC V8V 1C4
(On sea front)

On a corner lot facing the famous view across Juan de Fuca Strait to the snow-capped Olympics, this revitalized 1921 home far exceeds its modest outward appearance. Inside, common areas are possessed of a beautifully refurbished Craftsman-like charm. Each of the four spacious, luxurious view suites is outfitted with a modern private bath, fridge, wet bar, and TV. All are light, airy, and particularly soothing. Guests may come and go as they please using the separate entrance adjacent to the rear parking lot. Host Karen Young keeps the premises immaculate top to bottom, dispenses all manner of assistance to guests, and prepares a palate-pleasing hot breakfast each morning. The Sea Rose is a pristine retreat offering genial hospitality, a great location, and exceptional comfort.

No pets, children, or smoking; full breakfast; coin-op laundry available; on bus route; off-street parking; major credit cards; inquire about off-season and senior rates. Brochure available.

ROOM	BED	BATH	ENTRANCE	FLOOR	DAILY RATES	
					S - D	(EP) +
A	1Q	Pvt	Sep	2	$85	
B	1K or 2T	Pvt	Sep	1G	$95	($20)
C	1Q	Pvt	Sep	1G	$95	($20)
D	1Q	Pvt	Sep	3	$125	($20)

Rates stated in Canadian funds

Sonia's Bed & Breakfast by the Sea   **(604) 385-2700**
                                               1(800) 667-4489

175 Bushby Street, Victoria, BC V8S 1B5   **FAX: 744-3763**
(East of Beacon Hill Park, one block from waterfront)

Sonia McMillan is as clear on her own identity as she is on that of her lodging establishment, so there's no mistaking this B&B for anyone else's. As she'll readily tell you, she doesn't do antiques. She offers quality lodgings at a good value; her breakfasts are as bountiful as the rest of the hospitality. Guests are invited to make themselves at home in the living room, the family room, or the deck (with ocean view) -- they're even free to use the good crystal from the display cabinet. Dusty, the African Grey parrot, usually hangs out in the family room and becomes a friend of guests who so choose. People who stay at Sonia's appreciate the extent to which she and her husband, Brian, open their comfortable home to guests. They have a *great* time, too.

No children under thirteen; smoking outside only; full breakfast; TV/VCR and fireplace in family room; good access to long walks along waterfront; on bus route; off-street and street parking; off-season rates (April); *closed October-March*. Brochure available.

ROOM	BED	BATH	ENTRANCE	FLOOR	DAILY RATES S - D (EP)
A	1Q	Pvt	Main	1	$75
B	1Q	Pvt	Main	1	$75
C	1K	Pvt	Main	1	$85

Rates stated in Canadian funds

282

Sunnymeade House Inn   Phone/FAX: **(604) 658-1414**
1002 Fenn Avenue, Victoria, BC V8Y 1P3
(At Cordova Bay; central to ferries, Butchart Gardens, and city)

The country English-style home of Nancy and Jack Thompson is, in a word, exceptional. The picture-perfect garden and patio are as well maintained as the house itself, and the Thompsons have clearly anticipated everything a guest might need or desire. A hallway leads from the foyer on the main floor up to the guest quarters. There is a lounge for guests, along with five bedrooms offering private or shared baths. Luxurious, tastefully appointed rooms have their own vanity/sinks, luggage racks, and other niceties. Enticing full breakfasts are served, with a choice of menu items. For a warm welcome, elegant accommodations, and first-rate hospitality, Sunnymeade House Inn is simply unsurpassed.

No pets; smoking outside only; full breakfast; single sofa bed extra in Rooms D and E; walking distance from beach, fine restaurants, and the new world-class Cordova Bay Golf Course; regular bus service to Victoria and Swartz Bay ferry; off-street parking; credit cards (V,MC) to hold rooms only; inquire about weekly and monthly rates. Brochure available.

ROOM	BED	BATH	ENTRANCE	FLOOR	DAILY RATES S - D (EP) +
A	1Q	Pvt	Main	2	$89-$95
B	1Q	Pvt	Main	2	$89-$95
C	1Q	Pvt	Main	2	$95-$105
D	1D	Shd*	Main	2	$79-$89 ($30)
E	1D	Shd*	Main	2	$79-$89 ($30)

Rates stated in Canadian funds

283

Top O'Triangle Mountain　　　　　　　　**(604) 478-7853**
3442 Karger Terrace, Victoria, BC　V9C 3K5　　　FAX: **478-2245**
(Between Victoria and Sooke)

Staying out of the city has its advantages -- peace and quiet, a slower pace, ease of parking -- but this B&B offers much more. Top O'Triangle Mountain is just twenty-two minutes out of Victoria, but the view from this elevation is wondrous: the city and inner harbor, Port Angeles, the Olympic Mountains, and a spectacular light show at night. The house is built of interlocking cedar logs, and the warm look of wood permeates the interior. There are plenty of windows, decks all around, and a solarium where ample breakfasts are served. The three guest accommodations, all with private baths, include a room on the main floor and, on the ground floor, a mini-suite and a suite with a TV/sitting room. Comfort and silence ensure a sound sleep. Hosts Henry and Pat Hansen encourage unrestricted relaxation and sincerely want guests to think of their B&B as home.

No pets; families welcome (children under twelve, $5); no smoking in rooms or dining area; full breakfast; off-street and street parking; credit cards (V,MC). Room A has a water and mountain view, a sliding glass door to the deck, TV, and ensuite bath; it is available May 15-October 15 only; otherwise, another room on the main floor is used. Brochure available.

ROOM	BED	BATH	ENTRANCE	FLOOR	DAILY RATES S - D (EP)	
A	1Q	Pvt	Main	2	$85	
B	1Q	Pvt	Main	1G	$75	($20)
C	1Q	Pvt	Main	1G	$65	

Rates stated in Canadian funds

The Vacationer (604) 382-9469
1143 Leonard Street, Victoria, BC V8V 2S3 FAX: **384-6553**
(Two blocks from waterfront, bordering Beacon Hill Park)

One glance at this B&B and you feel the promise of something good inside. Pass the manicured front lawn and flower beds, enter the front door, and you'll receive the heartiest of welcomes from hosts Anne and Henry DeVries. They raised their family here and now keep their home in top shape for B&B guests. The spacious living room with a fireplace of stone is so comfortable that you might feel like inviting friends in for a visit -- and you are welcome to do so. The adjacent dining area is the scene of beautifully presented, four-course breakfasts. Anne prides herself on coming up with a different specialty each morning, no matter how long you stay. Three pretty bedrooms with excellent mattresses and color TVs, along with two bathrooms, occupy the second floor. Hosts offer the use of their secluded back yard, bicycles, and a separate phone line. They have a wealth of budget-stretching tips that should help to maximize your resources while visiting lovely Victoria.

No pets, children, or smoking; full breakfast; robes provided; tennis courts nearby; walking distance from downtown; off-street parking; Dutch and German spoken; credit cards (V,MC); free pickup from downtown, ferries, and bus depot; off-season rates. Host also operates a B&B reservation service offering a variety of other accommodations. Brochure available.

ROOM	BED	BATH	ENTRANCE	FLOOR	DAILY RATES S - D (EP)
A	1Q	Shd*	Main	2	$45-$70 ($20)
B	1Q	Shd*	Main	2	$45-$70
C	2T	Shd*	Main	2	$45-$70

Rates stated in Canadian funds

285

A View to Sea   **(604) 388-6669**
626 Fernhill Road, Victoria, BC V9A 4Y9   FAX: 385-1962
(Five-minute drive from inner harbor)

Sharon and Michael Sutton's home, called A View to Sea for obvious reasons, is majestically set among towering old trees and thriving gardens. Individual attention to guests is the hallmark of the Suttons' generous hospitality. Their welcoming guest lounge has a beamed ceiling, a big stone fireplace, a wrap-around deck with color-ful flowers, ample windows, and a vista of city, water, and mountains. Guest accommodations are done in soft pastels with custom-made valances and bedcoverings, luxurious carpeting, and reading lofts (with view) reached by spiral staircases. The master bedroom has an ensuite bath with a sunken soaking tub for two. On the home's lower level, guests are invited to use the hot tub and sauna. Breakfasts are tailored to personal tastes and served in the gracious dining room or on the cheery deck. At A View to Sea, pampering guests is an art form.

No pets; children over fourteen welcome; smoking outside only; full breakfast; TV/VCR in guest lounge; hot tub; sauna; off-street parking; credit cards (V,MC); off-season rates. Brochure available.

ROOM	BED	BATH	ENTRANCE	FLOOR	DAILY RATES	
					S - D	(EP)
A	1Q	Pvt	Main	2	$96	
B	1K or 2T	Pvt	Main	2	$82	
C	1K & 1T (or 3T)	Pvt	Main		$76	($20)

Rates stated in Canadian funds

286

Viewfield Inn   **(604) 389-1190**
1024 Munro Street, Victoria, BC V9A 5N9
(Ten-minute drive from city, northwest of inner harbor)

With the ambiance of a small private estate, this 1895 country
Victorian was expanded in 1989 to accommodate guests. The blend of
old and new works unusually well here. An air of peaceful seclusion
is created by a velvety lawn met by beautiful rock and flower gardens
with tall shrubs at the outer edges. Tall trees in the background hide
all but a marvelous view across the strait to the entrance of the inner
harbor and on to the Olympic Peninsula. The inn's guest quarters
include a sitting/dining room endowed with warm Victorian charm as
well as such amenities as a wet bar, fridge, TV/VCR and movies, and
an array of parlor games, books, and puzzles. Two luxuriously
appointed, antique furnished bedrooms were individually designed to
be as lovely as they are comfortable. Fresh flowers, wonderful breakfasts, the park-like setting, and the view are just a few of the good
memories hosts Larry and Valarie Terry hope you'll take with you
from Viewfield Inn.

No pets, children, or smoking; full breakfast; walk to Olde England
Inn, Fleming Beach, and Macauley Point Park; off-street parking;
credit cards (V,MC); two-night minimum; one-bedroom suite, $140.
Brochure available.

ROOM	BED	BATH	ENTRANCE	FLOOR	DAILY RATES S - D (EP)
A	1Q	Pvt	Sep	2	$80
B	1Q	Pvt	Sep	2	$95

Rates stated in Canadian funds

Wellington Bed & Breakfast   **(604) 383-5976**
66 Wellington Street, Victoria, BC V8V 4H5
(Just east of Beacon Hill Park and a half-block from waterfront)

With her marvelous talent for design, Inge Ranzinger has coaxed every charming nuance out of her Fairfield character home. Its interior is fresh, artistic, and classy. In the main-floor common areas, tones of mauve, pink, and aquamarine contrast with lots of white -- a splendid setting for pretty patterned rugs, myriad collectibles and art objects, and very homey furnishings. Equal flair marks the upstairs guest quarters. The White Room is a vision of palest lilac, white, fresh and dried flowers, and lovely works of glass. The Hearth Room has colonial blue wallpaper, lace curtains, and a fireplace; The Antique Room is a bit smaller and more traditional. Inge and her daughter, Sue, offer hospitality to match the inspired design of Wellington Bed & Breakfast.

Cat in residence; no pets; no smoking; no children under twelve; full breakfast; ensuite bath in Room C; bath across hall from Room B; bath on first floor for Room A; Dallas Road waterfront, shops, bistros, and tearooms nearby; 25-minute walk to town, or 10 minutes by bus; off-street and street parking; credit cards (MC); German and Spanish spoken; off-season rates.

ROOM	BED	BATH	ENTRANCE	FLOOR	DAILY RATES S - D	(EP)
A	1Q	Pvt	Main	2	$45-$65	
B	1K	Pvt	Main	2	$55-$80	
C	1Q & 1T	Pvt	Main	2	$55-$85	($15)

Rates stated in Canadian funds

Wooded Acres Bed & Breakfast   (604) 478-8172 *or* **474-8959**
RR#2, 4907 Rocky Point Road, Victoria, BC   V9B 5B4
(Between Victoria and Sooke)

The rural municipality of Metchosin is becoming known as a center for organic farming and for arts and crafts. It is particularly fitting to find here Wooded Acres Bed & Breakfast where "made-from-scratch" finds full expression. In a majestic forest setting, Elva and Skip Kennedy's home was built with logs from their property, and the mellow beauty of cedar, oak, and fir has tremendous appeal. The warm, snuggly atmosphere is enhanced by a rustic stone fireplace, heavy beams at the ceilings, country antiques, and intriguing displays of artifacts recovered from the local area. In the second-floor guest quarters, welcoming touches abound; parties of one or two couples at a time enjoy complete privacy and their own hot tub. Breakfast is a literal feast of home-baked specialties, fresh brown eggs, old-fash-ioned slab bacon, and Elva's own jams and jellies. Country goodness is reflected in every facet of the romantic escape to be found at Wooded Acres.

No pets; adult-oriented; full breakfast at guests' convenience; spe-cial diets accommodated; private guest spa; golf, fishing, hiking, tennis, and beachcombing nearby; off-street parking; two couples, $170. Brochure available.

ROOM	BED	BATH	ENTRANCE	FLOOR	DAILY RATES S - D (EP) +
A	2Q	Pvt	Main	2	$95

Rates stated in Canadian funds

The use of travelling is to regulate imagination by reality, and instead of thinking how things may be, to see them as they are.

—Samuel Johnson

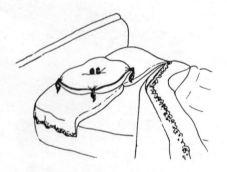

A guest never forgets the host who has treated him kindly.

—Homer

Please read "About Dining Highlights" on page *vii*.

ABBOTSFORD

Britannia Fish & Chips, 2-31205 Old Yale Road at Townline Road, Clearbrook; (604) 854-1815

Johlyn's Perogie Inn, 1-31813 South Fraser Way; (604) 855-7868

CAMPBELL RIVER

Charron's, 1376 Island Highway; (604) 286-0009; Continental

Gourmet-by-the-Sea, 4378 South Island Highway, Oyster Bay; (604) 923-5234; fresh seafood/creative Continental

Le Chateau Briand, 1170 Island Highway; (604) 287-4143; Continental

The Royal Coachman Inn, 84 Dogwood Street; (604) 286-0231; Continental

The Willows Neighbourhood Pub, 521 Rockland Road; (604) 923-8311

COURTENAY

La Cremaillere Restaurant, 975 Comox Road; (604) 338-8131; French

DELTA

Greek Village, 7953 - 120 Street; (604) 594-6524

Portofino, 9493 - 120 Street; (604) 581-7555; steak/prime rib/Greek

Wimaan Thai Restaurant, 8665 - 120 Street; (604) 594-6524

GIBSONS

Chez Philippe, Bonniebrook Lodge, 1532 Ocean Beach Esplanade, Gower Point; (604) 886-2887; French/West Coast

El Nino Seafood House; 1500 Marine Drive; (604) 886-3891; waterfront dining

MOUNT CURRIE

Country Bistro & Bakery; main highway through Mount Currie; (604) 894-6622

NARAMATA (northeast of Penticton)

The Country Squire, 3950 First Street; (604) 496-5416; fine dining by appointment (allow up to four hours)

NEW WESTMINSTER

des Gitans, 83 Sixth Street; (604) 524-6122; Swiss

OLIVER

Jacques French Cuisine, Main Street; (604) 498-4418

OSOYOOS

Barry's Neighbourhood Restaurant, 8311 - 78th Avenue; (604) 495-2224; varied menu

Chalet Helvetia Restaurant, 8312 - 74th Avenue; (604) 495-7552

Diamond Steak & Seafood House, Main Street near 89th Avenue; (604) 495-6223; Italian/Greek

The Old Vienna, Main Street; (604) 495-6621

PARKSVILLE

Creek House Restaurant, #1-1025 Lee Road; (604) 248-3214; Italian/Greek/fresh seafood/more

Kalvas Restaurant, 180 Molliet; (604) 248-6933; seafood/European

PEMBERTON
Willy G's Cafe, 1359 Aster; (604) 894-6411; Mediterranean/West Coast/fresh seafood/pasta

PENTICTON
Theo's, 687 Main Street; (604) 492-4019; Greek

PORT HARDY
Brigg Seafood House, Market and Granville Streets; (604) 949-6532

Sportsman's Steak & Seafood House, Market Street; (604) 949-7811

QUADRA ISLAND
Tsa-Kwa-Luten Lodge, Cape Mudge; (604) 285-2042; Northwest Coast/salmon barbecues

QUALICUM BEACH
The Carvery, 2775 West Island Highway; (604) 752-2131; German

G. Willies, 710 Memorial, in village; (604) 752-1050; deli/cafe with varied menu for all appetites

Old Dutch Inn, 110 Island Highway; (604) 752-6914; Dutch

Sand Pebbles Inn, 2767 West Island Highway; (604) 752-6974

REVELSTOKE
Alphaus, 604 Second Street West; (604) 837-6380; German

Black Forest Inn, TransCanada Highway West; (604) 837-3495; Bavarian dishes and seafood

Manning's, 302 MacKenzie Avenue; (604) 837-3258; Chinese

Zala's Pizza & Steak House; 1601 Victoria Road; (604) 837-5555

The 112, Regent Inn, 112 East First Street; (604) 837-2107; Continental

ROBERTS CREEK
The Creekhouse, Roberts Creek Road and Beach Avenue; (604) 885-9321; Continental

SECHELT
Blue Heron Inn, East Porpoise Bay Road; (604) 885-3847; waterfront fine dining

SIDNEY
Blue Peter Pub & Restaurant, 2270 Harbour Road; (604) 656-4551; waterfront seafood

Cafe Mozart, 2470 Beacon Avenue; (604) 655-1554; fine dining

Deep Cove Chalet, 11190 Chalet Road, Deep Cove; (604) 656-3541; Continental with a light touch/fine dining

The Latch, 2328 Harbour Road, Sidney; (604) 656-6622; Continental/seafood in elegant historic waterfront home

Marg's Bleue Moon Cafe, 9535 Canora Road; (604) 655-4450; pub-style restaurant

Newport House, 9853 Seaport Place; (604) 656-3320; waterfront pasta/seafood/lunch/dinner

Odyssia Steak House, 9785 Fifth Street; (604) 656-5596; pasta/steaks/pizza

Pelicano's Cafe and Bakery, 9851 Seaport Place; (604) 655-4116; coffee/muffins/lunch on waterfront

The Stonehouse Pub, 2215 Canoe Cove; (604) 656-3498; pub fare in old English character house

SOOKE

The Breakers, West Coast Road, Jordan River; (604) 646-2079; varied seafood

Good Life, A Bookstore Cafe, 2113 Otter Point Road; (604) 642-6821; fresh local specialties

Margison House, 6605 Sooke Road; (604) 642-3620; lunch and afternoon tea

Mom's Cafe, 2036 Shields Road; (604) 642-3314; hearty house-made dishes

Sooke Harbour House, 1528 Whiffen Spit Road; (604) 642-3421; Pacific Northwest/fresh local seafood/fine dining

SUMMERLAND

Schaefer's at the Winery, Sumac Ridge Winery, 17403 Highway 97; (604) 494-0038; varied menu and Heart Smart specialties

Shaugnessy's Cove, 12817 Lakeshore Drive; (604) 494-1212; seafood restaurant/pub

TOFINO

Orca Lodge Restaurant, 1200 block of Pacific Rim Highway; (604) 725-2323; Northwest coastal

VANCOUVER

Anton's Pasta Bar, 4260 East Hastings Street, North Burnaby; (604) 299-6636

Athene's Restaurant, 3618 West Broadway; (604) 731-4135; Greek

Bishop's, 2183 West Fourth Avenue; (604) 738-2025; contemporary home cooking

Bridges Seafood Restaurant, 1696 Duranleau Street, Granville Island; (604) 687-4400

Cafe Norte, 3108 Edgemont Boulevard, North Vancouver; (604) 255-1188; Mexican

Cafe Roma, 60 Semisch Street North at Esplanade, North Vancouver; (604) 984-0274; Italian

The Cannery, 2205 Commissioner Street; (604) 254-9606; fine seafood dining on waterfront

Capers, 2496 Marine Drive, West Vancouver; (604) 925-3316; cafe/deli/market emphasizing organic, vegetarian dishes

Chesa Restaurant, 1734 Marine Drive, West Vancouver; (604) 922-2411; Continental/West Coast

Cin Cin, 1154 Robson Street; (604) 688-7338; Mediterranean

Daisy Garden Restaurant; 2163 East Hastings Street; (604) 255-6783; authentic Chinese cooking

Deep Cove Pizza, 4385 Gallant Avenue, North Vancouver; (604) 929-6123 or 929-5712

Isadora's, 1540 Old Bridge Street, Granville Island; (604) 681-8816; seafood/meats/vegetarian/child-friendly

Kameros Restaurant, 2422 Marine Drive, West Vancouver; (604) 922-5751; Greek

Kettle of Fish, 900 Pacific Street; (604) 682-6661; fresh seafood

DINING HIGHLIGHTS: BRITISH COLUMBIA

Lalibela Restaurant, 2090 Alma Street; (604) 732-1454; Ethiopian

La Cucina, 1509 Marine Drive, North Vancouver; (604) 986-1334; Northern Italian

La Toque Blanche, 4368 Marine Drive, West Vancouver; (604) 926-1006; Continental

Le Crocodile, 818 Thurlow Street; (604) 669-4298; fine dining/French

Maria's Taverna, 2324 West Fourth Avenue; (604) 731-4722; Greek

Montri's, 2611 West Fourth Avenue; (604) 738-9888; Thai

Naam, 2724 West Fourth Avenue; (604) 738-7151; vegetarian

Nyala Ethiopian Restaurant, 2930 West Fourth Avenue; (604) 731-7899

Orestes, 3116 West Broadway; (604) 732-1461; Greek

Pasparos Taverna, 132 West Third Street, North Vancouver; (604) 980-0331; Greek

Quilicum West Coast Indian Restaurant, 1724 Davie Street; (604) 681-7044; West Coast native cuisine

Raga, 1177 Broadway; (604) 733-1127; Indian

Raintree, 1630 Alberni Street; (604) 688-5570; Northwest Coast

Salmon House on the Hill, 2229 Folkestone Way, West Vancouver; (604) 926-3212

Sawasdee, 4250 Main Street; (604) 876-4030, and 2145 Granville Street; (604) 737-8222; Thai

Scoozi's, 808 West Hastings Street; (604) 684-1009; French cafe/great soups

Shijo, 1926 West Fourth Avenue; (604) 732-4676; Japanese

Sophie's Cosmic Cafe, 2095 West Fourth Avenue; (604) 732-6810; eclectic menu

Star Anise, 1485 West Twelfth Avenue; (604) 737-1485; local ingredients with a French flair

Szechuan Chongqing Restaurant, 2495 Victoria Drive; (604) 254-7434

Tojo's, #202-777 West Broadway; (604) 872-8050; Japanese specialties by master sushi chef

Tomato Fresh Food Cafe, 3305 Cambie Street; (604) 874-6020; healthful, tasty, homemade dishes in one of city's oldest diners

Top of Vancouver Revolving Restaurant, Harbour Center, 555 West Hastings Street; (604) 669-2220; international

Vong's Kitchen, 5989 Fraser Street; (604) 327-4627; Chinese

Water Street Cafe, 300 Water Street; (604) 689-2832; West Coast

VICTORIA

Adrienne's Tea Garden Restaurant, 5325 Cordova Bay Road; (604) 658-1515; Continental

Banana Belt Cafe, 281 Menzies Street; (604) 385-9616

The Bird of Paradise Pub, 4291-A Glanford Avenue; (604) 727-2568; Mediterranean/pub fare

Blethering Place, 2250 Oak Bay Avenue; (604) 598-1413; British

Camille's, 45 Bastion Square; (604) 381-3433; West Coast contemporary

294

Chantecler Restaurant, 4509 West Saanich Road; (604) 727-3344; Continental

Chauney's, 614 Humboldt Street; (604) 385-4512; seafood

Chez Pierre, 512 Yates Street; (604) 388-7711; French seafood

The Clubhouse at Cordova Bay Golf Course, 5333 Cordova Bay Road; (604) 658-4075; casual dining for breakfast/lunch/dinner

Columbo's, 7855 East Saanich Road; Saanichton; (604) 652-3936; Greek pasta dishes/more

Colwood Corners Pub, 1889 Island Highway; (604) 478-1311

Da Tandoor, 1010 Fort Street; (604) 384-6333; Indian

Four Mile House, 199 Island Highway; (604) 479-2514; tea room/pub/restaurant in historic roadhouse

Green Cuisine, 5-560 Market Square; (604) 385-1809; vegetarian

Harbour House Restaurant, 607 Oswego Street; (604) 386-1244; seafood/steaks

Herald Street Caffe, 546 Herald Street; (604) 381-1441; Italian/Continental

Il Terrazzo, 555 Johnson Street; (604) 361-0028; Italian

James Bay Tea Room, 332 Menzies Street; (604) 382-8282; British

John's Place, 723 Pandora Avenue; (604) 389-0711; fresh, house-made, innovative breakfast/lunch/dinner

Kaz, 1619 Store Street; (604) 386-9121; Japanese

Oak Bay Beach Hotel, 1175 Beach Road; (604) 598-4556; afternoon tea/pub fare in The Snug

Olde England Inn, 429 Lampson Street; (604) 388-4353; English/prime rib

The Oxford Arms Pub & Restaurant, 301 Cook Street; (604) 382-3301; international/pub fare

Pablo's, 225 Quebec Street; (604) 388-4255; French Continental

The Parsonage, 1115 North Park; (604) 383-5999; country-style Scottish home cooking

Periklis, 531 Yates Street; (604) 386-3313; Greek

Re-bar, 50 Bastion Square; (604) 361-9223; vegetarian

Rebecca's, 1127 Wharf Street; (604) 380-6990; view dining

Romeo's Pizza, four locations: downtown at 760 Johnson, at 1581 Hillside, in Langford at 2945 Jacklin, and at Quadra and Mackenzie

Sam's Deli, 805 Government Street; (604) 382-8424; soups/sandwiches

Siam, 1314 Government Street; (604) 383-9911; Thai

Soho Village Bistro, 1311 Gladstone Avenue; (604) 384-3344; eclectic menu

Spinnakers Brew Pub, 308 Catherine Street; (604) 386-BREW; brewpub/lunch/snacks/dinner

Swan's Pub, 506 Pandora Avenue; (604) 361-3310; pub fare

The Swiss Neighbourhood Restaurant; 1280 Fairfield Road; (604) 384-6446; Swiss/European

The Tudor Rose Tea Room, 253 Cook Street; (604) 382-4616; light meals/afternoon tea/weekend dinners

If you reject the food, ignore the customs, fear the religion, and avoid the people, you might better stay home. You are like a pebble thrown into water; you become wet on the surface, but you are never a part of the water.

—James A. Michener

Voyage, travel, and change of place impart vigour.

—Seneca

301

B&B TRAVELERS REPORT

Knighttime Publications would like to receive any comments you may have about your experiences while using this directory. Please report any comment, suggestion, compliment or criticism as indicated:

Name and location of B&B _____

Date of visit _____

Length of stay _____

Comments _____

_____

_____

_____

_____

_____

_____

_____

_____

_____

_____

_____

Your name _____

Address_____

City/State/Zip _____
City/Province/Postal Code

Telephone _____

CUT HERE

From _____

_____

_____

FIRST
CLASS
POSTAGE

Diane Knight
Knighttime Publications
890 Calabasas Road
Watsonville, CA 95076-0418

- - - - - - - - - - - - - - - FOLD HERE - - - - - - - - - - - - - - -

CUT HERE

STAPLE OR TAPE

B&B TRAVELERS REPORT

Knighttime Publications would like to receive any comments you may have about your experiences while using this directory. Please report any comment, suggestion, compliment or criticism as indicated:

Name and location of B&B _____

Date of visit _____

Length of stay _____

Comments _____

_____

_____

_____

_____

_____

_____

_____

_____

_____

_____

_____

_____

Your name _____

Address_____

City/State/Zip _____
City/Province/Postal Code

Telephone_____

CUT HERE

From _____

FIRST
CLASS
POSTAGE

Diane Knight
Knighttime Publications
890 Calabasas Road
Watsonville, CA 95076-0418

- - - - - - - - - - - - - - - - FOLD HERE - - - - - - - - - - - - - - - -

CUT HERE

STAPLE OR TAPE

B&B TRAVELERS REPORT

Knighttime Publications would like to receive any comments you may have about your experiences while using this directory. Please report any comment, suggestion, compliment or criticism as indicated:

Name and location of B&B _____

Date of visit _____

Length of stay _____

Comments _____

_____

_____

_____

_____

_____

_____

_____

_____

_____

_____

_____

Your name _____

Address _____

City/State/Zip _____
City/Province/Postal Code

Telephone _____

CUT HERE

From _____

_____

_____

FIRST
CLASS
POSTAGE

Diane Knight
Knighttime Publications
890 Calabasas Road
Watsonville, CA 95076-0418

CUT HERE

- - - - - - - - - - - - - - - FOLD HERE - - - - - - - - - - - - - - - -

STAPLE OR TAPE

ORDERING ADDITIONAL BOOKS

Please send me: (I enclose payment with order)

____additional copies of *BED & BREAKFAST HOMES DIREC-TORY - WEST COAST* (8th edition) at **$12.95** each. Include **$2.00** postage and handling for first copy, plus **$1.00** for each additional copy to the same address. *California residents add current sales tax.*

Canadian residents, please send payment in U.S. funds using the above pricing.

Name _____

Address_____

City/State/Zip _____
City/Province/Postal Code

Send as a gift to: (Use extra paper for additional gifts)

Name _____

Address_____

City/State/Zip _____
City/Province/Postal Code

Gift card should read: _____

Mail this form with payment to:

KNIGHTTIME PUBLICATIONS
890 Calabasas Road
Watsonville, CA 95076-0418

CUT HERE

From _____

FIRST
CLASS
POSTAGE

Diane Knight
Knighttime Publications
890 Calabasas Road
Watsonville, CA 95076-0418

- - - - - - - - - - - - - - - - FOLD HERE - - - - - - - - - - - - - - - -

CUT HERE

STAPLE OR TAPE